COOKING THE ROMAN WAY

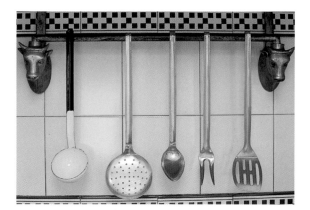

COOKING THE

HarperCollinsPublishers

ROMAN WAY

AUTHENTIC RECIPES FROM THE HOME COOKS AND TRATTORIAS OF ROME

DAVID DOWNIE

Photographs by

ALISON HARRIS

PAGES II—III: *Gino's Trattoria*

PAGES VI—VII: *Eating out in Rome*

HarperCollins books may be purchased for educational, business, or sales promotional use. For information, please write: Special Markets Department, HarperCollins Publishers Inc., 10 East 53rd Street, New York, NY 10022.

FIRST EDITION

Designed by Joel Avirom and Jason Snyder
Design assistant: Meghan Day Healey

Printed on acid-free paper

Library of Congress Cataloging-in-Publication Data

Downie, David.
   Cooking the Roman way : authentic recipes from the home cooks and trattorias of Rome / David Downie ; photographs by Alison Harris.
      p. cm
   Includes biographical references and index.
   ISBN 0-06-018892-8 hardcover
   1. Cookery, Italian. 2. Cookery—Italy—Rome. 3. Rome (Italy)—Social life and customs.
   I. Title.

   TX723 .D6878 2002
   641.5945—dc21   2002027279

02 03 04 05 06 ❖/TOP 10 9 8 7 6 5 4 3 2 1

enthusiasm and advice; Peggy Knickerbocker for the keen taste buds and all the good times; Dr. Abbie and Mr. Jerome Salny for being geniuses and sharing their brilliance; Barbara Bray for being a peerless guinea pig, a dear friend and an invaluable research assistant; the Kuhl and Labadie families for their enthusiasm, appetites and feedback on oil and spice; Caterina Howard for the recipe-testing and generosity; Anne and Charles Smith for the technical support; Meghan Day Healey and Jason Snyder for their professionalism and enthusiasm; Monica Meline, for her coordinating skills and assistance; Malcolm Ginniver and Alice Stewart for the *garofolato;* the late Fausto Frattini, coffee-roaster extraordinaire, for his kindness and wisdom; the great Claudio and Emilio Volpetti, friends and mentors, and their many wonderful helpers at Volpetti: Donato Salzarulo, Anselmo Blasilli and Muktar Hossein; Valentina and Mario Sassara for the recipes, the wine and olives and wild fennel flowers shared with spontaneous affection; Giuseppe and Alberto Simoni, and Danilo Sordi, of l'Antica Norcineria for the guanciale; Silvia Broggi at the Quirinale for her help researching the queen's visits; Anna Mangioli for the recipes; Carlo Dossi, Italian wine importer and food lover of renown in Paris, for sharing his address book; Daniela Maggioni for her ravioli and her warmth and for all the wonderful times together; the courageous, cheerful and indefatigable market people of Rome who gave us recipes and shared moments with us: Ettore and Armanda Graziani, Claudio Zampa and Lina De Clemente, Marcella Banco, Mirella Angelini, Mauro Berardi, Orlando Renzetti, Mario Capriotti, Anna Elisa Scipioni, Ugo Pantano and his aunt Fernanda Pantano, Maria Amato, Maria Assunta, Fabio Angelini; cheese-maker Giuseppe Brunelli for ushering us into the world of Pecorino Romano; Marco and Pierluigi Roscioli and their family and staff at Forno Roscioli for the fantastic recipes and the spontaneous generosity; Raimondo Ricci for his *Gran Caffès* and hospitality, and his helpful staff, at Sant'Eustachio; Luigi del Grosso, alias Gino, and his crew at Da Gino, for his enthusiasm and wonderful recipes; Alberto Ciarla for the fabulous fish recipes and the city lore; Alfredo Di Lelio for his fettuccine and his warm heart; Nando and Marco Ciampini for their recipes and anecdotes; Basilio, Anna and Mirka Fortini of La Taverna dello Spuntino in Grottaferrata for the delicious tiramisù; Aurelio and Jane Mariani at Antico Ristorante Pagnanelli for the kindness and the wonderful recipes, and their crew: Daniela Rezza, Carlo Cavallo and Francesco Coppola; Alberto Lombardi and Adriana Montellanico and their chef Fabio Cardia at La Briciola in Grottaferrata for the great recipes, the city lore, the music, the enthusiasm; the late Ninetta Ceccacci Mariani, her sons and the current team at Checchino dal 1887; Andreina Salomone at La Carbonara and her chef Eduardo Derose and maitre d' Sergio d'Antonio; Maria-Pia Pontani for the recipes all those years ago; Aldo Trabalzi at Sora Lella; Giacomo and Grazia Lo Bianco and chef Eugenio Velardi and his assistant Giulio Ciccotelli at La Matricianella; Fausto Simmi at La Cisterna, the Ceccarelli family at Da Giggetto and especially son Stefano Ceccarelli, master pastry-maker at La Dolce Roma; owner Valentino Seri and smiling Marzia Fabi of the Café du Parc; Silvano Giovanucci of La Tazza d'Oro; Stefania Porcelli at Checco er Carrettiere; owner Gianni Benedetti and his smiling helper Maria Alessandra Martinelli at Cacio e Pepe; Margherita Tomassini alias Sora Margherita and Gianna Agostinetti, pasta-maker extraordinaire; Giovanni Coletti and the staff of Osteria ar Galletto; Rosalena Trimani for the advice on Latium wines; Marino Matterazzi for the concise history of Roman baking; Piera and Marcello Proietti of Confetteria Moriondo & Gariglio for their Easter eggs, and Roberta di Paolo for her smiles; the team at Angelo Feroci; baker Fabio Albanesi for the pizza bianca; Gianni Cavaletti for the generous assistance with recipes, the millefoglie and the anecdotes; the team at Pasticceria Sacchetti; the norcini at Iacozilli; Massimo Arnese, baker at La Renella, for the flour and the tips; the Giolitti family and their excellent ice-cream makers at legendary Giolitti; Angelo Troiani, chef and co-owner of Il Convivio, and Agata Parisella, chef and co-owner of Agata e Romeo, for the amatriciana and the onions; the Alongi brothers and crew of Il Gelato di San Crispino, for the ice cream and the recipes and the precious time; Dr. Fabrizio Crespi, gourmet water engineer at ANEA; Dr. Jeremy Cherfas, science writer, and Stefano Padulosi, hulled wheat expert, at the International Plant Genetic Resources Institute (IPGRI), for their help with farro; Mario Mozzetti of Alfredo alla Scrofa, for the fettuccine and the friendly chat; Simona Patrizi for her recipes, and Fabio, Sandro and Luca at the Tortuga Bar for the coffee; historian Caterina Napoleone for Fellini and the snails; Loraine Toth for testing and eating with appetite; Garth Bixler for the stuffed lettuce and Steven Barclay for eating it so many times; Carole and Frank Lalli for their friendship and encouragement; Ulderico Munzi for that unforgettable flight, and for the other time; Andrew Dalby for artichokes and cherries, good cheer and scholarship; Dr. Graziano Ruffini for the many etymologies and wonderful communiqués; Ida Boncioli for saving me from allergies, and sharing her cookbooks; Carmen Scarpitta for the hospitality; Professor Massimo Bacigalupo for G. G. Belli; Raffaele Fiore, Paris president of Laziali nel Mondo, and Eleanor Bertino, for sharing their address books; Silvana Mangione, a helpful Roman in New York; Harriet Welty and Philippe Rochefort for tasting and testing; Eveline Taylor for the shopping, sharing and warmth; Stefania Barzini and Mita Vicavio for the views, the visits and the encouragement; Maria Cristina Biagi, curator of the Museo dei Poeti Romaneschi, for the books and the research; Efisio Espa for the learned views on Roman cooking and chefs.

INTRODUCTION

The Cooking of Rome

CLOSE YOUR EYES and imagine you're in Rome, seated al fresco in the sun on a rooftop terrace, smack in the center of town. Michelangelo did the decor on the Palazzo Farnese, framing the square below, and an ancient Roman sculptor, followed by several Renaissance architects, handled the mossy bathtub fountains poised like chess pieces in front of it. You hear the water splashing, accompanied by operatic voices and spluttering Vespas. It's early spring so there's still a bite in the air, but a thousand rooftop terraces and sidewalk tables already are filled with eager eaters. What, after all, can beat tucking into the pyramids of stuffed zucchini flowers fried golden in olive oil, the mounds of fresh fava beans and Pecorino Romano cheese, the braised artichokes *alla romana* and platters of rosemary-perfumed spring suckling lamb arranged before you? The answer is simple: Nothing.

Easy to make, good for you, gutsy, flavorful and fun to eat—that's my one-line definition of Roman food. This cookbook brings you the luscious cuisine of the Eternal City, a rich culinary heritage built up over the last 2,800 years.

The enduring cliché that "all roads lead to Rome" should have a corollary: Roman food has traveled down all roads. You might not realize it, but you've probably been enjoying Roman specialties for years. That's because some of the classics of Italian cooking come from Rome and the surrounding Latium region: bruschetta, *spaghetti alla carbonara, bucatini all'amatriciana,* fettuccine Alfredo, saltimbocca, buttery *crostata* (jam tart), *tartufo* (ice cream) and zabaglione. There are dozens more recipes of equal excellence in the Roman repertoire, and I hope you will be enticed to try them, too.

It's important to note that Roman food includes ingredients from many parts of Italy, notably Parmigiano-Reggiano and mascarpone cheeses from the north, balsamic vinegar from Modena, marsala from Sicily, pork products from Norcia to the northeast, fish from the Adriatic, San Marzano tomatoes from the Naples area and *savoiardi* (ladyfingers) from the Valle d'Aosta, bordering France. Rome's cooking has been enriched by an overlay of influences, with several shared recipes from the adjoining regions of Campania, Abruzzi, Tuscany and Umbria. Above all, it encompasses specialties from throughout Latium (*il Lazio* in Italian), a pocket-size region wrapped around the city. Roman cooking is Lazio cooking adopted and adapted by the capital's cooks. The result: You needn't stray beyond the city walls to experience the regional foods of Viterbo, La Tuscia and Sabina north of Rome; Amatrice and Rieti to the east; the Alban Hills, Ciociaria, Latina, Gaeta and Frosinone to the south. Thousands of provincials from these districts have been pouring in and out of town for the last three millennia, bringing with them a bounty of produce and cooking styles. Consequently, the food of Rome includes anchovies, shark or dogfish, skate, scorpion fish, squid, octopus and mussels from the Mediterranean coast 10 miles from Rome at Ostia. Lamb and ewe's milk cheeses, including Pecorino Romano, come from the rolling pasturelands that make much of Lazio look like a dreamy golf course. Cow's or water buffalo's milk mozzarella arrives daily from the hills of inland Frosinone or coastal Sperlonga, both south of Rome. The farmers of the rich fields of Fondi, a flat farm town on the way to Naples, and the volcanic Alban Hills overlooking Rome, flood the city's markets daily, year-round, with pale green, fluted Romanesco zucchini and their flowers, broccoli, broccoli rabe and peas. Olive groves spread from Lake Bolsena, bordering Tuscany, to Gaeta, edging Campania. Market gardens in the city's suburbs supply fresh herbs—spearmint, basil, rosemary, sage—plus several kinds of chicory and the numerous varieties of lettuces and field greens that go into *misticanza* salad (see page 244). The towns of Ladispoli to the north and Sezze to the south vie for the title of "Artichoke Capital" of Lazio. Artichokes are a Roman specialty, not to say an obsession. There are dozens of recipes for them. Thanks to imports from other regions, plus hothouse production, they're available year-round, and just in case the supply of fresh or pickled artichokes happens to run out, every Roman liqueur or medicine cabinet contains a bottle of the artichoke-based, dark, bitter and aromatic digestive liqueur called Cynar, or that other perennial favorite, Fernet-Branca, also made with artichoke essence.

Despite the inevitable social and economic upheavals Rome has undergone in its long history as a capital city, the cooking remains largely traditional. Historians point out that almost none of the dishes the ancient Romans ate are still prepared in the same way today, but many of the ancient cooking techniques, flavor combinations and favorite ingredients of centuries past are still popular. Take the celebrated ancient condiment *garum,* made from partly fermented anchovies or other fish mixed with sea salt. Romans today use salted anchovies (usually desalted and soaked in olive oil) to jazz up countless recipes. Country folk in the time of the emperors made dough, rolled it into various shapes, dried it, then tossed it into soups to thicken them. This proto-pasta was called *tracta,* and Romans today emulate their forebears by thickening their soups with *pasta asciutta*—dry pasta. Eating habits are similar, too. The ancient Romans organized their menus much like contemporary Romans, calling the courses *gustum* (*antipasti*), *mensa prima* (*primi*), *mensa secunda* (*secondi*), with the *dulcis in fundo* (a surprise sweet or *dolce* at the end). Romans reach over the millennia to share a passion for pork fresh and cured, Pecorino Romano cheese, a wide range of herbs, grilled meats, bittersweet combinations, stuffing, eggs, frittatas, certain vegetables (fava beans and chickpeas, cardoons, chicory, zucchini and their flowers) and fruit (cherries, figs), pizza and flatbread. If you want to see how the Romans made bread two thousand years ago, just ride a streetcar to the monumental city gate called Porta Maggiore and, as you slink by the so-called Baker's Tomb, take a look at the low-relief sculptures. Then step into any bakery and buy a round *ciambella* loaf, seemingly lifted off the tomb. The ancient Romans were as obsessed as modern-day greengrocers about not letting their vegetables (especially artichokes) oxidize while being prepared, so they used *aqua nitrata* (natron) just as Romans today employ lemony water to achieve the same results. I give a recipe for wine-dunking cookies (see page 267) called *ciambelline* that's only a couple hundred years old; the older version, possibly from Imperial times, used concentrated grape must instead of young Frascati wine for the flavoring.

The sources of written recipes and descriptions of ancient Roman foods and lifestyles are many. Cato wrote the farming treatise *De agricultura* in circa 180 B.C., giving, among other things, a recipe for the first documented layer cake. Columella wrote *De re rustica*, another agricultural treatise with many recipes, between A.D. 35 and A.D. 45. It was published in A.D. 60 and from it we can learn much about Roman foods and early wine-making. Marcus Gavius Apicius was the first-century author of the widely quoted *De re coquinaria* (sometimes erroneously given as *De arte coquinaria*). In reality the book is a ninth-century copy of a fourth- or fifth-century compilation of the original two-part, ten-volume work, which was lost. The title in English is usually *The Art of Cooking*, but for the sake of precision, I refer to it with its most widely accepted Latin name. A mine of culinary information, the writings of Apicius influenced umpteen generations of cooks throughout Europe. Pliny the Elder lived from A.D. 23 to A.D. 79 and wrote the *Naturalis historia*. Among other remarkable things, Pliny credited Apicius with the invention of foie gras (Apicius force-fed geese with figs, *ficatum* in Latin, from which comes the modern Italian word *fegato* and the French *foie*). It's not known when Petronius was born; he committed suicide in A.D. 66, having won fame for writing the Satyricon, with its famous banquet scene, "Trimalchio's Feast," set during the reign of Emperor Nero (A.D. 54 to A.D. 68). Petronius has taught historians much about feasting rituals and, incidentally, inspired Federico Fellini to make his wild 1969 film, *Fellini Satyricon*. The poet Martial lived circa A.D. 40 to A.D. 104. Author of a collection of works entitled *Epigrams*, he described Roman festivals and banquets galore. Of considerable importance as a source on Roman food was Juvenal. This poet and irreverent jokester lived from circa A.D. 60 to A.D. 130. His *Satires* poked fun at imperial excesses, above all the gluttony for which upper-class ancient Romans were renowned.

What survived the barbarian invasions as the Roman Empire fell was the even older, and extremely simple, cooking of the Etruscan shepherds and swineherds who inhabited the region before the Romans arrived. It's the base upon which the Roman peasant cooking of the Middle Ages and succeeding periods, broadly called *cucina povera* (poor people's food), was built. Contemporary Roman historian Caterina Napoleon calls this economical, survivalist cuisine "siege-cooking," because embattled post-Imperial Romans in their walled city, cut off from the rest of Italy for centuries, fed on whatever they could grow or gather within Rome's towering walls. That included chicory, figs, wild mint, bay, capers, courtyard animals, Tiber fish and eels, plus the goats, sheep and cows pastured until the late 1800s in the Forum, known for a thousand years as Campo Vaccino—the cow pasture. In the nineteenth century, as Rome shook off the shackles of the Papal States and grew into the capital of an industrialized nation, the working class and specifically the slaughterhouse workers of the Testaccio neighborhood on the then-southern edge of town created their own cooking style, cryptically dubbed *Quinto-Quarto* (the Fifth Quarter), based on organ meats, oxtails and cheap cuts totaling about a quarter of the animal's weight.

With the exception of a few recipes, the rich cuisine of the Vatican's papal court has never stuck, changing as it does with the comings and goings of popes and cardinals. Early papal cookbooks such as *De honesta voluptate et valetudine,* published in Rome in 1474 and written by Bartolomeo Sacchi, alias Platina, chef of Pope Sixtus IV, or *l'Opera* (1570) by Bartolomeo Scappi, "secret chef of Pope Pious V," had enormous influence in the courts of Europe. But like the writings of Apicius, these cookbooks were not targeted at either a popular or what we'd now call a middle-class audience and consequently had little trickle-down effect. The Papal States' true legacy in Rome is the canonical calendar of lean days and feast days: On Fridays, Christmas Eve and throughout the 40 days of Lent, strict Roman Catholics still eat fish or other lean foods, while during carnival anything goes (*carne vale* means "meat's okay").

Rome is a luscious layer cake of civilizations, each layer melding into the next without ever fully covering it or canceling the past. Perhaps the greatest single force in maintaining culinary traditions over the city's 2,800-year history has been the Roman-Jewish community. Its members have handed down dozens of recipes, some of them very old. Fried artichokes (*Carciofi alla Giudia,* page 37) is only the best known of them. Many other favorites that are either straight out of the Roman-Jewish tradition or inspired by it and believed by Romans to be of Jewish origin include fried stuffed zucchini flowers (*Fiori di Zucca Fritti,* page 46), artichokes braised in white wine and olive oil (*Carciofi alla Romana,* page 34), semolina gnocchi with butter and cheese (*Gnocchi di Semolino alla Romana,* page

68), spaghetti with tuna and dried porcini (*Spaghetti alla Carrettiera*, page 112), risotto with curly endive (*Risotto con l'Indivia*, page 129), anchovy gratin (*Graté di Alici o Sogliole*, page 194), sweet-and-sour salt cod (*Baccalà in Agrodolce alla Romana*, page 198), stuffed lettuce (*Lattughe Farcite*, page 234), pan-fried zucchini (*Concia di Zucchine*, page 251) and ricotta cheesecake (*Torta Ebraica di Ricotta*, page 294).

Like many subject peoples subdued by the ancient Romans, Jews first came to Rome in large numbers as prisoners of war following the annexation of their lands by General Pompey the Great in the first century B.C. The Roman-Jewish community grew and flourished under Herod Agrippa II, a prince who moved from Judea to Rome with his entourage around A.D. 70, after Titus's destruction of Jerusalem. The original Jewish neighborhood in Rome stretched along the Tiber River's west bank in Trastevere and remained focused there until the thirteenth century. By the time Pope Paul IV created the infamous walled Ghetto across the river from Trastevere, in central Rome, in 1556, most of Rome's Jews had already shifted into the Ghetto area. The Ghetto is defined today as the city block where the synagogue stands, and the surrounding streets sandwiched between the Theater of Marcellus, Via Arenula and the Tiber River. Rome's Jews were locked up there after sunset each night, suffering periods of persecution and poverty alternated with periods of tolerance and prosperity. The original Jewish population that arrived from Judea in ancient Roman times was supplemented but not supplanted over the centuries, particularly in the 1400s to 1600s, by Sephardim and Ashkenazim from other Mediterranean countries and central and eastern Europe. The Ghetto's walls came down in 1848, and the wrecker's ball removed much of the area's medieval architecture in the decades that followed, in part to make way for the synagogue. The Jews of Rome again experienced horrors and deportation during Fascism and the Nazi occupation. But some families held out and the spirit of this age-old community lives on, though most Roman Jews now live scattered around town and have fully integrated into Italian society.

The cooking of Rome is the product of a continuum stretching back millennia, but Romans began codifying their urban home cooking and regional peasant recipes only about two hundred years ago. Astoundingly, most of the dishes the Roman dialect poet Giuseppe Gioachino Belli describes in his sonnets written in the 1830s and 1840s are still popular today. Of the 225 Roman recipes collected in legendary cookbook writer Ada Boni's seminal 1929 *La cucina romana,* you'll still find perhaps 150 on Roman tables. But loving and respecting certain venerable recipes and cooking techniques doesn't mean Romans are hidebound traditionalists. When Romans speak of tradition, they mean the transmission from the past of elements worth preserving. They are not advocates of a rigid traditionalism, a retrograde fixation with the past and fear of the present and future. Roman food is lighter and more healthful now than it was in ancient times, or in Belli's and Boni's day. Olive oil has replaced suet across the board, meats are leaner than before, cooking times reflect a rediscovered respect for ingredients' natural qualities, and the sheer volume and richness of foods of all kinds have been reduced without compromising their lusciousness.

How to Compose a Roman Meal

Happily almost every component of a Roman meal can be plucked from the shelves of American supermarkets, produce stands and Italian specialty shops, and those that can't are easily substituted. A list of sources at the back of the book will help you to buy premium products and to track down the handful of them that can pose a challenge for some shoppers. Many ingredients the Romans and other central and southern Italians use lie at the foundation of Italian-American cooking: plum or cherry tomatoes, hot chili pepper, zucchini, salted capers and anchovies, Pecorino Romano and Parmigiano-Reggiano cheeses, table olives and extra-virgin olive oil, and a myriad of pasta shapes, including the globe's two most popular and most deeply Roman, spaghetti and fettuccine. What you cook is as good as the ingredients you use, so buy only the best.

No special tools are needed to make any of these recipes, unless you want to buy a square *tonnarelli* extruder die or cutting attachment for your pasta machine. Romans are physical, lusty cooks who do an awful lot by hand, from crushing garlic to deboning anchovies; shredding hot chili peppers; seeding and peeling sweet peppers and tomatoes; kneading dough for pasta, pizza and bread; pinching and rolling out lifesaver-shaped dunking cookies; smashing ripe fruit with a wooden spoon for *cremolato* and hand-molding ice-cream "potatoes" (studded with finger-broken bits of chocolate) and then calling them "truffles." That's why wherever appropriate I give a manual version of the recipe, plus instructions on how to achieve the same or better results with a food processor, standing mixer or other modern kitchen appliance. Throughout I refer to primary sources—home cooks and professionals of all kinds—because I want this book to be a photograph of Rome's cooking traditions today, and also because of the peculiar nature of many Italian cookbooks. The first guiding principle of most Roman food writers and anyone involved in kitchen tasks appears to be *quanto basta,* abbreviated as QB, meaning "as much as needed." The second is *come al solito,* "the usual way." Naturally these genial glosses have ancient roots. In Apicius's recipe #184 for lentils with chestnuts, he blithely writes: "*si quid deest, addes.*" If something's missing, add it. I wish life were that simple. Roman cooks generally make notes and lists. With few exceptions, most of their cookbooks are glorified scrapbooks or rosters of ingredients, usually incomplete, without reference to tools, technique or timing because, after all, you're expected to know what to do when and how, the way your grandmother did. A typical example is Valentina Sassara, a wonderful home cook who lives north of Rome on Lake Bolsena and makes everything from preserves, pickles and pastry to cured pork products entirely by hand, from scratch. When Valentina dusted off her personal collection of recipes, carefully copied from countless sources into an old agenda, I went through each, step-by-step with her, filling in the pieces of what would otherwise have been a culinary conundrum. My approach was to systematically compare the classic Roman recipes in their various incarnations in a dozen or more Italian or Roman cookbooks, then rework them, testing and retesting them in Rome and in the United States.

Some recipes collected here come from *trattorie*—the city's quintessential family-style eating establishments—restaurants, delis, creameries and bakeries, but that doesn't mean they're difficult to make or fussy. The first thing I asked chefs, butchers, bakers, pastry chefs and other pros was, "How would you make this at home?" Usually they answered, "This *is* the way we make it at home—there's no difference." In fact, Roman professional cooks are just as apt as Roman grandmothers to keep traditions alive. Whereas French restaurant cuisine descended from the cooking of the royal court, Italian food, in general, and the Roman trattoria, restaurant or food-artisan recipes I've included here, in particular, are humble, homey and straightforward.

I present the recipes course by course, as they would most likely appear on a Roman trattoria menu. That's because in Rome you really do eat in a trattoria as you do at home,

from appetizer to starter, main dish and vegetable side to fruit and dessert. The Italian
terms for this tantalizing succession of
courses are *antipasti, primi, secondi, contorni, frutta*
and *dolci.* Tidily dividing dishes is a habit with
roots several thousand years deep, prefigured
by the Latin expression "*Ab ovo usque ad malum*"
(from the egg to the apple), the soup to the
nuts, or, put in layman's terms, the whole she-
bang in careful order. Some of the antipasti

Cavaletti's recipe book

included here arguably could be placed among the vegetable sides—fried or
braised artichokes, for instance. When served generously, all of the pastas,
soups and rice-based dishes listed as *primi* can be served as *secondi* (main courses). Nothing prevents you from eating your *rustici* (turnovers) filled with spinach and ricotta not as
antipasti but as starters or even main courses. I've followed Roman tradition in the recipe
breakdown because it makes sense and reflects my personal taste when I cook a multiple-
course meal. The proportions of individual servings are gauged accordingly and are devised as part of a crescendo of dishes, with the total servings per recipe based on
practicality and enjoyment. For instance, I prefer frying small quantities of whole artichokes or mixed seafood, to maintain perfect control of the oil temperature and get the
food to the table crisp and piping hot. To me, making perfect carbonara for more than
four is a challenge I can live without. Each recipe therefore is devised for an ideal yield
and serving number. Most will satisfy four to six eaters, while a few for big-batch foods
like bread, pickled produce, stews, sauces, cookies and especially *pizza bianca* (flatbread),
which ideally should be made in bakery-sized quantities, will serve eight to ten.

The uninhibited animation around Roman tables is part of what makes the eating
experience so pleasant. Conviviality is a great condiment; you can rarely use too much of
it. It's the hidden ingredient in all the recipes I've chosen, something you'll have to supply yourself.

When I had doubts about classic Roman recipes, ingredients or the traditional way
of putting together a Roman meal, I asked my mother, Romana Anzi-Downie, for guid-

ance. She taught me the basics of cooking as soon as I grew tall enough to stir the pot of bubbling *garofolato* (beef stew) (see page 146) for Tuesday dinner, leftovers of which became pasta sauce for the great Wednesday spaghetti feed at our Bay Area home. She let me punch and push the pasta dough around on the kneading board built into our kitchen while she told me about her food-loving father's friendship with Alfredo Di Lelio of fettuccine Alfredo fame (see page 104), and how in the 1930s she ate with maestro Alfredo's solid gold fork and spoon. My mother's name tells a tale too long to recount in these pages: Roman by birth and upbringing (*romana*), married to a GI named Charles Downie who wound up in Rome in 1944. My mother has lived, cooked and worked as an artist and teacher in northern California since 1950, with a brief interlude back in her native city in the mid-1960s with children in tow. That's when I came, saw and was conquered by Rome, discovering a culinary bounty I could scarcely imagine in San Francisco, even with the benefit of an Italian immigrant mother who hit the specialty shops of North Beach several times a week for bottled artichokes, canned plum tomatoes, salt cod, skate, shark and tripe—her personal talismans of happiness. Since those magical childhood years, I have lived on and off in Rome and in other Italian cities or villages and have always delighted in cooking Roman specialties wherever I might find myself. My wife, Alison Harris, took the photographs that illustrate this book and helped to test the recipes and improve the manuscript, drawing on her knowledge of and love for Rome, where she lived for six idyllic years while growing up. We hope *Cooking the Roman Way* expresses our passion for Rome and its food and conveys a sense of the natural enthusiasm of Romans for the daily rituals of the table.

COOKING THE
ROMAN WAY

Pizza bianca, fresh out of the oven at Roscioli Bakery

ANTIPASTI

APPETIZERS

THE ANCIENT ROMANS often started a banquet meal with a *gustum,* an appetite-stimulator or appetizer, what contemporary Romans would refer to in standard Italian as an antipasto or a *stuzzichino,* or, in *Romanaccio* dialect, a *svogliatura.* The term antipasto simply means "something eaten before the main meal" and covers a pan-Italian selection of preparations, from cured pork to pickled fish, vegetables preserved in olive oil to baked goods. A *stuzzichino* is an appetizer or hors d'oeuvre that you pick at with your fingers or a toothpick; that's what the verb *stuzzicare* means. Such items would include olives, chunks of salami or cheese, crostini and other finger foods. The most Roman of the three terms, used only in the city and its region, *svogliatura* refers to any of the above eaten either before a meal or as a snack; *svogliare* means to satisfy hunger or quench thirst. Hors d'oeuvres is what we would call them. *Svogliature* and *stuzzichini* are the specialty of Rome's *osterie* (wine bars), which also serve simple food, institutions that in various incarnations have been around for centuries and predate the trattoria.

The most typically Roman and popular of all *osteria* hors d'oeuvres are sweet-and-sour pearl onions (see *Cipolline in Agrodolce alla Romana,* page 5) and tiny artichokes bathed in olive oil (see *Carciofini Sott'Olio,* page 42). Salted anchovies on thin slices of buttered bread and toasted crostini with melted anchovy butter are two other favorites. The list of authentically Roman antipasti is short and includes several recipes that are difficult if not impossible to reproduce outside the region let alone in the United States, and are therefore not in this cookbook. Among them are eel or *lattarini* (a kind of sand smelt) flash-fried, then pickled in vinegar for up to two weeks, and snails from the vineyards of the Alban Hills in a garlicky tomato sauce.

Besides the salted anchovies referred to above, and platters of raw mollusks and shellfish squirted with lemon juice, Roman fish appetizers are limited to battered and fried salt cod fillets sprinkled with salt (*filetti di baccalà*) and a handful of more or less authentically regional seafood salads of recent invention. I've included one such salad of shrimp and calamari (*Insalata di Gamberetti e Calimaretti,* page 48) because it uses authentic Roman seasonings, such as bay and black peppercorns, mixed with local produce, and therefore stands out from other, similar recipes made up and down the coasts of Italy.

Romans adore three vegetable antipasti, in particular: braised or fried artichokes (see *Carciofi alla Romana,* page 34 and *Carciofi alla Giudia,* page 37) and zucchini flowers stuffed with mozzarella and anchovy (see *Fiori di Zucca Fritti,* page 46). Simple antipasti not unique to Rome but enjoyed here nonetheless are platters of translucent Parma ham with sliced cantaloupe melon, and thickly sliced rounds of salami (the local variety is called *corallina*) flanked by fresh figs, mounds of freshly shelled fava beans, or pecan-sized chunks of aged or fresh pecorino sheep's cheese.

Baked goods hold pride of place: Romans consume extravagant quantities of *pizza bianca* (olive oil–perfumed flatbread), served plain or with various toppings, and *rustici* (turnovers) filled with such delicacies as ricotta and spinach. *Rustici* double as snacks, or a light lunch food, served instead of a *panino* or *tramezzino* (sandwich).

Cipolline in Agrodolce alla Romana

SWEET-AND-SOUR BABY PEARL ONIONS, ROMAN STYLE

1½ pounds fresh pearl onions

2 cloves garlic

2 tablespoons extra-virgin olive oil

¾ cup white wine vinegar

¼ cup balsamic vinegar

Water

Kosher salt or coarse sea salt

1 tablespoon sugar

SERVES 4

One of the classics of the Roman trattoria and *osteria* (wine-bar-cum-eatery) repertoire, this recipe makes an addictive, thirst-inducing *svogliatura* (snack) served in a bowl bristling with toothpicks. The ancient Romans loved onions, garlic, olive oil and vinegar. It's just possible this concoction has been around since Hannibal wowed the legions with his elephants. Some contemporary Romans, like our friend Anna Mangioli, a home cook and part-time guard at the ancient ruins of Trajan's Market (a temporary art exhibition space nowadays), make huge batches of *cipolline* and store them in jars of vinegar, a process known as *sott'aceto*. The vinegar creates tartness and astringency, so much so that if you eat more than half a dozen onions at a time—and I usually gobble twice that many—they will pucker your mouth. That's why I prefer this recipe for small batches of fresh sweet-and-sour onions made with a mix of white wine and balsamic vinegars diluted with water.

1   Cut the root-end off the onions. Pick up each onion with the fingertips of one hand and with the other hand use the knife to gently lift the flaky skin and remove it with a spinning motion. Rinse the onions in a colander under cold running water. If you find the peel difficult to remove, blanch the onions in boiling water for 2 to 3 minutes. Run cold water over them until they are easy to handle. The peel should slip off easily.

2   Peel the garlic, removing any green shoots and imperfections, and mince it with three of the onions.

3   Heat the oil in a medium-sized nonreactive pot over medium-low heat. Add the minced onions and garlic and sauté until the garlic begins to brown, 2 to 3 minutes.

4   Add the whole peeled onions, and sauté for 2 minutes, stirring with a wooden spoon or spatula. Pour in the vinegars and enough water to barely cover the onions. Add a large pinch of salt and the sugar. Stir while bringing the liquids to a boil. Lower the heat to minimum and simmer, covered, until the onions are tender when poked with a fork, 15 to 20 minutes.

5   With a slotted spoon or spatula, transfer the onions to a serving dish. Increase the heat to high and reduce the onion juices and vinegar, stirring often, until the liquid is thick but not syrupy, 15 to 20 minutes.

6   Spoon the juices over the onions and serve warm or chilled. You can keep the onions for up to a week in the refrigerator in a sealed container.

Good cooking in a Roman trattoria is not merely
a necessity, but a philosophical imperative.

William Murray, *Italy: The Fatal Gift*

Supplì al Telefono

FRIED TOMATO-FLAVORED RICE CROQUETTES WITH MOZZARELLA AND HAM

1 carrot

1 small onion

1 celery stalk

2 small tomatoes

2 cloves

3 tablespoons extra-virgin olive oil

Salt and freshly ground black pepper

Water

Pinch of sugar

2 tablespoons (1 ounce or ¼ stick) butter

1 cup rice, preferably carnaroli, arborio, vialone nano or other high-quality Italian risotto rice

4 ounces prosciutto cotto (Italian boiled ham)

2 heaping tablespoons freshly grated Parmigiano-Reggiano

1 (4-ounce) fresh mozzarella ball, preferably *fior di latte*

1 large egg, at room temperature

6 to 8 heaping tablespoons coarsely ground polenta or fine bread crumbs

Olive oil for frying

SERVES 6 (10 TO 12 CROQUETTES)

Roman fry-shops, snack bars, school cafeterias and *tavole calde* dispense thousands of these potato-shaped croquettes daily. You have to eat them hot, with your fingers. When you bite into them, the melted mozzarella makes a taffylike cord that resembles—according to locals—a telephone cord, so that you and the croquette are on the phone: *al telefono.* The name hints at the period when *supplì* became popular: the 1950s. Most Italians had no access to telephones until then. Suddenly their rice croquettes were talking! Once upon a time, grandma made them with leftover risotto, stuffing them with just about anything edible: tomato or meat sauce, ham, chicken. Surprise! And that's where the first part of the name comes from: *supplì* is a bastardization of the French word *surprise,* which entered the Roman vocabulary with Napoleon and his troops circa 1797—truly a surprising event.

1   Peel the carrot and onion and remove the stringy parts of the celery. Roughly chop the tomatoes, carrot, onion and celery and combine them in a food processor. Crush the cloves with the blade of a knife and toss them in with the vegetables. Process for 1 minute to make a runny paste.

2   Heat the 3 tablespoons oil in a large pot over medium-low heat. Add the vegetable mixture, a generous pinch each of salt and pepper and sauté for 10 minutes, stirring often.

3   Bring a kettle of water to a boil.

4   Add the sugar and butter to the vegetables, stirring until the butter melts. Stir in the rice, sautéing for 1 minute, and cover it with boiling water. Lower the heat and simmer, stirring occasionally, until the rice is tender, about 25 minutes.

5   With a wooden spoon or spatula, scoop out the risotto and spread it to cool on a baking sheet for 1 hour, or chill it in the refrigerator for 30 minutes.

6   Mince the ham. You should have ¾ cup. Scatter the ham and Parmigiano-Reggiano over the cooled risotto. Work the cheese and ham into the risotto with your fingers.

7   Drain the mozzarella and slice it into sticks about 2 inches long and ¾ inch thick.

8   Beat the egg in a small bowl. Pour the polenta into a second small bowl. Cover a large platter with waxed paper.

9   Make one *supplì* at a time. Scoop up a handful of risotto and form it into a tight oval about 3 inches long and 1½ inches thick. With your index finger, poke a hole about 2½ inches deep into the center of the lump. Insert 1 mozzarella stick and seal the end, squeezing gently to compact it. Dunk the *supplì* in the beaten egg and roll it in the polenta until thoroughly coated. Place it on the platter. Repeat until the risotto and mozzarella are used up. Loosely cover the *supplì* with plastic wrap and chill them for at least 1 hour, preferably overnight.

10 Pour about 2 inches of oil into a narrow, high-sided frying pan or saucepan. Heat over medium-low heat to 325° F, or use a deep fryer set to 325° F. To check the oil temperature approximately without a thermometer, flick a drop of water onto the surface, making sure you don't get splattered. The water should sizzle, dance and evaporate within seconds. Do not allow the oil to smoke.

11 Cover a large platter with several layers of paper towels.

12   With tongs, lower one *supplì* at a time into the hot oil, frying batches of three to five *supplì,* turning often, for about 5 minutes. Transfer the fried *supplì* to the paper towels to absorb excess oil.

13   Serve hot.

NOTE: In Italy, mozzarella made with cow's milk is called *fior di latte*. According to Italian law, only mozzarella made with water-buffalo milk can be sold as mozzarella. Water-buffalo-milk mozzarella has a lot more liquid and fat (8–9 percent compared to 3–4 percent) and consequently a shorter shelf life than the cow's-milk product. That and the cost are why most Romans use *fior di latte* for cooking and buy buffalo mozzarella as a table cheese. Good *fior di latte* is increasingly easy to find in America but travel-shy buffalo-milk mozzarella remains problematic, turning soft and acidic in a matter of days. The essential thing is to buy top-quality fresh water-buffalo-milk mozzarella or *fior di latte* and avoid industrial, rubbery imitations, which aren't appropriate for the recipes in this book.

Farro: How's it Spelt?

Farro is a variety of hulled wheat, a group of primitive grains grown since neolithic times and widely used by the ancient Romans. The first polenta was made from farro. The word gives us the modern term *farina,* meaning flour. Italy is probably the only place in the Western world where farro has been cultivated continuously for the last two thousand years, though similar grains grow throughout the Mediterranean and Middle East, especially in Syria.

According to the International Plant Genetic Resources Institute (IPGRI), an independent, international research institution, there are basically three kinds of hulled wheat that can go into Italian farro, and this gives rise to considerable confusion when it comes to marketing the grain.

Farro medio (medium farro) is called emmer or starch grain in English. Its Latin binomial is *Triticum dicoccum* or *dicoccon.* It's grown in the Garfagnana region of northern Tuscany and in the Latium and Abruzzi regions. This is the kind of farro you want: It works in any recipe for farro you'll find in any cookbook.

Here's where the confusion arises: In the northern United States and Canada, *Triticum spelta,* or spelt, has become an important crop, thanks to the organic food industry. This is the kind of hulled wheat often sold in health food stores labeled as "spelt," "*dinkel*" (its German name), or, less helpfully, farro. It has very low gluten content and, unlike emmer, does not make a starchy paste. North American growers go out of their way to advertise it as the same thing as Italian farro, which is confusing, since it is in fact only one of the three main varieties of farro and has limited uses. Don't get me wrong: Spelt is delicious. But anyone who cooks and compares American spelt and Italian emmer will soon discover that the difference goes beyond the spelling.

Of course, there's more to this tale; each of the main types of farro has dozens of variants. If you're interested in this grain's fascinating story, from its agricultural history to disputes about its modern taxonomy, you can order *Hulled Wheat, Proceedings of the First International Workshop on Hulled Wheats,* a detailed, 262-page report published by International Plant Genetic Resources Institute, 142 Via delle Sette Chiese, 00145 Rome, Italy (*www.ipgri.cgiar.org*).

Arancini di Farro alla Volpetti

FARRO RISOTTO BALLS WITH BASIL AND PARMIGIANO-REGGIANO

8 ounces whole Italian imported farro (*Triticum dicoccum,* or emmer) (1 cup)

1 carrot

1 celery stalk

1 small onion

1 clove garlic

2 tablespoons extra-virgin olive oil

Salt and freshly ground black pepper

Water

6 tablespoons minced fresh flat-leaf parsley

¾ cup minced fresh basil

6 heaping tablespoons freshly grated Parmigiano-Reggiano

3 large eggs, at room temperature

1 cup coarsely ground polenta or fine bread crumbs

Olive oil for frying

SERVES 6 TO 8 (12 TO 15 ARANCINI)

Arancini are a Sicilian specialty made with rice. They are called "little oranges," not because of their color, but because of their shape and golf-ball size. *Arancini di farro* are made with farro, a primitive kind of hulled wheat. The farro is cooked like rice to make a risotto-style paste redolent of basil and parsley. It's then cooled and rolled into balls that are fried golden in olive oil. Claudio and Emilio Volpetti, co-owners of the celebrated Volpetti delicatessen and *tavola calda* in Rome's Testaccio neighborhood, and their head chef, Donato Salzarulo, invented this recipe a decade or so ago. Their *arancini di farro* are now widely imitated.

1   Rinse the farro in a basin in several changes of cold water. Skim off and discard any chaff or husks. Strain through a sieve and rinse the farro under cold running water for several minutes, turning and stirring with your fingers.

Emilio and Claudio Volpetti (foreground)

2   Peel the carrot and remove the stringy parts of the celery. Roughly chop both and combine them in a food processor. Peel the onion and garlic, removing the garlic's green shoots. Chop and add them to the food processor. Process for 30 to 45 seconds to form a runny paste.

3   Heat the 2 tablespoons oil in a large pot on medium-low. Add the vegetable mixture and a generous pinch each of salt and pepper. Sauté, stirring often, for 5 to 6 minutes, or as long as it takes to boil a kettle of water.

4   Bring a large kettle of water to a boil. Add 6 cups boiling water to the vegetable mixture. Increase the heat to high and bring the mixture to a boil.

5   Add the parsley. Add the farro, stir thoroughly, cover the pot, and bring the mixture to a boil. Cook, covered, over medium heat for 15 minutes. Lower the heat to minimum and simmer, stirring often, for 45 minutes. It should have the consistency of creamy oatmeal or thick risotto and almost hold the spoon or spatula upright. If it becomes too dry, add warm water $1/4$ cup at a time.

6   Stir in the basil and remove the pot from the heat. Stir in 2 heaping tablespoons of the Parmigiano-Reggiano.

7   With the wooden spoon or spatula, scoop out the farro and spread it to cool on a baking sheet for 1 to $1^{1}/_{2}$ hours. Sprinkle the remaining 4 heaping tablespoons of Parmigiano-Reggiano over the farro.

8   Beat the eggs in a small bowl with a generous pinch each of salt and pepper. Pour the polenta into another small bowl. Cover a large platter with waxed paper.

9   Make one *arancino* at a time. Scoop up a handful of farro and form it into a tight ball the size of a golf ball. Dunk it in the beaten eggs and roll it in the polenta until coated. Place it on the waxed paper. Repeat until the farro is used up. Loosely cover the *arancini* with plastic wrap and refrigerate for at least 1 hour, preferably overnight.

10 Pour about 2 inches of oil into a narrow, high-sided frying pan and heat it to 325° F, or use a deep fryer set to 325° F. To check the oil temperature without a thermometer, flick a drop of water onto the surface, making sure you don't get splattered. The water should sizzle, dance and evaporate within seconds.

11 Cover a large platter with several layers of paper towels. With tongs, lower one to three *arancini* at a time into the hot oil. Fry until golden and crispy outside, 3 to 5 minutes, turning several times. Transfer the fried *arancini* to the paper towels to absorb excess oil.

12 Let the *arancini* cool to room temperature before serving. Cover the *arancini* with a clean cloth or dish towel, and you can keep them for several days; there is no need to refrigerate them.

Torta Salata con Olive e Prosciutto Cotto
ROMAN EASTERTIDE BREAD WITH OLIVES AND BOILED HAM

Romans have a charming, subtle way of saying that a person is nice, simple and decent—someone whom we might describe as "the salt of the earth." The saying is *buono come il pane:* "as good as bread." Romans are sociable people. The words "company" and "companion" in most Western languages derive from the Latin *cum panis,* meaning, literally, "with bread." Italians in their various dialects designate whatever they eat as a *companatico,* something to eat with bread. It's said that people do not live on bread alone. But here is a Roman loaf that might make the pundits rethink old sayings. This is bread and more. You might say it combines both the *panem* and *circenses* (the "bread and circuses" or food and entertainment) that the Roman satirical poet Juvenal (A.D. 60 to A.D. 130) wrote about when poking fun at Imperial mores. With a few figs, some salami or a boiled egg, you can make a meal of this particular loaf. Of course, the Romans I know wouldn't dream of doing that; they eat this bread as a snack or an antipasto accompaniment (there's *companatico* again) to that other ancient Roman foodstuff, a glass of chilled Alban Hills white wine, generically though incorrectly known today as Frascati. This recipe comes from the Mariani family at the Antico Ristorante Pagnanelli in Castel Gandolfo, a hill town about 10 miles from central Rome, where the popes have had their summer residence for centuries. The Marianis serve *torta salata* at Eastertide, when Romans indulge in a variety of rich breads incorporating hard-boiled eggs, olives or pork products (bits of prosciutto, pancetta or guanciale, cracklings, etc.).

¾ cup extra-virgin olive oil

4 cups all-purpose flour

1½ tablespoons baking powder

1½ cups Italian dry white wine, preferably Frascati or Marino

About ½ cup cool water

6 large eggs

8 ounces prosciutto cotto (boiled ham), sliced and cut into 1-inch squares (about ¾ cup)

¾ cup pitted, chopped Gaeta or other Italian or Greek black olives

¾ cup pitted, chopped green olives ·

½ cup freshly grated Pecorino Romano

Freshly ground black pepper

SERVES 10 TO 12

1   Preheat the oven to 350° F. Grease with olive oil and flour a 7-by-12-inch baking pan.

2   Combine the flour and baking powder in a large mixing bowl, and stir with a fork. Make a well in the middle and slowly add the oil, wine and water. Blend the ingredients for 2 minutes with an electric beater or whisk them by hand for about 5 minutes, until homogenous.

3   In another bowl, beat the eggs thoroughly with a fork or whisk. Stir the eggs into the flour mixture and whisk for about 1 minute.

4   Add the ham, olives, Pecorino Romano and a generous pinch of pepper. Whisk until the batter is almost thick enough to hold the whisk upright.

5   Pour the batter into the prepared pan. Bake until the bread turns golden, 50 to 60 minutes. To test for doneness, poke the bread with a strand of spaghetti; it should come out dry.

6   Serve at room temperature. Wrap this loaf in a clean cloth or dish towel and keep it fresh in a breadbox for several days. Don't refrigerate it or it will dry out.

Chi mmagna senza bbeve ammura a ssecco.
(He who eats without drinking dies dry.)

Old Roman saying

Bruschetta Classica
Toast Rubbed with Garlic and Drizzled with Olive Oil

Bruschetta is one of the simplest, yet addictively mouthwatering Roman recipes I know. In its most basic form, it's a rough slice of bread charred and rubbed with raw garlic, dribbled with lots of olive oil and sprinkled with salt. Of course, there are ways and ways of making bruschetta. You can top it with just about anything you want, from crushed boiled eggs to anchovies, puréed fava beans with dill, to artichokes, sweet peppers or eggplant preserved in olive oil. This is peasant food. Once upon a time it represented a big part of country folks' diet. They'd slap on it whatever they could lay their hands on, and eat thankfully.

By merging two Italian terms, the recipe's Roman dialect name tells a lot about the origin of bruschetta: *brusco* means "brusque," as in quick, and *brustolito* (from the verb *abbrustolire*) indicates something toasted over an open flame. Our friend Paola Savi, a food-loving Roman with a country house, showed us how she, her family and her ancestors have been making *bruschetta all'antica* for the last few thousand years. She cuts peasant bread into slabs, pours lots of oil (pressed from the fruit of her own olive trees) into a shallow bowl, dips the slabs of bread in one at a time and lets the oil drip back into the bowl. Only then does she grill the bread over the roaring, wood-burning fire in her big, ancient fireplace. When the bread is crisp, rough-surfaced and blackened, she rubs it with fresh garlic from her garden, drizzles it with more sweet, greenish oil and sprinkles it with coarse salt. "Anything else isn't bruschetta," she insists, and she's probably right.

If you have a fireplace designed for cooking, or a barbecue, I heartily recommend making *bruschetta all'antica* the way Paola does. If you don't—unfortunately not everyone has easy access to a roaring, wood-burning fire, a villa and attached kitchen garden—try this recipe for the next best thing. It also happens to be lighter. One of the keys to making great bruschetta is getting the surface of the toast rough so that it acts like a grater when rubbed with garlic.

8 thick slices fresh country bread

4 cloves garlic, peeled

8 to 10 tablespoons extra-virgin olive oil

Kosher salt or coarse sea salt

SERVES 4

1 Broil or toast the bread until medium-dark. Put two slices on each of four plates.

2 Rub the hot toast vigorously with the whole garlic cloves. Drizzle at least 1 tablespoon of oil over each slice and sprinkle with salt.

3 Eat immediately, mopping up any spilled oil off the plate and licking your fingers.

VARIATION: Despite what Paola and other purists say, bruschetta with diced fresh tomatoes has become a staple of modern Rome. No university student or night owl could survive without it. Follow steps 1 and 2 above. Dice 8 ultra-ripe small Italian plum tomatoes and top the bruschetta with them and a sprinkle of freshly ground black pepper.

Pizza Bianca

ROMAN FLATBREAD FLAVORED WITH OLIVE OIL AND SALT

Roman *pizza bianca* isn't pizza in the usual sense at all, but rather a leavened flatbread with a rough, uneven texture, varying in thickness from ¼ to ¾ inches and incorporating olive oil to give it a unique texture: crispy outside and silken inside. There are family-run bakeries on practically every street in Rome, most with multigenerational experience, and most of them make great *pizza bianca.* So it figures that few locals bother to bake their own. The satisfaction of making *pizza bianca,* though, is the most delicious condiment of all, compensating for minor imperfections or technical drawbacks—the lack of a wood-burning brick oven with slabs of stone in it, for example, or the ability to make 100 pounds of dough at a time (the ideal quantity to get *pizza bianca* to leaven just right).

Flatbreads like *pizza bianca* come out best when baked on an oven stone or thick terra-cotta tiles. Lay them out in your oven and place the pan on top or, better yet, get two oven stones, put one below the baking tray and one on a rack above it. You can even

Roscioli Bakery (left to right) Shelby Valikodaqt, Pierluigi Roscioli, Luigi Cocciolo, Tamara Napoleoni, Marco Roscioli, Sebastian Giano, and Anna Laura Concotelli (front)

use your oven grill or broiler to get the top stone especially hot, thereby approximating the heat radiated in a bakery oven (a trick the great cookbook writer Paula Wolfert taught me). The next best thing to oven stones is a heavy, thick-bottomed baking tray.

Italians almost universally use soft, fresh yeast instead of active dry yeast. The flour is different from what we have in the United States—with less gluten or "strength." I have made this recipe both with and without a starter or sponge, using all different kinds of flour-and-yeast combinations on both sides of the Atlantic. I'm now convinced that the Romans are right: The dough is pleasanter to the tooth and closer to the original only-in-Rome texture when it's made in the following way. The small amounts of sugar and milk in this recipe encourage the yeast to grow and are especially helpful in cold weather or in locations where the water is soft or has a high chlorine content. Rome's water is spring water, and it's hard—full of flavorful calcium and minerals—with almost no chlorine at all.

Anyone who visits a few Roman bakeries soon learns that there are as many ways to make *pizza bianca* as there are Roman bakers. Different recipes result in softer, puffier, oilier or saltier pizzas than others, but this is my favorite, an adaptation for the home cook of Giorgio and Pierluigi Roscioli's secret formula from l'Antico Forno, a cult bakery that's constantly mobbed, despite being hidden down a narrow street between the outdoor market at Campo de' Fiori and the former Jewish Ghetto. The Roscioli family are part of a baking clan. All of the clansmen are from the village of Rocca di Montemonaco in the Marches region, or the nearby town of Foligno in Umbria, northeast of Rome. Foligno and Rocca di Montemonaco are believed by many Italians, particularly Romans, to be the homeland of Italy's greatest *fornari* or *fornai* (bread bakers). The term *forno* means "oven" but is used in Rome and other parts of Italy as shorthand for "bakery."

The Roscioli's *pizza bianca* is especially delicate—light, crispy and redolent of olive oil. As Pierluigi says, "The less yeast you use, and the longer you let the dough rise, the more delicate the flavor of the *pizza bianca* will be." Most Romans don't particularly like yeasty breads; they consider the smell or taste of yeast the mark of a sloppy baker. But if you enjoy yeast, and need to shorten the rising time in this recipe, double the amount given and cut the rising time in half. Romans love olive oil and love to mop it up with *pizza bianca,* and they often ask the baker to brush their *pizza bianca* with extra oil at the bakery counter just before they wolf a serving down, so don't hesitate to brush on more oil if you like your *pizza bianca* that way.

This recipe can also be used to make *rustici* (turnovers), page 22.

FOR THE DOUGH:

5 to 5½ cups all-purpose flour

½ teaspoon active dry yeast or ½ cube (0.3 ounces) fresh live yeast

1 teaspoon sugar

1 cup tepid water

½ cup whole milk, at room temperature

Kosher salt or coarse sea salt

5 tablespoons extra-virgin olive oil

FOR THE TOPPING:

6 tablespoons extra-virgin olive oil

Kosher salt or coarse sea salt

1 tablespoon tepid water, plus more as needed

SERVES 8 (1 LARGE OR 2 SMALL PIZZAS)

TO MAKE THE DOUGH:

Hand-kneaded method:

1   Pour 4 cups of the flour into a mound in a large mixing bowl and form a well in the center.

2   Dissolve the yeast and sugar in ½ cup of the water, stirring gently with a fork. Stir in 3 heaping tablespoons of flour and the milk. Let the yeast mixture sit for 15 to 20 minutes in a warm, draft-free spot, until it foams and bubbles. Pour the yeast mixture slowly into the flour well, stirring with a wooden spatula. Mix gently, slowly adding the remaining ½ cup water and a generous pinch of salt.

3   Knead the dough in the mixing bowl for about 10 minutes by hand, until the dough is smooth, elastic and easy to roll into a ball. Incorporate 4 tablespoons of the oil, kneading and squeezing the dough between your fingers, 3 to 4 minutes. Roll the dough into a ball and leave it in the bowl.

Standing-mixer method:

1   Combine the yeast, sugar and ½ cup of the water in the bowl of a standing mixer fitted with a dough paddle or hook. Add 3 heaping tablespoons of flour and mix for 15 seconds at low speed. Pour in the milk and mix at low speed for 15 to 30 seconds. Turn off the mixer and, with a rubber spatula, scrape the sides of the bowl, stirring the yeast mixture. Set the bowl in a warm, draft-free spot for 15 to 20 minutes, until the yeast foams and bubbles.

2   Return the bowl to the mixer. Add 4 cups of the flour while mixing at low speed for about 1 minute, slowly incorporating the remaining ½ cup water. Increase the speed to medium-low, and mix for about 2 minutes, while adding 4 tablespoons of the oil and a pinch of salt. Continue to mix until the dough cleans the sides of the bowl, 3 to 5

minutes. If it is too tacky, sprinkle in additional flour; if it is too stiff, drizzle in tepid water a tablespoon at a time.

3   Transfer the dough to a flour-dusted marble slab or board and knead it vigorously by hand for 2 minutes. Roll it into a ball and put it in a clean large bowl.

TO FINISH:

4   Brush or rub the surface of the dough ball with the remaining oil. Sprinkle about ½ tablespoon of salt on top of and around the dough and cover the bowl with a clean dish towel. Let the dough rise in a warm, draft-free spot for 2 to 3 hours, until porous and nearly doubled in volume. The dough can now be used for *pizza bianca,* or to make *rustici* (page 22).

TO MAKE THE *PIZZA BIANCA:*

5   Preheat the oven to 450° F. Oil a shallow 10½-by-15½-inch baking sheet.

6   Uncover and punch down the dough. Transfer it to a marble slab or board generously dusted with flour. Knead for about 1 minute, incorporating any oil and salt left in the bowl. The dough should be only slightly sticky.

7   With a rolling pin, roll out the dough to about the size of the baking pan. Stretch it with your fingertips, pulling and patting until the dough is about ½ inch thick. Lift the edge and slide the baking sheet underneath. Stretch the dough evenly over the baking sheet, pressing down here and there with your fingertips as if you were giving a gentle massage, creating dozens of dimples.

8   Partially dissolve about 1½ teaspoons salt in 1 tablespoon warm water. Add 4 tablespoons of the remaining oil and stir. Drizzle or brush the oil-and-water mixture over the dough. Smooth it evenly over the surface with your fingers or a pastry brush, making sure it goes into the dimples and over the ridges.

9   Let the dough sit in a warm, draft-free spot for 20 minutes.

10 Bake for 15 to 20 minutes, until golden and crispy in spots, pale in others.

11 Turn out the *pizza bianca* onto a baking rack or cutting board while still hot. Let it cool for a few minutes before serving. If you like lots of olive oil on your pizza as Romans do, brush it with the remaining 2 tablespoons of oil.

Rustici con Ricotta e Spinaci

RICOTTA AND SPINACH TURNOVER

1 recipe *Pizza Bianca* dough (pages 20 to 21, up to step 4)

2 heaping tablespoons flour for dusting

2 tablespoons extra-virgin olive oil

3 pounds fresh young spinach, well rinsed

1 tablespoon butter

1 large egg, at room temperature

2 cups ricotta (about 1 pound), preferably Italian ewe's milk ricotta

Kosher salt or coarse sea salt and freshly ground black pepper

2 heaping tablespoons freshly grated Pecorino Romano

SERVES 4 TO 8 (8 SMALL APPETIZER TURNOVERS OR 4 LARGE FIRST-COURSE TURNOVERS)

These mini pizzas are Rome's version of the Neapolitan calzone or folded, filled turnover-like pizza. They're pretty rustic in appearance, hence their name, and are made with the same dough used for *pizza bianca.* The fillings range from the classic spinach and ricotta, to ham and cheese, or spicy pan-fried chicory with garlic and hot chili pepper. I've even tasted *rustici* with sautéed artichokes tucked inside. Romans eat these turnovers primarily as snacks or in lieu of a sandwich at lunch. This *rustici* recipe comes from Pierluigi Roscioli of l'Antico Forno bakery.

1   Prepare the *pizza bianca* dough through step 4.

2   Uncover and punch down the dough. Transfer it to a marble slab or wooden board generously dusted with flour. Knead for about 1 minute, incorporating any oil and salt left in the bowl. The dough should be slightly sticky.

3   Divide the dough into eight (or four) equal-size pieces. Dust a rolling pin with flour and roll out the pieces of dough into rough squares about ⅛ inch thick, tugging with your fingers. Place the squares side-by-side on a large work surface and let them rest for 10 to 15 minutes.

4   Preheat the oven to 400° F. Oil two shallow 10½-by-15½-inch baking sheets.

5   Place the spinach, still dripping, in a large stockpot. Stirring frequently, cook, covered, over medium heat until it wilts, 8 to 12 minutes. Drain in a colander, pressing down firmly with the bottom of a water glass and your fingers to eliminate as much liquid as you can.

6   Melt the butter in the stockpot over medium-high heat. Return the squeezed spinach to the stockpot and sauté, stirring constantly, for 2 to 3 minutes. Transfer the spinach to a cutting board and mince it. Transfer the spinach to a large mixing bowl. Thoroughly beat the egg into the spinach.

7   If the ricotta is runny, strain out the excess liquid through cheesecloth. Stir the ricotta into the spinach, adding a generous pinch each of salt and pepper. Stir in the Pecorino Romano, which will also help absorb any remaining liquid, in addition to providing flavor.

8   With a slotted spoon, scoop up the mixture 1 tablespoon at a time and make equal mounds in the centers of each of the dough squares, until the mixture is used up.

9   Prepare one turnover at a time. With your fingers, spread the filling evenly over the dough surface, leaving a ½-inch border of plain dough all around. Lift a corner of the square and fold it over until it aligns with the corner opposite, forming a triangular turnover. Pinch firmly along the edges or press down crisply with the tines of a fork to seal the turnover.

10   Dip a pastry brush into the remaining oil and brush the surface of each turnover. With a spatula transfer the turnovers to the baking sheets. Bake for 12 to 18 minutes, until the crust is golden.

11   Serve hot or at room temperature.

Freshly unmolded ricotta

Desalting Anchovies

$\mathcal{B}$efore using salted anchovies, you might have to clean them (some are not fully gutted) and desalt them, to better control the amount of salt in the recipe you're making. Here's how: Brush off the salt with your fingers and quickly rinse the fish under cold running water. If the anchovies need cleaning, with a paring knife, your fingers and a pair of tweezers, scrape off the skin. Remove the innards, the spine, dorsal fin and any small bones. Separate the anchovies into fillets. Rinse them again and pat them dry with paper towels. If you're going to be using anchovies often, say six fillets twice a week, you can desalt and clean batches of a dozen fish, yielding twenty-four fillets, and keep them at the ready under oil for up to 2 weeks. Coat the bottom of a sterilized jar or glass or Pyrex container with extra-virgin olive oil and lay the fillets on top. Pour in more oil, building layers of fillets if necessary, making sure the fish are always totally submerged in the oil. Seal or cover the container with plastic wrap and refrigerate it for up to 2 weeks. Use the anchovy fillets still dripping with oil or pat them dry on paper towels, as called for by the recipe.

Crostini di Provatura e Alici

TOASTS WITH ANCHOVY BUTTER AND MELTED PROVOLONE

4 large slices country-style white bread

4 anchovy fillets

2 tablespoons unsalted butter

12 ounces provola, caciocavallo or provolone cheese, in approximately ¼-inch-thick slices, each 1½ inch square

SERVES 6 TO 8
(12 TO 16 CROSTINI)

This simple combination seems so exquisite to the Roman palate and soul that saying "like butter-and-anchovies" means "like peas in a pod." For an appetizer Romans often spread a slice of fresh bread with sweet butter and top it with an anchovy in olive oil plucked from a jar—that's it. This cocktail party recipe adds provola, caciocavallo or provolone cheese to these basic ingredients and transforms the fresh bread into toast. Crostini are also a popular *svogliatura* (snack) served in wine bars to keep the Frascati flowing. The Romans use a baguettelike white bread loaf called *ciriola* for their crostini but any top-quality white bread will do.

1   Preheat the oven to 350° F.

2   Toast the bread medium-dark. Cut it into roughly 1½-inch squares and put them on a baking sheet.

3   If you are using salted anchovies desalt them (see Desalting Anchovies, page 24). If you are using anchovy fillets packed in oil, remove them with a fork and drain them on paper towels. Chop the anchovies.

4   In a small sauté pan over medium-low heat, melt the butter. Add the anchovies, stirring and crushing with a wooden spoon or spatula for 3 to 4 minutes. Remove the pan from the heat.

5   Spoon the melted anchovy butter over the squares of toast and top each with a square of cheese. Bake until the cheese melts and crisps, 8 to 10 minutes.

6   Transfer the crostini to a platter and serve hot.

Pizza Bianca con Prosciutto e Fichi

ROMAN FLATBREAD WITH PROSCIUTTO AND FRESH FIGS

1 baked *Pizza Bianca*
(page 17)

8 ripe figs

8 very thin slices Parma
ham (about ¼ pound)

SERVES 8

There are two expressions in Rome that say "hey, everything is hunky-dory"—happily a common refrain in this upbeat town. They are *come burro e alici* (like butter and anchovies) and *come pizza e fichi* (like pizza and figs). These are considered the perfect taste combinations, and by extrapolation the best metaphors for amiable harmony in the universe. No surprise then that the most frequently served snack or appetizer in summer when fresh fruit abounds is *pizza bianca* topped with peeled split figs and translucent strips of Parma ham, an unbeatable trio if you ask me, and one that might someday rate its own refrain.

1   Slice the *pizza bianca* into eighths.

2   Rinse the figs under cold running water, pat them dry on paper towels, peel them with your fingers and a paring knife and split them open.

3   Place 1 slice of Parma ham atop each strip of pizza, crown it with a freshly peeled, split fig and serve.

Christmas in Rome

Once upon a time, nomadic *zampognari* shepherds playing their primitive *zampógne* (bagpipes) swarmed into Rome from nearby pasturelands and posted themselves on every street corner at Christmastide, among the traditional potted or dried palms. But nowadays you're more likely to see a forest of mini fir trees and an army of unlikely Santa Clauses.

At Rome's outdoor markets, greengrocers pick the dry leaves off recently harvested bunches of hot *peperoncino* (chili peppers), their stands a kaleidoscope of white turnips, orange squash and persimmons, variegated Sicilian winter melons, violet Romanesco broccoli, crinkly cabbage and candid cauliflower, pale cardoons, mounds of fresh walnuts, bundles of zucchini flowers and spiky Sardinian or plump Apulian artichokes. Pastry shops, such as Sacchetti in Trastevere, make thousands of *pangiallo,* deliciously dense loaves of walnuts, almonds, hazelnuts, pine nuts, candied fruit, raisins and almond paste. At Valzani, an eighth-generation rival Roman pastry shop, also in Trastevere, the *pangiallo* is flanked by the related Christmastide specialty *panpepato,* which contains spoonfuls of black pepper and a coating of dark chocolate around a nutty, honey-sweet heart. Sweet buns, either brimming with whipped cream or chock-full of raisins and pine nuts, and chestnut-flour cake (see *Castagnaccio Romano,* page 274) put a smile on Roman kids' faces.

On Christmas Eve, a time of lean eating for those respecting Roman Catholic traditions, you might start with slivered fresh vegetables battered and fried golden (see *Pezzetti Natalizi,* page 28), followed by skate-and-broccoli soup (see *Minestra di Arzilla e Broccolo Romano,* page 63), or giant *paccheri* (tube pasta) and ricotta, fried salt cod fillets and *lattarini* (lake fish), or fried artichokes (see *Carciofi alla Giudia* or *Carciofi Fritti Dorati alla Romana,* page 237 or page 252). To pass the time until midnight Mass, you might play bingo and snack on nuts, dates, figs stuffed with ricotta and almonds (see *Fichi Ripieni,* page 270) or mandarins, using snippets of crinkly peel as bingo markers.

For Christmas lunch, you might eat boiled capon or chicken in its broth (see page 62) or egg-drop soup (see *Stracciatella,* page 61). More lavishly, you might stuff a capon, chicken or young turkey with chestnuts and truffles (see *Pollo Ripieno alla Papalina,* page 184), or apples and sausages. Lentils bring good luck and prosperity while bacon-wrapped, herbed pork roast (see *Maiale Porchettato,* page 172) brings shouts of gluttonous joy to one and all, whether locals or pilgrims, pious or profane.

Pezzetti Natalizi

CHRISTMASTIDE VEGETABLES FRIED IN OLIVE OIL

1 package active dry yeast
or 1 cube (0.6 ounces)
fresh live yeast

¼ cup tepid water

6 large eggs, at room
temperature

1½ cups all-purpose flour

Freshly ground black
pepper

1 medium-sized
cauliflower (about
1 pound)

1 pound broccoli

1 large purple eggplant

1 pound zucchini

Kosher salt or coarse
sea salt

8 ounces fresh button
mushrooms (*champignons
de Paris* or Cremini)

Fine salt

4 to 6 cups light extra-
virgin olive oil for frying

SERVES 6 TO 8

On Christmas Eve, Romans snack on platters of
irresistible seasonal vegetables dipped in a delicate batter
and fried in extra-virgin olive oil. Favorite ingredients
include cardoons, eggplant, zucchini, artichokes, borage,
parsley, nettle tips, mushrooms, cauliflower and broccoli.
Some families enrich this mixed vegetable-and-herb fry
with salt cod or lamb brain. Zucchini and most green
produce are available year-round in Rome because of the
mild climate and imports. But if you can't find a specific
vegetable mentioned below because of the season, just
increase the quantity of one of the others.

1 In a large mixing bowl, dissolve the yeast in the water,
   stirring with a fork for about 1 minute. Add the eggs
   and with a whisk or electric mixer, beat until foamy.
   Whisk or beat in the flour and a generous pinch of
   pepper until the mixture has the consistency of thick
   pancake batter. Cover the bowl and refrigerate it for 30
   minutes or more.

2 Rinse the cauliflower, broccoli, eggplant and zucchini
   under cold running water. Shake them dry. With a
   paring knife, cut away any woody sections or
   imperfections. Slice the eggplant into thin rounds, cut
   the rounds in half and place them in a colander in the
   sink. Sprinkle with a generous pinch of kosher salt and
   let the eggplant sit for 30 minutes. Brush off the salt
   (do not wash it off). Cut the cauliflower and broccoli

into florets and dice their stems into bite-sized chunks. Slice the zucchini into rounds about ¼ inch thick. Combine the zucchini, cauliflower and broccoli in a bowl and set aside.

3   Clean the mushrooms carefully with moistened paper towels. With a paring knife, cut off the bases of the stems and thinly slice the mushrooms and attached stems. You should have 2 cups.

4   Remove the batter from the refrigerator and stir gently but thoroughly with a wooden spoon or spatula, adding a generous pinch of fine salt.

5   Pour about 2 inches of oil into a large, high-sided frying pan or medium saucepan. Heat over a medium-low heat to 325° F, until bubbling-hot but not smoking. To check the oil temperature without a thermometer, flick a drop of water onto the surface, making sure you don't get splattered. The water should sizzle, dance and evaporate within seconds.

6   Spread several layers of paper towels on a large platter.

7   Drop the vegetables, four to six pieces at a time, into the batter. Use a slotted spoon, slotted steel spatula, or tongs to stir and coat them. Slowly lift them out of the batter and slip into the hot oil. Fry in batches of four to six pieces, turning and flipping several times until crisp, 3 to 4 minutes. Drain the fried vegetables on the platter covered with paper towels. Continue to batter and fry the vegetables until all have been cooked. Add oil to the pan and adjust the heat to maintain the starting level and temperature.

8   Remove the paper towels from the platter, arrange the vegetables, sprinkle them with fine salt and pepper and serve immediately.

An Obsession with Artichokes

*D*eft gestures with blackened, expert fingers, rich cries in *romanaccio* dialect, flying leaves, squirting lemons, bared hearts and flashing knives . . .

Gladiators grappling in the Coliseum?

No, a gaggle of Rome's animated artichoke women—for some mysterious reason Roman men rarely prepare artichokes—at any open market in town, most picturesquely at the daily fruit, vegetable and flower market at Campo de' Fiori just south of Piazza Navona.

Artichokes are the single most popular green vegetable in Rome, a culinary icon as ancient and revered as wild mint, or *mentuccia* (its scientific name is *Calamintha nepeta* or *Nepitella*). The two are often eaten together, as in *carciofi alla romana* (see page 34). All Roman households possess at least one special curved-blade artichoke knife, called a *spellucchino da carciofo.* Professionals at produce stands and Rome's open markets get their knives sharpened at least once a week by itinerant knife sharpeners.

Romans believe that artichokes possess formidable aphrodisiac, digestive and diuretic powers—stripping out bad cholesterol, acting like a liver tonic and generally filling the body and soul with vim and vigor. Maybe that's why locals have been obsessed since ancient times with the growing, preparation and eating of them. The emperors of old probably ate primarily small, wild, spiky artichokes similar to those still found near Rome and called *carciofini selvatici.* Some scholars claim the ancients knew only cardoons, a related plant. Whether they were artichokes or cardoons, the ancient Romans grew them in a variety of Mediterranean places, particularly in what's now Tunisia. Apicius in *De re coquinaria,* the famous first-century recipe book, refers repeatedly to artichoke (or possibly cardoon) bottoms as *sfondilos* (in recipes #112, #113; elsewhere he calls cardoons, *carduos*). What he probably meant to describe was what we call artichoke hearts, as anyone who's tried to carve out the bottom of a tiny, tough cardoon flower would discover. Further support for the existence of artichokes in antiquity comes from archeological finds. I've seen ancient mosaics showing artichokes (or cardoons) and even found a low-relief sculpture of one amid the tombs of the Via Appia Antica (about 100 yards south of the intersection with Via Erode Attico).

The round, blunt-leafed *Cynara scolymus,* or globe artichoke, called *carciofo romanesco* in Rome, probably came onto the scene about five hundred years ago. These *romaneschi* artichokes are eaten by the ton, especially in spring. In their raucous cries, Rome's artichoke women hawk their best, most-flavorful artichokes as *cimaroli* (tip-toppers) or *mammole* (big mammas). They brandish them with maternal pride. That's because these plumpest and tastiest of Rome's *carciofi* are always the first to sprout from the top (the *cima*) of the plant's main stem. The nickname *mammole* (or *mamme,* depending on which neighborhood you come from) derives instead from the belief that the largest artichoke on the top of the plant is said to give birth to the slightly smaller ones below, called *figli* (offspring).

Cimaroli or *mammole* are sold by the piece, not the bunch. Because they're so flavorful, they cost twice as much as the offspring from lower branches (also called *braccioli,* or arms). The children may be exquisite but, to the Roman palate, they're not nearly as delicious as the single tip-topper of a mother.

Romans don't let their artichokes—either the plants themselves or their edible inflorescences—get old and woody, which explains, in part, why botanically similar globe artichokes grown just about anywhere else are rarely as tender or flavorful. For this same reason, artichokes from the market gardens around Rome are usually easier to clean than their American counterparts, and, ironically, while a greater portion of them is edible, the Romans systematically whittle them down to their hearts, leaving only stubby tender inner leaves attached. Few Romans would dream of chewing on, scraping at or spitting out tough leaves French-style, no matter how tasty the accompanying dipping vinaigrette (the exception to this rule is rustic barbecued *carciofi alla matticella;* see page 256).

Truth be told, most but by no means all Romans buy their fresh artichokes ready to cook from the master artichoke cleaners known as *carciofàre* at every city marketplace. Seated among tubs of lemony water, the *carciofàre* quickly pare away outside bracts (leaves), turning the artichokes as if they were on a lathe. Speed competitions are held in the spring at some Roman markets, and during the second week of April at the big annual artichoke fair in the town of Ladispoli north of Rome. The lemon juice in the tubs keeps the artichokes from turning black once cut and imparts a nice lemony taste. Many *carciofàre* wear rubber gloves to protect their hands from the lemon and artichoke juices—in a matter of minutes, the natural dyes in artichokes can make you look like a rabid smoker, with tobacco-stained fingers.

Once the artichokes have been trimmed and cleaned, they're bagged in plastic with a squirt of lemony, acidulated water to keep them pale green until cooked. Most are sold with about 4 inches of pared stem attached. They're deep-fried as *carciofi alla giudia* (see page 37), coming out looking like bronze sunflowers, or braised as *carciofi alla romana* (see page 34). This latter dish is the most popular way in Rome to cook the vegetable: The artichokes are simmered stem up, head down, in a bath of olive oil, white wine and water, and look like so many upturned wineglasses without feet.

Since American globe artichokes are often bigger and tougher than Roman ones, with vulcanized, unsalvageable stems only a few inches long, the best cleaning method is to start by lopping off the stems entirely. You'll need a sharp, short-bladed paring knife plus a heavy, long carving knife that's also very sharp. Be careful but ruthless in eliminating every tough part of the artichoke, even if it means leaving only the heart intact. Italians trim away and discard about 65 percent of every artichoke they buy, according to nutritionist Renzo Pellati, author of the popular food encyclopedia, *Tutti I Cibi Dalla "A" Alla "Z"* (Mondadori, Milan, 1997).

Artichoke Recipes in this Book

Artichokes show up as the main or, at least, an important ingredient in dozens of Roman dishes, from appetizers to first and main courses. Here's a list of all the recipes in this book that call for artichokes:

Carciofi alla Romana (Artichokes, Roman Style, Braised with Garlic and Mint), page 34

Tip: Use slivered, sautéed artichokes (see *Carciofi Fritti Dorati alla Romana,* page 252) to fill a frittata, page 216.

Special Cases: Cleaning and Trimming Tough, Huge or Tiny Artichokes

To clean and trim artichoke varieties other than globe artichokes (see page 40), including small violet-leaved artichokes, first use scissors to snip off the sharp leaf tips. With your fingers and a sharp, short-bladed paring knife, pinch and cut off the outer leaves. Once the tender pale green, purplish or yellowish inner leaves appear, place the artichoke on a cutting board and with a large, sharp carving knife lop off the upper ends of the leaves, leaving only the tender bottom sections of the leaves and the heart. Be draconian. With your fingers and the short-bladed knife, whittle the artichoke right down to the heart if necessary, leaving only tender, edible inner leaves attached. Use the knife or a vegetable peeler to remove all the fibrous, woody parts remaining. Discard them and scoop out the hairy choke if there is one, using a serrated spoon. Cut the artichoke into quarters or slices, or cook it whole, as directed by the recipe.

Carciofi alla Romana

ARTICHOKES, ROMAN STYLE, BRAISED WITH GARLIC AND MINT

1 lemon

6 young, tender globe artichokes, preferably with long stems

4 cloves garlic

3 heaping tablespoons minced fresh spearmint, nepitella or pennyroyal

3 heaping tablespoons minced fresh flat-leaf parsley

Kosher salt or coarse sea salt and freshly ground black pepper

1 cup extra-virgin olive oil

2 cups Italian dry white wine, preferably Frascati or Marino

1 cup cold water

SERVES 6

Romans adore artichokes. The *alla romana* suffix of the recipe's name indicates this is a recipe developed in Rome, and it is the Romans' favorite way to cook the vegetable, with fried Carciofi alla Giudia (page 37) coming in a close second. The ancient gourmet Apicius (first century A.D.) describes a strikingly similar dish in *De re coquinaria* (recipe #113), but many think this recipe originates with the Jewish population of Rome's Trastevere neighborhood about two thousand years ago.

As with many primal Roman dishes, there is lively disagreement about how best to prepare *carciofi alla romana:* in a bath of olive oil only, or in oil mixed with water and/or wine, with or without stem attached, top side up or down, and so forth. All Romans agree, though, that you should use tender young globe artichokes seasoned with garlic and mint, preferably a variety of cultivated or wild spearmint similar to the Romans' own wild *mentuccia* (nepitella).

My approach to this classic incorporates the wisdom of various artichoke experts and home cooks, including my mother Romana, who has been making *carciofi alla romana* successfully in California for the last fifty years, using American artichokes. While most Romans leave the artichoke stems attached, I find that with American artichokes, it's easier to cut the stems off and cook them along with the artichokes.

1   Halve the lemon. Juice one half into a bowl of cold water big enough to hold the artichokes and their stems. Use the other half to rub the artichokes as you work.

2   Clean and trim the artichokes to remove all inedible parts (see How to Clean a Globe
    Artichoke, page 40).

3   Peel the garlic, discarding the green shoots, and mince. Combine the garlic and herbs in
    a small bowl. Add a generous pinch each of salt and pepper. Pour in 3 tablespoons of the
    oil and stir.

4   Remove the artichokes and stems from the lemony water and shake them dry. Fill each
    with the moist herb-and-garlic mixture. With your fingers, open the stubby leaves wide,
    filling between, until the mixture is used up.

5   In a pan large enough to hold all the vegetables, arrange the artichokes, base down,
    surrounded by stems. Pour the remaining oil directly over the artichokes. Pour the wine
    and water over the stems. Bring the braising liquids to a boil. Lower the heat to
    minimum and simmer, covered, until the artichoke bases and stems are tender when
    poked with a fork, 15 to 20 minutes.

6   Sprinkle with salt and pepper and serve hot or at room temperature.

■   Globe artichokes usually have harmless rounded tips. If the leaves of your artichokes
    have sharp tips, use scissors or a knife to snip or lop them off before you begin the
    cleaning process.

■   Don't throw away the leftover oil
    and juices from this dish. Save and
    use them like a vegetable stock for
    other artichoke-based recipes, such
    as *Vignarola* (page 259). The juices
    can be refrigerated, covered, for up
    to a week.

Artichokes, Roman style

A Greedy Desire for Mint

"The smell of mint stirs up the mind
and appetite to a greedy desire for food."

—Pliny the Elder

Romans make lavish use of mint in their cooking. They employ two main types, which they call *menta romana* and *mentuccia*. *Menta romana* is a kind of spearmint (there are countless varieties of spearmint worldwide). Roman spearmint is not exactly the same as American spearmint but the two are close enough to be interchangeable. *Mentuccia* is another story. Its scientific name is *Calamintha nepeta,* but in Italian and English it is known as *nepitella* (though in most English dictionaries the word does not appear). *Calamintha nepeta* is a variety of calamint; herbalists sometimes call it "lesser calamint." In America, it is very difficult to find.

A closely related mint with a smell and taste very similar to that of *Calamintha nepeta* is *Mentha pulegium,* commonly called pennyroyal. There are actually several subspecies of pennyroyal, including mock pennyroyal (*Hedeoma pulegioides*); they are close enough to be interchangeable. Nurseries and some produce markets sell pennyroyal. It is not exactly an everyday household herb.

For braised artichokes, Roman style (*carciofi alla romana,* page 34), the authentic recipe calls for *Calamintha nepeta* (i.e., mentuccia or nepitella). If you can find *Calamintha nepeta,* definitely use it. Pennyroyal is a good substitute, if you can get hold of some. Spearmint, easy to find, works fine with braised artichokes and all other recipes in this book calling for mint.

Carciofi alla Giudia

FRIED ARTICHOKES, JEWISH STYLE

Stroll through what used to be the Jewish Ghetto in the heart of old Rome—an atmospheric few hundred square yards of weathered *palazzi* and ruins near the Tiber River, Synagogue and the Theater of Marcellus—and you're pretty much guaranteed to catch the irresistible scent of artichokes frying in olive oil.

Simple the recipe may be—the only indispensable ingredients are artichokes, oil and salt—but getting it right is tricky. The trick is to fry the artichokes twice, the first time in hot oil, the second time in extremely hot oil, and to let them cool in between. It's the temperature differential—what the Italians call the "thermal shock"—of the second frying that causes the artichokes to spread open effortlessly. There's no need to pound or press down on them.

Let's be honest. Cleaning and trimming artichokes is no fun, whether they're the tender round Roman type or the spiky, tough kind sold at most supermarkets in the United States. No recipe for *carciofi alla giudia* will work if you make it with anything but very fresh, young artichokes. Woody or rubbery artichokes will soak up the oil, burn or lose their leaves while being fried, so don't even try this recipe with them.

You need a quart of oil to make a batch of up to twenty artichokes, so some cooks economize by frying their artichokes in seed oil instead of olive oil. My feeling is that if you're going to attempt making this exquisite delicacy at home, do yourself a favor and buy an inexpensive light-bodied extra-virgin olive oil for frying. The gains in flavor and digestibility are well worth it. Olive oil burns at 400° F and loses its wholesomeness. So don't exceed 375° F and you'll get flavorful, healthful results. Always heat olive oil slowly, allowing it to accumulate heat, over a medium burner. Once cooled, the oil can be filtered and reused to fry the next batch of artichokes, provided you do so within 3 to 4 days, after which the oil starts to spoil because of the suspended artichoke bits in it.

Timing is the hardest part of this recipe. Cooking at home without professional equipment, I have never managed to accurately fry more than two artichokes at a time, because the leaves need plenty of room to spread open like flower petals, which is precisely what they are—the bracts of an inflorescence or budding flower. Unless you are willing to fill a huge pot with quarts of oil, my suggestion is to use a narrow pot and start by frying one artichoke at a time. Once you've got the hang of it, try doing two or more. If you want to get fancy, fill an atomizer with water and spray the artichoke during the second frying. The tiny water droplets reinforce the crisping process. But be careful and wear kitchen gloves to avoid burns; the water can cause splattering.

1 lemon

6 young, tender globe artichokes, preferably with long stems

4 cups extra-virgin olive oil for frying

Fine salt

SERVES 6

1 Halve the lemon. Juice one half into a bowl of cold water big enough to hold the artichokes and their stems. Use the other half to rub the artichokes as you work.

2 Clean and trim the artichokes to remove all the inedible parts (see How to Clean a Globe Artichoke, page 40).

3 Pour at least 5 inches of oil into a tall, narrow pot. Heat over medium from 310° to 325° F so that the oil is bubbling-hot but not smoking.

4 Place 2 large platters near the stovetop. Spread several layers of paper towels on one of them.

5 Fry one artichoke at a time. Jab the prongs of a long, two-pronged cooking fork into the base of the artichoke. Lift and grip the end of the stem with a pair of tongs. Using the fork and tongs, slowly lower the artichoke into the hot oil. The artichoke will float. You must keep it submerged and turn it while frying it. Remove the prongs of the fork from the artichoke, and with the tongs gently keep it submerged in the oil and turn while frying, 8 to 10 minutes, until barely tender. Remove the artichoke to the platter without paper towels. Fry the remaining artichokes one or two at a time and place them on the platter. Let them cool for 10 to 15 minutes.

6   Top up the frying oil and increase the heat to bring the oil temperature to 350° F. To check the oil temperature approximately without a thermometer, carefully flick a drop of water onto the surface, making sure you don't get splattered. The water should sizzle, dance and evaporate within seconds.

7   With the cooking fork and tongs, gently lower the artichokes into the oil a second time in batches of one or two, and fry until the leaves have spread open, crisped and turned golden, 2 to 3 minutes. If you like, wear kitchen gloves and use the tools to lift the artichokes while frying, to spray them several times with an atomizer filled with water for increased crispness.

8   Transfer the artichokes to the platter covered with paper towels, sprinkle them with a generous pinch of salt and serve immediately.

How to Clean a Globe Artichoke

Here's how 40-year Campo de' Fiori veteran greengrocer Marcella Banco cleans her globe artichokes. This method works on American artichokes, too, as long as they're not too huge or tough. First, Marcella squeezes lemon juice into a tub of cold water big enough to hold all the artichokes she's working on. She halves another lemon and uses it to rub the artichokes, their stems and even the razor-sharp paring knife she wields to pare them down.

If the stems are too woody or shorter than about 4 inches, Marcella lops them off and discards them. Otherwise she leaves the stems attached and, rotating the artichoke while holding it stem-outward away from her body, peels or cuts the stems down to their pale pith, discarding any tough or stringy parts. If the customer calls for detached stems, she cuts them off flush with the base of the artichoke and drenches them with lemon juice or floats them in acidulated water. Some cooks prefer to make *carciofi alla romana* with the stems separate. Some mince the stems and add them to the mint and garlic used to flavor the recipe.

Next, Marcella removes the artichokes' scaly outer leaves—usually three or four layers of them. She breaks off the tops of each by holding the artichoke stem-end outward, away from her body, gripped firmly in her left hand while she pinches the lower section

of each leaf between the thumb and forefinger of her right hand. She gives a short tug outward to snap the leaf free. The meaty lower swellings of each leaf stay attached to the artichoke's heart.

Once the dunce cap of tender pale green, purplish or yellowish inner leaves appears, Marcella inserts the blade of her paring knife behind the outside layer of leaves and begins to cut, rotating the artichoke counterclockwise with her left hand. This is the deft spinning you see going on in Roman markets, and in restaurants and homes where people prefer to clean their artichokes themselves. The object is to eliminate all inedible parts so that the remaining artichoke heart and the surrounding, buttery-soft leaves are all that go into anyone's mouth. There simply are no big, leathery leaves left by the time the job is done.

Most *carciofi romaneschi* sold in Rome do not have a hairy, inedible choke in their center—they're harvested before the choke has a chance to grow. However, almost all American ones do. So do as Marcella does when she comes across one with a choke: She uses her knife or a spoon, preferably a serrated-edge spoon, to gently scrape out the fluff, tugging with her fingers to remove any recalcitrant tufts. Then she flips the artichoke over in her left hand, so that the base now points inward toward her body, and uses her knife to cut away any remaining woody dark green portions, spinning the artichoke again while paring.

As Marcella works, she rubs halved lemons on the artichokes and stems, then tosses the finished artichokes into the lemony water to keep them nice and green. Once all her artichokes are cleaned and trimmed of all inedible, fibrous matter and have soaked in the lemony water, she shakes them dry one by one and uses them whole, or cuts them into quarters or slices as called for by her customers.

Carciofini Sott'Olio

Baby Artichokes in Olive Oil

When I was a small child my mother would drag me several times a month to the Italian shops in the North Beach neighborhood of San Francisco not far from where we lived. There she would stock up on the exotic Italian foods then unavailable in supermarkets. Festooned with pontoon-sized provolone cheeses and ranks of stiff, smelly salt cod, the deli counters were always stacked with giant jars of colorful vegetables pickled in vinegar or preserved in olive oil. There were red sweet peppers and purple eggplants, rainbow-colored capers and white onions, but it was the thimble-sized artichoke hearts that my mother was never able to resist. When we moved to Rome in the mid-1960s I discovered why: Romans are artichoke-mad. For my mother, those *carciofini* floating in oil in a North Beach deli were a ticket home on the nostalgia express.

Over the years I too have developed an addiction to artichokes under oil, so I was delighted to finally learn from Anna Mangioli in Rome how to preserve them *alla romana* (Roman style). Anna is a great home cook and sometime-volunteer guard at the 1,800-year-old Trajan's Market (now a temporary art exhibition space) overlooking the Forum. She spends several days a week in what probably used to be an Imperial-period fishmonger's stall and, ignoring the artworks around her, gazes over Rome's columns and cupolas thinking of food—her passion. That's where I met her. The mere mention of Emperor Trajan's efforts to make this covered marketplace the ancient world's best got her talking about artichokes. I told her about my mother, and she told me about her vegetables. At the end of their season Anna pickles huge batches of tiny artichokes, which she and her husband enjoy the rest of the year.

This recipe is good for anywhere from 25 to 100 baby artichokes or the quartered hearts of 10 to 25 medium-sized globe or other artichokes. Once trimmed, the artichokes should be no bigger than an egg and ideally the size of a thimble so that you can pop them in your mouth whole.

1 lemon

25 to 100 baby artichokes (or the quartered hearts of 10 to 25 medium-sized artichokes)

1 cup white wine vinegar

4 cups water

Kosher salt or coarse sea salt

2 cloves garlic

4 whole sprigs fresh parsley

Bay leaves or cloves (1 for each jar)

4 to 6 cups extra-virgin olive oil

You'll need to pack the artichokes in glass jars, so before making this recipe, sterilize the jars and their lids by boiling them in water to cover for about 10 minutes. Let them drip and air dry thoroughly before using them.

As a general guideline, an 18-ounce ($2\frac{1}{4}$-cup) jar holds about twenty to twenty-three whole tiny artichokes or fifty to sixty quarters of large artichoke hearts, and you'll need about 1 cup of oil to cover them. A 12-ounce ($1\frac{1}{2}$-cup) jar should hold from fourteen to sixteen whole tiny artichokes or thirty-five to fifty quarters of large artichoke hearts, and holds about $\frac{3}{4}$ cup of oil. It's difficult to resist gobbling the artichokes up right away, but you should try to let them sit for at least 5 days before you begin eating them. They're even better after 10 days and best of all after a month. If you want to eat your artichokes right away, make *Carciofi alla Romana* (page 34) instead, or see the note at the end of this recipe.

1   Halve the lemon and juice half into a basin of cold water big enough to hold all the artichokes.

2   Clean and trim the baby artichokes, removing all the inedible and woody parts but leaving the artichokes whole (see How to Clean a Globe Artichoke, page 40). If you are using large artichokes, cut the trimmed hearts into quarters.

3   Combine the vinegar, water, a generous pinch of salt, the whole unpeeled garlic cloves, and the parsley sprigs in a medium saucepan. Squeeze in any remaining lemon juice, drop the squeezed lemon halves into the pot and bring the liquid to a rolling boil.

4   Drop batches of ten to twelve artichokes or quartered hearts and the bay leaves, if using, into the boiling liquid and boil for 12 to 15 minutes, until tender. Remove the artichokes and the bay leaves with tongs or a slotted spoon, allowing the cooking liquids to drain back into the pot, and transfer to a colander. If needed, add more water and vinegar in equal proportions and bring the pot back to a boil to cook additional vegetables.

5   Let the vegetables drain and cool in the colander. Transfer them to a rack and let them air-dry for 1 hour, preferably in a breezy, sunny spot.

6   Drop 1 clove or 1 bay leaf into each sterilized jar. Drop in the artichokes, one at a time, without packing them down, leaving about $1/2$ inch of space free between the tops of the last layer of artichokes and the rim. Pour in enough oil to cover the artichokes fully. It should reach to $1/4$ inch below the rim of the jar. With a wooden spoon, tap the side of the jar to dislodge air pockets before sealing. Repeat the operation until all the ingredients are used up.

7   Store the jars in a cool, dark spot. Let the artichokes sit for at least 5 days before eating them. They will last for months if properly stored. Once opened, refrigerate the jar and use the contents within a week.

VARIATION: You can make eggplant under oil (*melanzane sott'olio*) in much the same way. Instead of artichokes, substitute several large purple eggplants, thinly sliced, sprinkled with several generous pinches of kosher salt or coarse sea salt and left to drain in a colander for 2 hours. Remove them from the colander, brush off the salt (do not wash it off) and cut the slices into strips about 3 to 4 inches long and 1 to $1^1/2$ inches wide. Prepare the eggplant strips as per above, boiling, straining, air-drying and packing them into jars. Instead of bay leaves or cloves, put 1 garlic clove, 1 hot chili pepper (or $1/4$ teaspoon crushed red pepper flakes) and a pinch of dried marjoram into each jar.

In a hurry? You can make artichokes or eggplant in olive oil for same-day eating by using 2 tablespoons of vinegar per 4 cups water and boiling the vegetables for 18 minutes. With this method you can even use frozen artichoke hearts if you wish. Make sure the vegetables marinate, totally submerged in oil, for at least 4 hours before serving. Prepared this way, they're delicious but must be eaten within several days and cannot be stored for long periods.

Peperoncino
(Hot Chili Pepper)

Though chili peppers, like sweet peppers, are from the New World and not Italy, the *peperoncino* (*Capsicum annuum annuum* Linné) was actually created in Italy, probably in the 1600s, and is immensely popular in Rome, especially in recipes with vegetables, poultry, lamb, cured pork and anchovies. About 1 to 1½ inches long, curved like a sickle and bright cherry red when fresh, *peperoncino* is usually sold and used dried, when it has shrunk and straightened to ½ to 1 inch, and faded several shades. Because of the color and shape, the reformed Italian Communist Party has adopted the *peperoncino* as a symbol for its annual Festa dell'Unità bash (*right*), with the slogan "the pleasure of being antagonists." That's one way to put some pep in tired politics.

For these recipes, *peperoncino* is the perfect chili in the perfect package, because of its uniform size and potency. I urge you seek it out in Italian specialty food shops or by mail order. If you can't find the authentic item, the equivalent of one *peperoncino* is usually about ¼ teaspoon crushed red pepper flakes. The Anaheim chili is *peperoncino*'s closest American relative.

Remember, whenever you touch *peperoncino* or other chili peppers, make sure to wash your fingers thoroughly before touching your eyes or any other sensitive areas. If you find shredded *peperoncino* makes recipes too spicy for your taste, add the *peperoncino* whole instead, remembering to remove it before serving. One whole *peperoncino* is about a third as powerful as a shredded one.

Fiori di Zucca Fritti

FRIED STUFFED ZUCCHINI FLOWERS

When I was very young and living in San Francisco, my mother astonished me by plucking blossoms from our backyard—peppery nasturtium or mild fava bean flowers, the blooms of a purple wisteria or a white acacia—then popping them into her mouth or rushing to the kitchen to fry them in olive oil. Later, when I lived in Rome, I began to understand that many Romans are compulsive flower-eaters.

Rome's outskirts and the rich farmland known as the Salto di Fondi near Anzio, south of town, teem with market gardeners who specialize in the growing of squash flowers—the Romans' favorite edible bloom. The best flowers for stuffing do not grow from the shoots that bear the zucchini themselves, but are separate entities on long, hairy stems with no fruit attached. The plant uses these apparently "barren" or "male" flowers for the purpose of pollination. A curious fact I learned from a Roman vegetable farmer is that zucchini flowers have thicker, longer pistils than other kinds of squash flowers. All zucchini or squash flowers work fine for this recipe, as long as they're fresh. In the United States you can buy them at specialty produce markets and farmers' markets, or you can grow your own; even if your zucchini plant doesn't bear fruit, it's sure to flower. Remember: zucchini flowers last only hours after they've been picked, so plan carefully before buying them.

There is no more exquisite antipasto or finger snack than stuffed, fried *fiori di zucca* Roman style, especially in spring, true zucchini season. What makes them so good is the combination of piquant anchovy and mild mozzarella. Some of the best I have eaten come from Antico Ristorante Pagnanelli, a country restaurant near the Pope's summer residence in Castel Gandolfo, atop the Alban Hills. With a few modifications, this is their classic recipe, made with a rich egg-based batter.

24 zucchini blossoms

12 ounces fresh mozzarella, preferably cow's milk *fior di latte* (three 4-ounce balls)

12 anchovy fillets

4 large eggs, at room temperature

2 cups all-purpose flour

Freshly ground black pepper

Olive oil for frying

Kosher salt or coarse sea salt

SERVES 6

1   Use a narrow-tipped paring knife or your fingertips to carefully remove and discard the stamens from the flowers without tearing the petals. Remove and discard the stems. Rinse the flowers gently under cold water and pat them dry with paper towels.

2   Cut the mozzarella into 24 slivers the size and length of a baby finger—about 2 inches—and place them in a colander. Press down gently to squeeze out as much liquid as possible.

3   If you are using salted anchovies, desalt them (see Desalting Anchovies, page 24). If you are using anchovy fillets packed in oil, remove them with a fork and drain them on paper towels. Slice each anchovy fillet in half lengthwise. Wrap 1 anchovy strip around 1 finger of mozzarella and slip them together into a zucchini blossom. Gently twist the petal tips closed; they will stay closed themselves (and if they open slightly, it doesn't matter). Repeat the operation until all the ingredients have been used. Set the zucchini blossoms on a platter as you finish each.

4   Beat the eggs in a medium-sized mixing bowl.

5   Pour 1 cup of flour into each of two shallow bowls. Grind some pepper into the second bowl of flour.

6   Heat the oil in a large frying pan over medium heat until bubbling-hot, but not smoking.

7   Dredge each stuffed zucchini flower in the first bowl of flour, dip it into the beaten eggs and dredge it in the pepper-seasoned flour.

8   Add 6 flowers at a time to the oil and fry for 3 to 5 minutes or until crisp, turning gently with a spatula 2 to 4 times. Remove the flowers to paper towels to drain.

9   Sprinkle with salt and serve hot.

Insalata di Gamberetti e Calamaretti con Finocchio e Sedano

SEAFOOD SALAD WITH SHRIMP, CALAMARI, FENNEL AND CELERY

2½ cups water

¼ teaspoon fresh or dried thyme

1 bay leaf

2 tablespoons white wine vinegar

6 to 8 black peppercorns

1 pound fresh or frozen shelled shrimp (about 1⅓ pounds unshelled)

1 pound fresh or frozen calamari rings

3 stalks celery

1 fennel bulb

3 tablespoons freshly squeezed lemon juice

4 tablespoons extra-virgin olive oil

Fine salt and freshly ground black pepper

SERVES 6

*C*risp and refreshing thanks to the fresh fennel and celery in it, this Roman seafood salad is made with two local delicacies, shrimp and calamari, usually caught by day boats from Rome's port, Ostia. It's easy and quick. You can use fresh or frozen seafood to make it, and the typically Roman herbs—bay leaf and thyme—can be either fresh or dried. You rarely see fish appetizers in Rome, except those with lots of mayo or aspic offered in touristy international-style restaurants. But this recipe is authentic—all the ingredients are Lazio regional old-timers. It's a hot-weather favorite, served at room temperature or, better yet, chilled.

Note: For cleaning instructions for calamari or squid, see page 133.

1   Pour 2 to 2½ cups cold water into a medium-sized saucepan. Add the thyme, bay leaf, vinegar and peppercorns. Bring the water to a boil over high heat.

2   Drop the seafood into the boiling liquid, stirring with a wooden spoon. Bring the liquid back to a boil, lower the heat to medium and simmer for 10 minutes, stirring occasionally.

3   Dice the celery and fennel bulb and combine them in a serving bowl. Dress them with the lemon juice, oil, salt and plenty of pepper.

4   Drain the seafood through a sieve or colander and let it cool to room temperature. Discard the bay leaf and peppercorns. Add the seafood to the bowl with the diced vegetables and toss thoroughly.

5   Let the salad sit for 15 minutes so the seafood can absorb the lemon juice and oil. Serve at room temperature or chilled. You can refrigerate this salad in a sealed container for up to 24 hours.

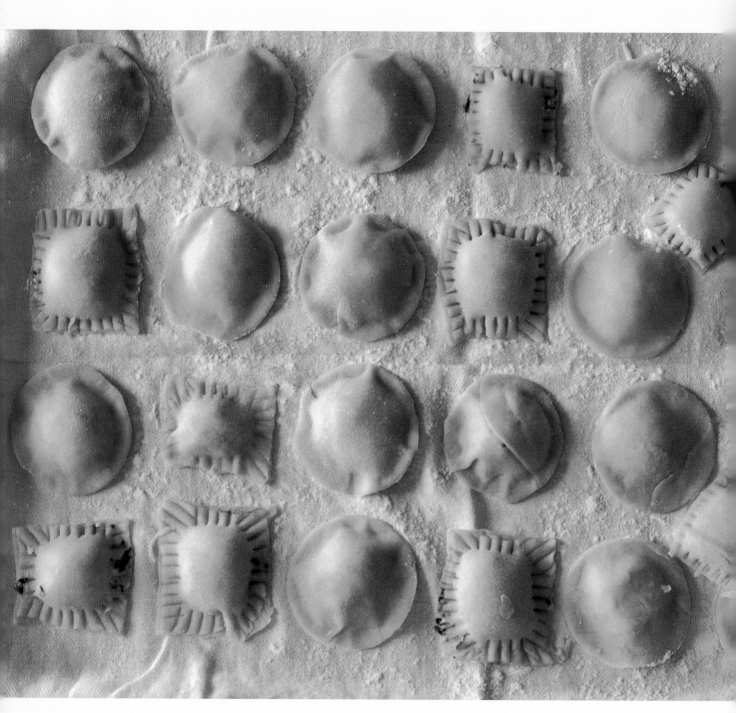

Roman Spinach and Ricotta Ravioli (page 72)

PRIMI PIATTI

Soup, Pasta and Risotto

IN HER SEMINAL 1929 BOOK, *La cucina romana,* cookbook writer Ada Boni listed forty-five Roman starters, of which about half were soup, labeled either *zuppa* or *minestra* (in Rome, usually a soup thickened with pasta or bread). Many Roman soups are so satisfying they could really be considered *piatti unici*—stand-alone, all-in-one dishes. In the booming *Dolce Vita* days of the 1950s and '60s, when a cosmopolitan, urbane lifestyle was the rage, *zuppa* and *minestra* went out of fashion because they were considered peasant foods. But humble, wholesome soup has made a big comeback in the last 15 years or so.

Roman soup recipes are remarkable for their earthiness and complex flavors, ranging from light-bodied but intensely herbal to thick, stewlike soups made with broccoli, skate and pasta; pasta and potatoes; onions and eggs; or chickpeas, hulled wheat and chestnuts.

Like the Neapolitans, Romans are big pasta eaters and have been so for a long, long time. There are dozens of homegrown Roman pasta recipes and a handful of typical pasta types, both dry (*pastasciutta*) and fresh (*pasta fresca*). Many of the Romans' favorite pastas are familiar to Americans because they were among the first to reach the United States with the late nineteenth- and early twentieth-century waves of Italian immigrants. The king of fresh egg ribbon pasta in Rome is fettuccine, flanked by its counterpart *tonnarelli,* which are made from the same ingredients and come out either plump and round or square-shaped. *Tonnarelli* are tough to find in America so in these recipes I recommend using fettuccine instead. For Romans, fresh filled egg pasta usually means ravioli stuffed with ricotta and spinach, or with ground beef or veal.

Fresh gnocchi (as opposed to the dry, packaged kind) are more dumpling than pasta but are nonetheless universally included among the pasta dishes in Roman trattorias, restaurants and Roman homes. There are two types of fresh gnocchi, one made with mashed potatoes mixed with flour, the other with semolina (medium-coarse milled durum wheat).

In Rome, all of these fresh pasta and gnocchi types are made at home or bought from *pasta fresca* stores found in every neighborhood. Since such stores are few and far between in the United States, I've included recipes for making fresh pasta from scratch. Most of the dry pasta types popular in Rome, made with durum wheat or regular flour and eggs, are easy to find in the United States. Ribbon or long pasta varieties typical of Rome (though not uniquely Roman) are spaghetti, *spaghettoni* (large spaghetti), fettuccine, *ricce* (wavy-edged fettuccine) and *bavette* (alias *trenette* or linguine). The long, hollow Roman pasta is *bucatini,* a very close cousin of *perciatelli,* also from Lazio, or *foratini, fidelini* and *fide bucate,* which are regional names for similar pasta shapes. Authentically Roman short, straight pastas are penne and rigatoni, which are also eaten in other parts of Italy. Uniquely Roman elbow or shell pastas are *maniche di frate* (friar's sleeves), *bombolotti* (big little pipes) and *paccheri* (giant elbows). Equally loved are *cannolicchi* (short little tubes), which you find in several central Italian regions. All of these short pastas are easily substituted with the universally popular *pipe rigate* (ridged pipes) or shells of various sizes. All Roman dry pastas are readily available from Italian specialty food shops and many supermarkets in the United States.

Pasta e Ceci

PASTA AND CHICKPEAS WITH ROSEMARY AND GARLIC

1 pound dry chickpeas (about 3 cups) or 2 (15.5-ounce) cans chickpeas

2 cloves garlic

1 anchovy fillet (optional)

4 tablespoons extra-virgin olive oil

3 heaping tablespoons fresh rosemary leaves

5 quarts water

Kosher salt or coarse sea salt and freshly ground black pepper

8 ounces elbow pasta (*cannolicchi, maniche di frate, bombolotti,* shells, *pipe rigate*)

About 1 cup freshly grated cheese, half Pecorino Romano and half Parmigiano-Reggiano

SERVES 6

Since Fridays—for Catholics the lean day of the week—were taken up by fish, chickpeas, also considered by the church a lean food, wound up having their "canonical day" of the week on Tuesdays. No one seems to know why—the choice of Tuesday is a mystery, though some say, "Tuesday is a semi-lean day." Perhaps it *was* back in the days of the Papal States before Italy was unified in 1860. *Pasta e ceci* appears on the menus of dozens of traditional trattorias like Da Gino, hidden down a dogleg alley near the Italian parliament building. Gino's real name is Luigi del Grosso, and he's run the place since the 1950s. His recipe is much older than that though, and it's as popular today as ever, even among the trendy cellular-wielding youngsters and brash politicians he has as clients. It's satisfying to catch powerful ministers and members of parliament bent over their bowls like humble human beings, happily slurping up Gino's thick, garlicky pasta-and-chickpea stew. The sight fills me with hope for the future of Italian food and politics.

The purist recipe for *pasta e ceci* banishes cheese and calls for an anchovy to give piquancy. But I find it comes out exquisite with or without the anchovy and/or cheese. The trick to getting this nutty-flavored pasta stew nice and thick is to crush 10 to 15 percent of the chickpeas with the spoon while stirring.

1 Soak the dry chickpeas, if using, in several changes of cold water for at least 8 hours, preferably overnight. Drain them in a colander. If you are using canned chickpeas, drain and rinse them.

2 Peel and mince the garlic, discarding any imperfections including the green shoot.

3 If you are using the anchovy fillet, desalt it (see Desalting Anchovies, page 24).

4 Heat 2 tablespoons of the oil in a large earthenware or stainless steel pot over medium-low heat. Add the minced garlic and sauté for 1 minute.

5 Stir the rosemary leaves into the pot. Add the chickpeas and sauté over high heat, stirring continuously for 3 to 4 minutes. Pour in the water and bring the liquid to a boil. Lower the heat and simmer the chickpeas until tender, stirring occasionally and crushing with a wooden spoon or spatula, about 2 hours (30 to 45 minutes for canned chickpeas). The stew should evenly coat the back of a wooden spoon or spatula.

6 Add several pinches each of salt and pepper, stir in the pasta and simmer until soft, about 15 minutes.

7 Serve the stew in soup bowls. Drizzle the remaining 2 tablespoons oil over the stew and pass a bowl of freshly grated cheeses on the side.

Zuppa di Ceci, Farro e Castagne

CHICKPEA, FARRO AND CHESTNUT SOUP

8 ounces dry chickpeas (about 1½ cups) or 1 (15.5-ounce) can chickpeas

8 ounces imported Italian farro or spelt (about 1¼ cups)

8 cups water

8 ounces fresh chestnuts (about 1½ cups) or 1 (16-ounce) can chestnuts packed in water

1 bay leaf

Pinch of sugar

1 medium-sized white onion

2 cloves garlic

2 heaping tablespoons minced rosemary leaves

6 tablespoons extra-virgin olive oil

Kosher salt or coarse sea salt

½ cup Italian dry white wine, preferably Frascati or Marino

Freshly ground black pepper

SERVES 6 TO 8

*T*he Alban Hills and Apennine slopes near Rome have long been cloaked with chestnut trees, some groves going back thousands of years. This rustic soup combines chestnuts with two other millennial ingredients, chickpeas (garbanzo beans) and farro, a hulled wheat that is called emmer or starch grain in English. This primitive grain is the ancestor of modern wheat (see Farro: How's it Spelt? page 10). The ancient Roman word for "farro" was *far*. When ground into flour, *far* was called *farina,* which gives us the modern Italian and English word "farina" (flour). So farro may well be the fountainhead of all wheat. It's still grown in its various primitive forms in Lazio and Tuscany and is widely available in Italy. Farmers in Canada and the northern United States grow a type of related hulled wheat, spelt (*Triticum spelta*). Although very different in texture and gluten content, spelt works fine in this recipe. Spelt is available in most health food stores and many supermarkets. You can find imported Italian farro in many Italian food shops and by mail order (see Sources, page 297).

A delicious, naturally sweet and nutty-flavored fall-winter soup still made in the Alban Hills by home cooks, it has been rediscovered thanks to a handful of chefs, such as Adriana Montellanico of La Briciola restaurant in Grottaferrata, who made the soup for me, explaining the venerable recipe's fine points.

1   Soak the dry chickpeas in several changes of cold water for at least 8 hours, preferably overnight. Drain in a colander. If you are using canned chickpeas, drain in a colander and rinse with cold water.

2   Pour the farro into a sieve, rinse it under cold water and let it drip dry.

3   Bring the water to a boil in a large pot. If you are using fresh chestnuts, scrub them under cold running water. Drop them into the boiling water and blanch for 1 minute. Keep the water boiling. With a slotted spoon, remove the chestnuts and rinse them under cold running water until they are cool enough to handle. With a paring knife, peel and quarter them, eliminating the hairy inner skin and any imperfections. Add the quartered chestnuts, bay leaf, and sugar to the boiling water and stir with a wooden spoon or spatula. Bring the water back to a boil. Lower the heat and simmer for about 10 minutes, until the chestnuts are tender. If you are using canned chestnuts, drain off the water, quarter them and add them with the bay leaf and sugar to the boiling water. Boil for 2 to 3 minutes only.

4   Fish out and discard the bay leaf. With a slotted spoon, fish out the chestnuts and reserve. Keep the cooking water simmering for later use.

5   Peel the onion and garlic and remove the garlic's green shoot. Mince them with the rosemary leaves.

6   Heat 4 tablespoons of the oil in a large earthenware or stainless steel pot over medium heat. Add a generous pinch of salt and the minced garlic, onion and rosemary. Sauté until the onion becomes translucent, stirring with a wooden spoon or spatula, about 2 minutes. Add the wine and boil to evaporate it, 1 to 2 minutes.

7   Stir in the chickpeas and sauté for 2 minutes. Ladle in enough of the boiling chestnut water to barely cover the chickpeas. Cover the pot and bring it to a hard boil. Add the farro, stir, cover the pot and bring the liquid to a boil.

8   Drop in the quartered chestnuts and ladle in another 4 cups of the chestnut water. Grind in plenty of black pepper. Bring the soup back to a boil. Lower the heat and simmer, covered, for at least 2 hours, stirring occasionally and crushing the chickpeas and chestnuts with a wooden spoon to thicken the soup. As the soup cooks, add chestnut water, 1 ladle at a time, to maintain the same level and chunky, fairly thick consistency.

9   Serve the soup hot in soup bowls. Swirl in the remaining 2 tablespoons extra-virgin olive oil, and serve with a peppermill on the side.

Zuppa di Finocchio e Fagioli

FENNEL AND BEAN SOUP WITH CHERRY TOMATOES, MINT, BASIL AND SAGE

1½ pounds dry red kidney beans (about 4½ cups)

Water

6 to 8 whole fresh sage leaves

Kosher salt or coarse sea salt

2 cloves garlic

2 medium-sized white onions

3 stalks celery

1 small bulb fennel

4 to 6 thin slices Parma ham (about 2 ounces) (optional)

1½ pounds cherry tomatoes

4 tablespoons extra-virgin olive oil

3 heaping tablespoons minced fresh spearmint

3 heaping tablespoons minced basil

4 heaping tablespoons minced dill

Freshly ground black pepper

1 heaping tablespoon aniseeds or fennel seeds

About 1 cup freshly grated cheese, half Pecorino Romano and half Parmigiano-Reggiano

SERVES 6 TO 8

Wild fennel grows like a weed in and around Rome, making it a cheap—or free—food. This peasant recipe for fennel, beans and lots of fresh herbs comes from the Alban Hills, a region of long-extinct volcanoes south of Rome, known for its vineyards, orchards and market gardens full of fresh herbs. The multi-herb treatment makes this simple recipe come alive with the wonderful flavors of sage, garlic, mint, basil and dill. Rome's southeastern city limits run right up to the foot of the Alban Hills nowadays, and a large number of talented chefs operate restaurants there. Adriana Montellanico, chef-owner of La Briciola in Grottaferrata, showed me how she makes this soup. Since wild fennel isn't easily found in America outside the San Francisco Bay Area, I use domestic fennel and fennel seeds instead, plus lots of fresh dill, and the results are delicious. To make this a vegetarian recipe, leave out the ham.

1   Soak the beans in several changes of cold water for 8 hours, preferably overnight. Drain and transfer the soaked beans to a large pot and barely cover them with cold water. Add the sage leaves and a pinch of salt, cover the pot and bring the water to a boil.

2   Boil, covered, for 20 minutes, stirring often. Lower the heat and simmer, partially covered, for 3 to 4 hours, stirring every 20 minutes or so and adding warm water by the ladle to keep the soup from boiling dry or excessive thickening.

3   Peel the garlic and onion, removing and discarding the garlic's green shoot. Coarsely chop both. Remove the stringy matter, stalks and leaves from the celery and fennel and thinly slice them. Mince the Parma ham, if using. Cut the tomatoes in half.

4   Heat 2 tablespoons of the oil in a frying pan over medium heat. Add the garlic, onion, celery, fennel and ham, if using, and sauté, stirring, until the onion becomes translucent, 2 to 3 minutes.

5   Add the tomatoes to the frying pan and sauté, stirring, for 2 to 3 minutes. Lower the heat and keep the mixture simmering. Add the mint, basil and dill to the frying pan with a pinch each of salt and pepper. Stir in the fennel seeds.

6   When the beans are tender, add the herb-and-vegetable mixture from the frying pan and stir thoroughly. Simmer for 2 to 3 minutes, uncovered.

7   Turn off the heat and let the soup sit for 1 to 2 minutes. Serve the soup in deep bowls with the remaining 2 tablespoons oil swirled in. Pass a bowl with the cheeses on the side.

The Arch of Titus in the Forum,
with the Coliseum in the background

In the Belly of the Poet:
G. G. Belli, Rome's Famished Bard

Giuseppe Gioachino Belli (1791 to 1863), Rome's best-loved dialect poet, exalted the language and ways of simple folk, though he himself was an educated member of the middle class. A virulent anti-papist like many Romans then and now, his works revolve around two major themes: the corruption of the church and the wonders of Roman food. Often the two are intertwined. And that's why, almost a century-and-a-half after his death, G. G. Belli remains a local hero, with a monument to his honor in Trastevere, Rome's institutionalized "popular quarter" inhabited by *romani di Roma*—authentic Romans from Rome.

At the highbrow end, the spirited Belli wowed members of the Tiberina Academy in 1840 by paraphrasing French savant Brillat-Savarin's *Physiologie du goût,* a revolutionary book on the marvels of the culinary arts. Brillat-Savarin had quipped that the discovery of a new delicacy was more important than the discovery of a new star in the heavens (this was 1840 and astronomy was all the rage). Noted Belli: "Gastronomy" is even more wondrous than "astronomy" because it encompasses it plus a "G."

Fellow anti-clerics applauded when Belli scorned the beatification of a certain Ippolito Galantini, whose miracle was to have resuscitated roasted songbirds that a poor countryman was about to eat. The happy birds took wing, leaving the man hungry. A miracle? It was a Friday, the lean day of the week, and by Vatican law no one in the Papal States could eat meat, red or otherwise. The starving sinner was thus punished. Where the Pope saw beatitude, Belli sniffed criminal interference and dietary dictatorship.

In what I think of as probably Belli's most delightfully subversive poem, "*La Cucina der Papa*" ("The Pope's Kitchen"), the narrator has just visited the papal kitchens while the pope's cook busily prepares a feast of veal, beef, chicken, eggs, fish, greens, pork and game. Impressed, the narrator asks, "Is the Pope expecting a regal guest?" The cook chuckles: "Nooooo, the Pope always eats alone."

It was Belli who nicknamed eggplants *marignani* (in Italian, they're called *melanzane*), because minor prelates were called *marignani,* and their robes were an eggplant color, their bodies an eggplant shape. The moniker has stuck to this day. Belli also may have been the first to call German seminarians *gamberi cotti* (cooked prawns) because they turned red in the Roman sun just as modern-day tourists do.

For culinary historians, Belli represents a bottomless gullet of gastronomical intelligence about the lifestyle and eating habits of Romans of all classes in the first half of the nineteenth century. In his thousand-plus sonnets, he describes a wedding feast, banquets (of the rich and the poor), the Christmas Eve delicacies a cardinal will eat while the poor folks look on, and an Eastertide meal that shows how much more Romans revered food than the Vatican's brand of religion. Amazingly, many of the dishes Belli describes are still popular today: crostini (see page 25); Roman artichokes (see page 34); *misticanza* salad (see page 224); pan-fried chicory; prosciutto and salami; gnocchi (see page 70); boiled chicken or beef and their broth (see page 62); roasted, stuffed or stewed chicken and turkey (pages 184 and 190); sweet-and-sour wild boar (see page 174); tripe (see page 149); *garofolato* (see page 146); fried fish; salt cod in tomato sauce; Christmas cake; *zuppa inglese* (see page 275); wine-dipping cookies (see page 267); *crostata* (see page 292) and dozens of other perennials. Belli may also have been the first Italian to use a dialect version of the term *trattoria,* derived from the French word *traiteur,* meaning "caterer." Like most Romans of his day, Belli didn't particularly love the French, since it was they who protected the Papal States and thwarted the Italian revolutionaries bent on unifying the country. And he didn't have much time for their food, either.

Stracciatella

ROMAN EGG-DROP SOUP

8 cups homemade chicken broth (see page 62)

2 large eggs, at room temperature

$^{1}/_{2}$ cup freshly grated Parmigiano-Reggiano

$^{1}/_{2}$ cup freshly grated Pecorino Romano

2 heaping tablespoons minced fresh flat-leaf parsley

1 tablespoon freshly squeezed lemon juice

Kosher salt or coarse sea salt and freshly ground black pepper

Pinch of nutmeg

SERVES 6 TO 8

Stracciatella stands for two things in Rome: chocolate-chip ice cream and egg-drop soup. The name derives from *straccetti* (little rags or tatters). The consistency of *stracciatella* depends on the ragged pieces of egg in it. The faster you stir, the finer they are. What makes this soup especially delicious is the squirt of lemon juice and pinch of nutmeg added at the end.

1   Bring the broth to a slow boil in a medium saucepan over medium heat. Reduce the heat to low and simmer.

2   Beat the eggs in a mixing bowl. Add the cheeses and stir in the parsley.

3   Whisk the boiling broth so it swirls clockwise. Pour in the egg mixture and whisk vigorously until the eggs tear into tiny shreds, about 1 minute. Add the lemon juice and season the soup with a pinch of salt, plenty of freshly ground pepper and a pinch of nutmeg.

4   Ladle the soup into soup bowls and serve immediately.

In the narrow little throat of street, beyond, a booth, dressed out with flaring lamps, and boughs of trees, attracts a group of sulky Romans round its smoky coppers of hot broth, and cauliflower stew; its trays of fried fish, and its flasks of wine.

Charles Dickens, *Pictures from Italy*

Brodo di Gallina

CHICKEN BROTH

3-pound chicken, hen or roaster, preferably range-raised, or 3 pounds beef, preferably a tough cut

12 cups cold water

2 celery stalks

2 carrots

1 medium-sized onion

Kosher salt or coarse sea salt

10 black peppercorns

SERVES 6 TO 8 (YIELDS 12 CUPS BROTH AND 3 POUNDS POULTRY OR BEEF)

*R*omans use broth and stock extensively. The most popular variety by far is made with chicken. Use this recipe for pasta sauces, meat, poultry and soups, such as *Stracciatella* (see page 61), whose prime ingredient is chicken broth.

You can make this recipe with either chicken or beef.

1   Combine the chicken and water in a large stockpot.

2   Rinse and scrape the celery and carrots. Peel the onion. Add them to the stockpot with a pinch of salt and the peppercorns.

3   Cover and bring the water to a boil over medium-high heat. Reduce the heat to low and simmer, partially covered, for about 1 hour, skimming off any fat and foam.

4   Remove the chicken from the broth and bone it. Keep the meat for other uses. Strain the broth, skim off the fat and serve it hot. Or, if it's very fatty, cool, chill, and remove the fat before reheating it.

NOTE: You can refrigerate chicken broth in sealed containers for up to 5 days or freeze it for several months. To make a quick substitute for broth or stock, bring 4 to 8 cups of water to a boil and add a peeled whole onion, several whole sprigs of parsley and a generous pinch of black pepper or 10 black peppercorns. Boil gently for at least 15 minutes. Strain before using. The difference between homemade broth and store-bought broth, or bouillon cubes, is enormous. If you must use cubes, I strongly recommend avoiding those containing MSG.

Minestra di Arzilla e Broccolo Romano

SKATE, BROCCOLI AND PASTA SOUP

2 cups peeled, seeded and chopped medium-sized fresh Italian plum tomatoes (about 1 pound) (see How to Peel and Seed a Tomato, page 93)

Kosher salt or coarse sea salt

2 pounds skate, cleaned and skinned

2 cloves garlic

2 anchovy fillets

4 tablespoons extra-virgin olive oil

1 *peperoncino* (hot chili pepper) shredded, or ¼ teaspoon crushed red pepper flakes

1 pound broccoli, preferably *broccolo romano* (Romanesco broccoli), cut into florets

1 cup penne, rigatoni, shells or other short pasta (about 4 ounces)

SERVES 6

*T*raditionally served on Holy Friday, this classic Roman soup often appears on trattoria menus on other Fridays—the lean day of the week—throughout the year. Skate was long considered a fish for the poorer classes, possibly because it's tricky to clean. A primitive creature like shark, skate has cartilage instead of bones. The cartilage makes wonderful stock and means there are no sharp little bones to fuss over. That's what makes skate ideal for this recipe, which merges soup, stew and pasta. The flavors are intense; the emulsifying process brings out the spiciness of the hot chili. The pasta cooked directly in the stock helps to thicken the consistency. Be warned: You won't see *minestra di arzilla* served by cooks concerned with the aesthetics of their plated masterworks. This is homely, homey food, but delicious. The word *arzilla* is Roman dialect for the Italian *razza* (ray fish). *Arzilla* also means "full of vim and vigor," and that explains why Romans consider this peppy recipe with lots of pungent broccoli and vitamin-packed tomatoes a real pick-me-up.

1   Bring 4 quarts of water to a boil in a large pot. (It can be the same water used for peeling the tomatoes.)

2   Add a generous pinch of salt and the skate to the boiling water. Lower the heat to medium and boil the skate for 10 minutes, stirring occasionally and skimming off any froth and foam.

3   With the heel of your hand or the flat part of a wide-bladed knife, crush the garlic on a cutting board. Spread the cloves open with your fingers. Discard the skins and green shoots. If you are using salted anchovies, desalt them (see Desalting Anchovies, page 24). For anchovy fillets packed in oil, remove them with a fork and drain them on paper towels.

4   Heat the oil in a large saucepan over medium-low heat. Add the garlic, sauté for 2 minutes and discard it. Add the *peperoncino*. Add the anchovies to the saucepan, crushing and stirring with a wooden spoon, about 1 minute.

5   Toss the tomatoes into the saucepan, stirring and crushing for about 5 minutes.

6   Stir the broccoli into the saucepan, sautéing for 2 to 3 minutes. Raise the heat to medium-high and begin incorporating the boiling skate stock into the tomato-and-broccoli mixture, one ladle (about 1 cup) at a time, letting it froth, reduce and emulsify. The process should take about 15 minutes and use 1½ to 2 cups of stock.

7   Carefully transfer the skate from the stockpot to a cutting board. Let it cool for a minute or so. Scrape the skate off the cartilage with a serrated knife, following the grain of the flesh. Discard the cartilage. Roughly chop the skate and add it to the saucepan.

8   Ladle 4 cups of skate stock into the saucepan, increase the heat to high and bring the contents to a hard boil. Toss in the pasta and cook it until it is about half done, 4 to 6 minutes. Cover the pot and let the soup sit for 4 to 6 minutes to finish cooking the pasta.

9   Transfer the soup to a large serving bowl or tureen and serve immediately in deep soup bowls.

How to Roast, Skin
and Seed a Sweet Pepper

Italians, in general, and Romans, in particular, object to eating the slippery, indigestible, translucent membrane that sheaths sweet (bell) peppers. It has an unpleasant consistency, "like a hair on your tongue" as one Roman friend of mine puts it. There are many ways to roast, skin and seed a *peperone*. Vegetable peelers are not part of the Roman sweet-pepper-peeling arsenal—for good reason. They're tricky to use on the waxy, rubbery skin and, above all, can't impart to the pepper that delicious caramelized flavor derived from scorching, grilling or roasting.

Some Roman cooks blacken their *peperoni* in the oven at high heat. Many cooks abhor this, because roasting renders peppers flaccid. That's why most Romans grill them whole on the stovetop, placing the peppers directly on the burners—a messy but straightforward method. Afterward, some cooks plunge the peppers whole into a deep pot of cold water and weigh them down under the surface until the skins start to detach. This can make the peppers watery, washing away their juices and diluting their concentrated sweetness.

Other practitioners wrap the grilled whole peppers, still scalding hot, in wet kitchen towels, while others drop them into pots with tight-fitting lids, or into brown paper or plastic bags, to let the natural steam inside the moist hot vegetables soften the peel.

Here are three ways of roasting and peeling peppers that combine the best of the above, plus a fourth way that's fast and easy with imperfect results.

1   The first-choice method for preparing any kind of pepper in any season uses the barbecue. Blacken the peppers on a grill over the flames or coals for 10 to 15 minutes. Transfer them to a Dutch oven or pot big enough to hold them and cover it tightly. Let the peppers steam for 15 to 20 minutes, until cool enough to handle. Rub and peel the skins off.

2   The second method features a standard kitchen gas range. You can use electric burners but the clean up is tedious because the peppers stick to the elements. This works best with ripe, summery-sweet yellow and red bell peppers. Start by covering your stovetop

with aluminum foil to protect it from sticky juices. Poke holes in the foil large enough so the gas burners come through. Soak one paper towel per pepper in cold water. Spread the towels on a countertop. Next to them, place a Dutch oven or other large pot with a lid, big enough to hold all the peppers. Carbonize the peppers directly on the flames, balancing them on the burners and turning every minute or so with metal tongs until thoroughly blackened, about 15 minutes. Transfer the peppers one by one to the wet paper towels, wrap them carefully but quickly and use the tongs to lower them into the Dutch oven or pot. Cover the peppers and let them steam for 20 minutes, until cool enough to handle. Using the damp paper towels, rub the skins off.

3   The third technique works best with out-of-season hothouse peppers and green bell peppers, which often have a slightly bitter edge. It's not the right technique if you want your peppers firm. Preheat your oven to 450°F. Place the peppers in an uncovered Dutch oven or on a baking sheet and roast them for 20 to 30 minutes, turning 4 to 6 times. Alternatively, if you have a broiler in your oven, use it to char the peppers for 10 to 15 minutes, turning often. Roasting and/or grilling indeed makes the peppers flaccid, but it also concentrates their sweetness, a nice trade-off. Transfer the peppers to a large pot and seal it. Let the peppers steam for 20 minutes, until cool enough to handle. Rub their skins off.

4   My sister Diane Downie, an avid eater of sweet peppers, favors another method when in a hurry. Here's how she puts it: "I clean out the seeds and ribs of each pepper as I would for making stuffed peppers. I cut out the top around the stem, reach in and pull out the seeds and ribs then rinse out the pepper. I use an older, heavy skillet over high heat and throw in the peppers, rotating them with tongs until blackened all around. Then I turn off the heat, cover them to steam for about 15 minutes and remove the skin with my fingers and a knife. It's fast and a lot less messy than some other methods, but usually leaves some skin on the pepper."

Whichever method you choose, you'll need to seed and finish cleaning the peppers on a cutting board set into a rimmed baking sheet to catch the juice that runs from them. Once you've removed and discarded the seeds and membranes, slice or chop the peppers or spread them flat, as called for by the recipe.

Bombolotti con Crema di Peperoni

ELBOW PASTA WITH SWEET PEPPER AND GARLIC PURÉE

4 cloves garlic

4 tablespoons extra-virgin olive oil

Kosher salt or coarse sea salt

I pound *bombolotti* (or *cannolicchi, maniche di frate, pipe rigate,* or other elbow or shell pasta)

6 large yellow and/or red sweet (bell) peppers, roasted, skinned and seeded (see How to Roast, Skin and Seed a Sweet Pepper, page 65)

Freshly ground black pepper

4 heaping tablespoons freshly grated Pecorino Romano

About I cup freshly grated cheese, half Pecorino Romano and half Parmigiano-Reggiano

SERVES 4

Ettore Graziani was born into a family of greengrocers who worked the Piazza di San Cosimato market in Trastevere for generations. Before giving up their stand recently, he and his mother Armanda shared with us this great summery recipe for sweet peppers puréed with garlic and swirled with Pecorino Romano and olive oil, a wonderfully simple and original sauce that goes especially well with short elbow pasta.

1   Bring 5 quarts or more water to a boil in a large pot.

2   With the heel of your hand or the flat part of a wide-bladed knife, crush the garlic on a cutting board. Spread the cloves open with your fingers. Discard the skins and green shoots.

3   Heat 2 tablespoons of the oil in a large, high-sided frying pan over medium. Add the garlic and sauté until it begins to color, 2–3 minutes. Remove the frying pan from the heat.

4   Add a generous pinch of salt to the boiling water. Toss in the pasta, stir and cover until the pot returns to a boil. Remove the lid.

5   Combine the garlic with its cooking oil and the peppers in a food processor and process to a thick, pulpy purée. Transfer the purée to the frying pan and reduce it over medium-low heat, stirring frequently while the pasta cooks.

6   Drain the pasta when it is barely al dente and toss it still dripping into the frying pan with the pepper sauce. Stir and toss vigorously, incorporating a generous pinch of freshly ground black pepper, the remaining 2 tablespoons oil and 4 heaping tablespoons of freshly grated Pecorino Romano.

7   Serve immediately with a bowl of freshly grated cheeses on the side.

Gnocchi di Semolino alla Romana

BAKED SEMOLINA GNOCCHI WITH BUTTER AND PARMIGIANO-REGGIANO, ROMAN STYLE

Two types of gnocchi, the first made with semolina, the second with mashed potatoes, vie for the hearts and stomachs of Romans. I've seen locals almost come to blows arguing over which is the older, more authentic, more Roman of the two. But since the potato didn't show up on Roman tables until about three hundred years ago, and semolina has been around a lot longer (though it was originally made with milled hulled wheat or other grains), I have a feeling the semolina gnocchi win out. This recipe's suffix, *alla romana,* would further militate for the seniority of semolina. Many Roman food writers and gastronomes now think that the potato dethroned the original version several centuries ago. But semolina has come back much improved, because it's now made from durum wheat. Happily both types of gnocchi are easily prepared and equally desirable for their luscious, melt-in-your-mouth butteryness. They are also very different: *Gnocchi di semolina alla romana* is a stand-alone dish—you don't need to sauce it. *Gnocchi di Patate* (page 70) is a vehicle for tomato or meat sauce.

Gnocchi di semolino alla romana is the archetypal comfort food, made by every Roman home cook I know. Our friend Carla Bertini, a lover of traditional Roman cuisine, took us into her kitchen in eastern-central Rome and showed us the tricks that she learned from her mother and grandmother for making these gnocchi.

4 cups whole milk

8 ounces semolina (about 1⅓ cups)

½ cup butter (1 stick)

2 cups freshly grated Parmigiano-Reggiano

2 egg yolks

Kosher salt or coarse sea salt

SERVES 6

1   Heat the milk in a medium saucepan over medium-high to just under a boil. Remove it from the heat and sprinkle in the semolina while stirring with a wooden spoon.

2   Lower the heat and return the pot to the burner. Simmer the semolina, stirring constantly, for 10 minutes. Add ¼ cup of the butter, ½ cup of the cheese and the egg yolks. Stir until they melt thoroughly into the semolina, 2 to 3 minutes. Remove the pot from the heat.

3   With cold water and a clean sponge or paper towel, moisten a large work surface, preferably a marble slab. Turn out the semolina and, with the wet blunt edge of a long-bladed knife, spread and flatten the semolina to a thickness of about ½ inch.

4   Let the semolina cool for 30 to 40 minutes, until firm. With a sharp knife, a cookie cutter or a medium-sized water glass, cut the semolina into 2-inch squares, rounds or other shapes.

5   Preheat the oven to 400° F. Butter a deep 7-by-12-inch baking dish.

6   Fill the baking dish with gnocchi set side by side and sprinkle them with about ¼ cup of the remaining cheese. Slice the remaining ¼ cup butter into very thin pieces and scatter about one-third of it over the gnocchi.

7   Lay a second layer of gnocchi atop the first. Sprinkle them with 4 more tablespoons of the cheese and scatter another third of the butter over them. Continue building layers until the gnocchi have been used up. Top the gnocchi with the remaining one-third butter slices and a tablespoon or two of cheese.

8   Bake for 10 minutes. If you have a broiler, top-brown the gnocchi for 2 minutes.

9   Serve hot in pasta bowls with the remaining cheese passed on the side.

Gnocchi di Patate

Potato Gnocchi with Tomato or Meat Sauce

2 pounds potatoes, preferably Yukon gold, yellow Finn or russet

2¼–2½ cups all-purpose flour

Kosher salt or coarse sea salt

1 recipe *Sugo Finto* (page 89) or *Garofolato e Sugo d'Umido* (page 146)

4 tablespoons butter (½ stick), thinly sliced

About 1½ cups freshly grated Parmigiano-Reggiano

Serves 6

These little potato dumplings are served in many a Roman trattoria, traditionally on Thursdays. A festive dish, home cooks make them for the big family lunch on Sunday, instead. They are not unique to Rome, but over the last three hundred years, they have become part of the Roman repertoire, to the point of having almost driven out of existence the older, more rustic *gnocchi di semolino alla romana* (see page 68). Potato gnocchi are like the stone rustication on the ground floor of Rome's grand *palazzi;* they're something solid to build on. Depending on how they're sauced, they can reach baroque heights (eggplant and tomato sauce with minced mint, or spicy lamb sauce) or remain neo-classically pure. They're delicious enough on their own with butter and cheese, but I like them best with a simple, fresh tomato sauce or a classic meat ragù.

1   Scrub the potatoes and remove any imperfections with a paring knife. Cover them with cold water in a large pot. Bring the water to a boil over high heat. Lower the heat to medium and cook until tender, 10 to 15 minutes. Drain the potatoes in a colander and run cold water over them for 15 to 30 seconds to loosen the skins. With your fingers and a knife, remove and discard the skins.

2   Run the potatoes through a food mill or potato ricer directly into a large mixing bowl. Pour in 2 cups of the flour and a pinch of salt and knead with your fingers for 3 to 4 minutes to make a thick, sticky dough.

3   Transfer the dough to a flour-dusted board or marble slab and separate it into four
    equal parts. Dust your hands with flour. With your palms and fingers, roll each piece of
    the dough into a baton about ¾ inch in diameter.

4   Cover a platter with parchment or waxed paper and dust it with flour.

5   Cut the batons into roughly ½-inch by ¾-inch round dumplings. Separate the
    dumplings. Working with one at a time, use the tines of a fork to lightly impress the
    dumpling until slightly concave. Sprinkle with flour and carefully place the dumpling on
    the platter. Continue to make gnocchi and dust them with flour, setting them on the
    platter so that they do not touch each other, until the dough is used up.

6   Heat the sauce in a saucepan over medium-low to just under a boil. Lower the heat and
    simmer while the gnocchi cook.

7   Bring at least 5 quarts of water to a slow boil in a large pot. Add a very generous pinch
    of salt. With a wooden spoon, stir the water so that it spins slowly clockwise. Use your
    fingers and a spatula to transfer one dumpling at a time to the boiling water. Cook no
    more than ten gnocchi at once, stirring often to keep the water spinning slowly. When
    the gnocchi float to the surface, they're cooked.

8   Remove the gnocchi one at a time with a ravioli skimmer or slotted spoon and place
    them in a deep serving bowl. Top them with a tablespoon or so of sauce, a slice of butter
    and a small pinch of cheese. Continue to boil and transfer the gnocchi until all of them
    have been cooked, sauced and sprinkled with butter and cheese. Add any remaining
    sauce and butter to the bowl and toss gently.

9   Serve hot with a bowl of the remaining Parmigiano-Reggiano on the side.

Ravioli Quaresimali con Burro e Salvia

Roman Spinach-and-Ricotta Ravioli Sauced with Melted Butter and Fresh Sage

Once upon a time, the forty days of Lent between Ash Wednesday and Easter Sunday were strictly a meatless time for Roman Catholics. That's ostensibly why this spinach-and-ricotta-based ravioli recipe was devised. In fact, spinach and ricotta make a great combination any time of year, anywhere, regardless of religious tenets, and that's certainly why this recipe has survived into modern times. The ravioli are so delicious as is that you don't need to sauce them elaborately. The simplest dressing is olive oil (or melted butter) and fresh sage leaves. But a light tomato sauce (*Sugo Finto*, page 89) is great too. If you want a hearty sauce, try Roman meat ragù (*Garofolato e Sugo d'Umido*, page 146).

The pasta that envelopes the ravioli filling is slightly different from the one used for making fettuccine (see *Fettuccine Fresche all'Uovo*, page 117) in that it has more all-purpose flour proportionally to the durum wheat flour, and more egg yolk, plus tiny amounts of olive oil and white wine. I'm a great believer in totally handmade pasta; the texture and taste are superior to machine-made, and sauces of all kinds stick to it better because it's porous and irregularly shaped.

For the filling, there's nothing like real ewe's-milk ricotta imported from Rome. If you use low-fat American ricotta, make sure to drain off all the liquid and add in several extra heaping tablespoons of freshly grated Pecorino Romano to stiffen the texture and improve the flavor.

This recipe comes from the celebrated trattoria Sora Lella. My Roman friend Daniela Maggioni, a gifted ravioli-maker, helped me to adapt it for home cooks.

Trevi Fountain

FOR THE PASTA:

1½ cups all-purpose flour

½ cup durum wheat flour, plus 3 to 4 heaping tablespoons for dusting

1 egg yolk

2 large eggs

½ teaspoon salt

1 teaspoon extra-virgin olive oil

1 teaspoon dry white wine

About 3 tablespoons cold water, or more as needed

FOR THE FILLING:

12 ounces fresh young spinach

1 tablespoon butter

1 cup ricotta (about 8 ounces), preferably Italian ewe's-milk ricotta, at room temperature

Fine salt and freshly ground black pepper

Pinch of nutmeg

1 large egg, at room temperature

3 to 5 heaping tablespoons freshly grated Parmigiano-Reggiano

FOR THE SAUCE:

½ cup butter (½ stick) or ¼ cup extra-virgin olive oil

4 to 6 whole fresh sage leaves

Fine salt and freshly ground black pepper

1 cup freshly grated Parmigiano-Reggiano

SERVES 6

BY HAND DOUGH-MIXING METHOD:

1   To make the ravioli entirely by hand, you'll need a pasta board or food-safe countertop or tabletop. Combine the all-purpose flour and ½ cup durum wheat flour in a large bowl, and stir them together with a fork until thoroughly mixed. With your fingers or a wooden spoon, dig a well in the center.

2   Pour the yolk and 2 whole eggs into the flour well. Sprinkle in the salt and dribble in the oil, wine and water.

3   With the wooden spoon, break the egg yolks and stir slowly clockwise until the flour absorbs the eggs and liquids. Squeeze and knead the dough with your fingers until the dough is stiff and uniform, about 10 to 12 minutes. Transfer the dough to a large wooden cutting board or marble slab. Let it sit for 30 minutes before rolling it out.

STANDING-MIXER OR FOOD-PROCESSOR MIXING METHOD:

1   Combine the all-purpose flour and ½ cup durum wheat flour in the bowl of the standing mixer fitted with a dough hook or paddle attachment, or in a food processor with a wide blade. Mix at low speed or process for 15 seconds. Add the

eggs, salt, oil, wine and water. Mix at low speed or process until the dough becomes granular in consistency, 2 to 3 minutes.

2   With about 1 tablespoon of the remaining durum wheat flour, dust a large cutting board or marble slab. Turn the grainy dough out onto the cutting board. Flour your hands with the durum wheat flour and squeeze and knead the dough until it is uniform and stiff, adding a tablespoon or so of cold water. Let it sit for 30 minutes before rolling it out.

ROLLING OUT THE DOUGH:

1   With a rolling pin, roll out the dough to make a stiff but elastic sheet of pasta no more than $1/8$ inch thick. With a sharp knife, slice the sheet in half. Dust each sheet with durum wheat flour on both sides. Lifting with your fingers, put one sheet out of the way on the edge of the work surface or on a flour-dusted platter.

2   Flatten the first sheet until almost translucent, rolling firmly outward from a central point in all directions, gently lifting and turning the dough a quarter turn at a time, to form a rough disk. Carefully put the pasta sheet to the side on a cutting board or platter. This will be the top sheet of ravioli pasta.

3   Transfer the other sheet to the work surface and roll it out in the same way so that it is as close as possible to the same size and thickness as the first sheet. This will be the bottom sheet of ravioli pasta.

MAKING THE FILLING:

1   If the spinach is not prewashed, soak it in a large basin of cold water. Change the water several times. Break off and discard any woody stems or imperfect leaves. Rinse the spinach in a colander under cold running water to elimate any remaining traces of dirt or grit. Transfer the spinach, still dripping, to a large stockpot. Cover and cook, stirring frequently, over medium heat until the spinach wilts and expels its liquid, 8 to 12 minutes. Drain the cooked spinach in a colander, pressing down firmly with the base of a water glass and your fingers to eliminate as much of the juice as you can. You should have about $1^1/4$ cups firmly packed cooked spinach.

2   Melt the butter in the stockpot over medium-high heat. Add the spinach and sauté, stirring constantly, for 2 to 3 minutes.

3   Transfer the spinach to a cutting board and mince it. Transfer the spinach to a large
    mixing bowl.

4   If the ricotta is runny, place it in a cheesecloth-lined strainer and squeeze out the excess
    liquid. Stir the ricotta into the spinach, sprinkling in a generous pinch each of salt,
    pepper and nutmeg. Add the egg. Stir thoroughly, adding the Parmigiano-Reggiano to
    absorb any remaining spinach or ricotta juices. The mixture should have the consistency
    of a grainy paste. If it seems too wet, add grated cheese as needed to thicken and dry it.

MAKING THE RAVIOLI:

1   Scoop up the spinach-and-ricotta mixture 1 teaspoonful at a time and make equal
    mounds in rows spaced about ½ inch apart atop the bottom sheet of pasta.

2   Carefully lift the top sheet of pasta and align it over the bottom sheet.

3   With a serrated-edge pasta wheel, cut lines lengthwise and crosswise over the pasta
    around the mounds. Alternatively, use a small water glass or cookie cutter to cut around
    the mounds. Press down firmly as you cut to crimp the top and bottom sheets of pasta
    together. With your fingers or the tines of a fork, press down along the edges of the
    ravioli to make a solid seal.

4   Cover a large platter with a dishcloth or waxed paper. Sprinkle several generous pinches
    of flour over the ravioli. With a spatula and your fingers, transfer the ravioli to the
    platter. Build layers of flour-scattered ravioli on the platter.

5   Let the ravioli sit in a cool place for at least 30 minutes before cooking them. To store,
    loosely cover the platter with another dishcloth—never with plastic wrap, which will
    make the ravioli limp—and refrigerate for up to 24 hours.

MAKING THE SAUCE AND COOKING THE RAVIOLI:

1   Bring at least 5 quarts of water to a boil in a large pot.

2   Heat the butter in a small saucepan over low heat. Add the sage leaves and a pinch each
    of salt and pepper. Stir and let the sage flavor the butter, 2 to 3 minutes. Turn off the
    heat and discard the sage leaves.

3　Add a generous pinch of salt to the boiling water. With a wooden spoon, stir vigorously clockwise. With a ravioli skimmer or slotted spatula, gently but quickly lower the ravioli into the spinning water in small batches. Cover the pot. When the water returns to a boil, cook the ravioli, uncovered, until they float to the top, 2 to 3 minutes.

4　With the slotted skimmer or spatula, quickly transfer the ravioli to a serving bowl, pour the sage-perfumed butter over them and stir gently. Serve with a bowl of Parmigiano-Reggiano on the side.

NOTE: To make the pasta using a pasta-making machine, combine the pasta ingredients and follow the manufacturer's instructions for making ravioli. To roll and cut pasta with a machine, see How to Use a Home-Style Pasta-Rolling Machine, page 121.

Flour

Italian home cooks almost universally use two kinds of wheat flour. Highly refined, low-gluten "00" (zero-zero) flour from *Triticum aestivum* wheat goes into bread, pizza and desserts. Soft and powdery, it is lower in gluten but otherwise very close to American all-purpose flour, a perfect substitute. American pastry flour and bread flour are comparatively gluten-rich and aren't right for these recipes. The other kind of flour in the Italian kitchen cupboard is finely milled durum wheat flour, *Triticum durum,* and is reserved for making pasta. Mix it with all-purpose flour to make fettuccine, *tonnarelli* and ravioli. You can buy durum wheat flour at some supermarkets, most Italian specialty food shops, some fresh pasta shops, or by mail order. Semolina for *gnocchi di semolina* is a medium grind of durum wheat, widely available in American supermarkets; use it for gnocchi (it is not suitable for making fettuccine, *tonnarelli* or ravioli). In Rome, chestnut flour (*farina di castagne*) is used exclusively for *castagnaccio* (flat-bread, see page 274). Italian specialty food shops and some supermarkets stock it, and it too is available by mail order (see Sources, page 297, for all types of Italian and domestic flour).

Spaghetti Aglio, Olio e Peperoncino

Spaghetti with Garlic, Olive Oil and Hot Chili Pepper

4 cloves garlic

8 to 10 tablespoons extra-virgin olive oil

2 *peperoncini* (hot chili peppers), shredded, or ½ teaspoon crushed red pepper flakes

Kosher salt or coarse sea salt

1½ pounds spaghetti

2 heaping tablespoons minced flat-leaf parsley (optional)

1 cup freshly grated Parmigiano-Reggiano (optional)

SERVES 6

*S*ome cooks sprinkle either minced parsley or grated cheese on it, and some add crushed anchovy fillets to make *spaghetti con le alici,* but I like these garlicky, spicy spaghetti as is. The amount of oil is really up to you—I like lots but you can cut the quantity down by a couple of tablespoons if you prefer, adding more oil at the end if you find the pasta too dry. Since garlic is the prime ingredient in this recipe, make sure the garlic you buy is fresh and firm.

1   Bring at least 5 quarts of water to a boil in a large pot.

2   With the heel of your hand or the flat part of a wide-bladed knife, crush the garlic on a cutting board. Spread the cloves open with your fingers. Discard the skins and green shoots.

3   Heat the oil in a very large, high-sided frying pan over medium. Add the garlic and *peperoncino.* Sauté for 1 to 2 minutes. Remove and discard the garlic. Lower the heat and keep the frying pan warm.

4   Toss a generous pinch of salt into the boiling water. Drop in the spaghetti, stir and cover the pot. When the water returns to a boil, remove the lid and cook, uncovered, until barely al dente, about 1 minute less than the time given on the package. Drain the pasta.

5   Transfer the pasta to the frying pan, raise the heat to medium and sauté it with the garlicky oil for about 30 to 60 seconds.

6   Serve immediately in pasta bowls, sprinkled with the parsley, if using. Pass a bowl of Parmigiano-Reggiano on the side, if using.

Rome's Canonical Daily Specials

*O*nce upon a time in Rome, people looked forward to their weekly Sacred Wheel of rotating Roman classics; the choice was limited, but the quality was high. Though habits have evolved, with freewheeling culinary liberalism gaining the upper hand, the menu-week still often features:

Monday: *Bollito* (boiled beef or chicken)

Tuesday: *Pasta e ceci* (pasta and chickpeas), fish of some kind

Thursday: *Gnocchi di patate* (potato gnocchi)

Friday: *Pasta e broccoli, minestra di arzilla, baccalà* (pasta and broccoli, skate soup, salt cod)

Saturday: *Trippa alla romana* (tripe)

Sunday: *Abbacchio e fettuccine alla romana* (suckling lamb and hearty fettuccine)

And what about Wednesday? "It's always been the only day of the week when anything could be served," says my Roman friend Carla Bertini, a talented home cook. Now every day is Wednesday, so to speak, since daily specials are flanked by a myriad of menu choices.

A Tale of Two Pecorini:
Pecorino Romano

Cheese-maker Giuseppe Brunelli rubs his massive, hairless head, seemingly lifted off a Roman general's bust in the Vatican Museum, as he leads us through the cool, barrel-vaulted aging tunnels in his vast Pecorino Romano facility at Prima Porta on Rome's northern outskirts. "Rome was founded by shepherds," he says, "not heroes." His voice echoes among the approximately 200,000 keglike cheese rounds, each weighing 45 to 75 pounds and each worth $500 to $600, stacked in the ancient tunnels. The tunnels were carved starting two thousand years ago from a limestone hill once part of the park of the Augustan-era Villa Livia Drusilla. Brunelli is among the biggest producers of Pecorino Romano, supplying many of Italy's top cheese shops and delis, and he bristles when asked why 80 percent of Pecorino Romano comes not from Latium but Sardinia, since 1955 headquarters of the Pecorino Romano DOC (protected origin) consortium. "The name Pecorino Romano doesn't mean pecorino made in Rome, it means sheep's cheese made in the Roman way, which happens to be the ancient Roman way."

In fact, recipes reported by Cato the Censor going back to the second century B.C. detail how pecorino was made, and the cheese is amply described by Columella and Pliny the Elder (both first century A.D.), as well as other Roman writers. It was among the main foodstuffs of ancient shepherds, city folk and legionnaires alike, and today features in dozens of Roman recipes.

At multigenerational, family-run plants like Brunelli's, the Pecorino Romano is basically made in the old way, with stainless steel and plastic for hygiene. The ewes are milked twice daily, morning and evening, in the October to July period (not in August or September). The milk is mixed, filtered, cooled, heated to 68° C and centrifuged. It's reheated to 47° C in a vat, curdled with natural rennet, formed into rounds, branded, salted and aged for up to a year, with periodic brining and cleaning, then coated with black nontoxic plastic.

Once upon a time, millions of sheep grazed in and around Rome, but the total number now stands at approximately 650,000 head. There are four to five times as many in Sardinia. Sadly, the number of Latium sheep is declining as the capital continues to sprawl outward, overrunning prime grazing land. Only one family of shepherds still lives and grazes their flock inside Rome's city limits, among the ancient ruins of the Marrana della Caffarella parklands near the Via Appia Antica. Their crumbling farmhouse and tiny cheese works is an anachronism destined to go the way of the most prized Latium sheep breed, Sopravvissana, now nearly extinct. The Sarda breed, which produces three times the quantity of milk, has taken over purely for economic reasons. For the same reasons, Pecorino Romano production was shifted largely to Sardinia in the late nineteenth century to take advantage of the island's vast undeveloped spaces and impoverished economy. The story no one tells about Pecorino Romano is that Sardinia's seemingly boundless grazing land was hacked out of primeval cork oak

Salting a wheel of Pecorino Romano

forests, an assault whose ecological consequences are still felt more than a century later, particularly in terms of topsoil erosion.

"A sheep is a tool for turning a meadow into milk," says Brunelli, lamenting yet downplaying the loss of the Sopravvissana breed. "The sheep here and in Sardinia are the same now. The biggest difference between Pecorino Romano made here or there is the meadowland, not the animal. Latium's dark, rich soil with lots of humus produces lush grasses and forage, and rich milk. Sardinia is harsh, rocky and full of wild herbs, and the milk and cheeses reflect this."

Experts, such as Claudio Volpetti in Rome, agree that Pecorino Romano from Latium is flakier and more delicate to the palate than its Sardinian Pecorino Romano-Sardo counterpart. Other differences between the two *pecorini* include salt content (slightly higher in Sardinia), color (white in Sardinia, yellowish in Latium), aging (5 to 6 months in Sardinia, about twice that in Latium) and cost (many Sardinian varieties are considerably cheaper). Pecorino Romano has been available in America for the last hundred years, though as Brunelli points out, the quality varies widely (the same can be said for domestic Pecorino Romano, which is often sold in chunks or, grated, in plastic tubs). A "DOC/DOP" label stamped into the waxy black or yellowish rind distinguishes authentic Italian Pecorino Romano—but it doesn't tell you if the cheese was made from Latium or Sardinian milk. Adding to the confusion, some Latium-based cheese companies import milk from Sardinia. The only way to tell the difference is to know the brand and use your eyes and taste buds.

When using Pecorino Romano in these recipes, be aware that Romans often consider it a salt substitute, so go easy with additional salt. The semisharp, mutton taste of the cheese is very different from that of creamy, smooth cow's-milk Parmigiano-Reggiano. Pecorino Sardo, a similar ewe's-milk cheese also made in Sardinia, comes in smaller rounds, is aged 2 to 12 months, has less salt if it is intended to be eaten fresh, and is a fine substitute for Pecorino Romano once it has been aged for 10 to 12 months.

Spaghetti a Cacio e Pepe
SPAGHETTI WITH PECORINO ROMANO AND BLACK PEPPER

This is the simplest and one of the tastiest pasta dishes in the Roman repertoire, served at home and at every trattoria offering *cucina romana* or *cucina povera* (poor folks' cooking), including Trattoria Gianni, a friendly place with a sidewalk terrace in the Prati quarter north of the Castel Sant'Angelo. In honor of this dish, Gianni's is nicknamed "Cacio e Pepe," which means "with cheese and pepper." The recipe lies at the root of many other Roman standards, including *Spaghetti alla Gricia* (page 84) and *Bucatini all'Amatriciana* (page 90). Romans use black pepper lavishly and always have: pepper saved the city from total destruction twice. In A.D. 408 Alaric the Visigoth lifted his siege after receiving a tribute of a ton and a half of peppercorns, and in A.D. 452 Attila the Hun largely spared Rome after accepting payment of an unspecified quantity of pepper (and cinnamon).

Kosher salt or coarse sea salt

1½ pounds spaghetti, *spaghettoni, tonnarelli* or fettuccine (*Fettuccine Fresche all'Uovo,* page 117)

About 2 cups freshly grated Pecorino Romano

1 heaping tablespoon freshly ground black pepper

SERVES 6

The trick to making this recipe work is to dilute the cheese and pepper with 1 tablespoon of pasta water per serving, and to amalgamate the ingredients in the pot the pasta water was boiled in, a technique called *mantecare,* meaning to mix and meld.

1   Bring at least 5 quarts of water to a boil in a large pot and add a tiny pinch of salt. Drop in the pasta, stir and cover the pot. When the water returns to a boil, remove the lid and cook, uncovered, until the pasta is al dente. Reserve about ½ cup of the cooking water and drain the pasta.

2   Return the still-dripping pasta to the pot in which it was boiled. Away from any direct source of heat, stir in the reserved pasta water and toss vigorously while sprinkling in about 1 cup of the cheese and the pepper.

3   Serve immediately in pasta bowls with the remaining 1 cup Pecorino Romano on the side.

Spaghetti alla Gricia

SPAGHETTI WITH GUANCIALE AND HOT CHILI PEPPER

8 ounces (about eight, ¼-inch-thick slices) guanciale, pancetta or bacon

¼ cup extra-virgin olive oil

1 *peperoncino* (hot chili pepper), shredded, or ¼ teaspoon crushed red pepper flakes

Kosher salt or coarse sea salt

1½ pounds spaghetti, *spaghettoni, tonnarelli* or fettuccine (*Fettuccine Fresche all'Uovo,* page 117)

About 1½ cups freshly grated Pecorino Romano

SERVES 6

You can usually guess the age bracket of Roman eaters by the name they give this dish. People over forty call it *un'amatriciana in bianco,* meaning "white *amatriciana*" sauce because it has no tomatoes. That's because when you remove the tomatoes from a classic *amatriciana,* what's left is cured pork jowl, hot chili pepper and Pecorino Romano cheese—in other words the components of this recipe. An ancient recipe from the Apennine mountains east and southeast of Rome, some people claim *spaghetti alla gricia* comes from the hill town of Grisciano, not far from Amatrice. Pronounced by Romans, the words Grisciano and *gricia* sound like they're plausibly linked. Others point out that the name is probably a mispronunciation of the word *grigia,* which means "gray," and refers to the fact that, without tomatoes, the sauce has a grayish coloring. Whatever the origin, this old-fashioned recipe has been popular in Rome for a long, long time. Purists don't use garlic to make *spaghetti alla gricia* because, they feel, it doesn't work in combination with hot chili pepper and Pecorino, two of the recipe's essential ingredients.

1 Bring at least 5 quarts of water to a boil in a large pot.

2 Roughly chop the guanciale. You should have about 1½ cups.

3 Heat the oil in a very large, high-sided frying pan over medium. Add the *peperoncino* and the guanciale and sauté, stirring until the guanciale is crisp, 1 minute. Remove the frying pan from the heat.

4 Add a pinch of salt to the boiling water. Drop in the pasta, stir and cover the pot. When the water returns to a boil, remove the lid. Cook, uncovered, until the pasta is barely al dente, about 1 minute less than the suggested cooking time on the package.

5 Return the frying pan to medium heat. Drain the pasta and toss it in still dripping. Sauté for about 30 seconds, tossing, stirring and scraping. Turn off the heat, stir in 6 heaping tablespoons of the cheese and let the pasta sit for 30 seconds.

6 Serve the pasta in bowls, passing the remaining 1 cup Pecorino Romano on the side.

NOTE: In the United States, guanciale may be sold as "cured pork jowl" or "hog mawls."

Maria Alessandra Martinelli at Trattoria Cacio e Pepe

Bringing Home the Bacon:
Rome's Divine Guanciale

While most of Italy favors pancetta—cured pork belly, very much like unsmoked American bacon—Rome and its region worship guanciale, salt-cured pork jowl. Every *salumeria* and *salsamenteria* deli in town, not to mention the *norcinerie,* whose name derives from Norcia, the Umbrian town famous for its pork, plus many *trattorie,* are festooned with these triangular-shaped, pepper-covered jowls, which go into dozens of recipes from *amatriciana* and *gricia* sauce to pan-fried zucchini. Guanciale is fattier, more elastic and sweeter than pancetta or bacon and imparts an inimitable, delicate flavor to whatever it's cooked with. The inhabitants of only one other Italian region love guanciale as much as the Romans: Umbria (see *Norcini:* Rome's Umbrian Pork Butchers, page 169).

Imported Italian guanciale is difficult to find in America. Salumeria Biellese in Manhattan, in business since 1925, is the only domestic guanciale producer I know of. Run by third-generation deli men Marc Buzzio and Paul Valetutti, Biellese's curing method reflects the family's northern-Italian ancestry. The jowls spend about 3 weeks in a vat, coated with plain fine salt and ground black pepper, bay, sage and rosemary, then are air-dried for 3 months. Salumeria Biellese sells whole jowls weighing approximately 1.5 pounds for about $20 plus shipping (2 to 3 days regular or overnight) (see Sources, page 297). If you can't find imported or domestic guanciale and don't have time to mail-order it, try using bacon or pancetta instead and tossing a few juniper berries into the frying pan with it. I find juniper imparts a note of sweetness approximating the taste of the real thing. Just make sure to remove the berries before serving.

Pipe Rigate alla Checca

ELBOW PASTA WITH RAW TOMATOES, BASIL, CAPERS, OLIVES AND FENNEL SEEDS

1/4 cup extra-virgin olive oil

4 1/2 cups chopped ripe fresh Italian plum or halved cherry tomatoes (about 3 pounds)

2 heaping tablespoons capers (see page 88)

3/4 cup pitted, chopped Gaeta or other Italian or Greek black olives

1 heaping tablespoon fennel seeds

4 heaping tablespoons minced fresh flat-leaf parsley

6 heaping tablespoons minced basil

Kosher salt or coarse sea salt and freshly ground black pepper

1 pound *pipe rigate* or other elbow or shell pasta (*maniche di frate, bombolotti, cannolicchi*)

SERVES 6

In his posthumously published opus, *La cucina romana e del Lazio,* Roman restaurant critic and food historian Livio Jannattoni details the birth and christening of this refreshing summertime recipe dreamed up in 1972 by Sora Ada, the chef of the Osteria dell'Antiquario near Piazza Navona, where antiques dealers feed to this day between deals (but not on this recipe, which disappeared along with the chef in the mid-1980s). I have to preface Jannattoni's story by saying that Romans love making off-color remarks. They're famous among less-scurrilous Italians as avid users of expletives, oaths and cryptic bastardizations of the language. The recipe's name, then, according to Jannattoni, comes from the inclusion of fennel seeds in it, called *semi di finocchio* in Italian. *Finocchio* is also an old-fashioned and inoffensive way to say homosexual, and so is the term *checca.* Etymology aside, the sauce is a wonderfully different, refreshing summertime salsa full of fresh basil and parsley. It relies on the ripeness of the tomatoes, so make sure to use only top-quality, ultra-ripe plum or cherry tomatoes. You can serve it hot or cold—it makes a great do-ahead pasta salad.

1   Bring at least 5 quarts of water to a boil in a large pot.

2   Pour the oil into a large serving bowl.

3   Combine the tomatoes with the oil and toss. Sprinkle in the capers. Add the olives. Sprinkle in the fennel seeds. Add the parsley and basil and toss thoroughly, sprinkling in a generous pinch each of salt and pepper. Let the salsa sit while you cook the pasta.

4   Add a generous pinch of salt to the boiling water and drop in the pasta. Stir and cover the pot. When the water returns to a boil, cook, uncovered, until the pasta is al dente.

5   Drain and transfer the pasta to the serving bowl and toss thoroughly. Serve immediately. Alternatively, drain the pasta in a colander, let it cool and toss it with the salsa in the bowl. Serve at room temperature or chilled. You can refrigerate the dish, covered, for up to 24 hours.

Capers

Rome's city walls and many of its stone monuments are home to countless clinging caper shrubs. Cognoscenti claim the Aurelian Walls between the Porta San Lorenzo gate and the Ministry of Aeronautics produce the most succulent specimens. Capers, called *capperi* in Italian (*Capparis spinosa* in Latin), thrive in cracks and crevices producing delicate white blossoms—that is, when the blossoms aren't nipped in the bud. That's because capers are the immature buds of the caper bush. Small, misleadingly named "nonpareil" capers are usually pickled in vinegar and sold in glass jars. The French name makes it sound as if these were the best kind of caper, but, in fact, they should be your last choice. Premium jumbo capers come from a handful of Italian and Greek islands. The best of all are a plump, tangy variety, *capperi di Pantelleria,* from the island of Pantelleria south of Sicily. Large, premium capers like them are usually preserved in sea salt and must be desalted before use. Soak them in cold water for 15 to 20 minutes, rinse them, then pat them dry with paper towels. Salted capers are more flavorful than vinegar-packed capers and worth the cost and effort of finding them. They're available at Italian specialty food shops and by mail order (see Sources, page 297).

Spaghetti col Sugo Finto

SPAGHETTI WITH FRESH TOMATO SAUCE

FOR THE SAUCE:

1 large onion

¼ cup extra-virgin
olive oil

Kosher salt or coarse
sea salt and freshly ground
black pepper

4 cups peeled, seeded and
chopped medium-sized
fresh Italian plum
tomatoes (about 2 pounds)
(see How to Peel and Seed
a Tomato, page 93)

4 to 5 whole basil leaves

FOR THE PASTA:

1½ pounds spaghetti (or
other dry or fresh ribbon,
filled or short pasta)

½ cup freshly grated
Pecorino Romano

About 1 cup freshly grated
Parmigiano-Reggiano
and/or Pecorino Romano

YIELDS ABOUT 4 CUPS
TOMATO SAUCE, ENOUGH TO
SAUCE 6 SERVINGS OF DRY
OR FRESH PASTA (SEE NOTE
AT END OF RECIPE)

Sugo finto means "fake meat sauce," and it is a favorite all over central-southern Italy, especially in the Rome and Naples areas, where the tomatoes are unrivaled. Like the Neapolitans, the Romans love the idea of a "fake" and, in this case, use cheap and abundant onion and basil instead of (formerly) expensive beef. Some recipes call for parsley, lard and tomato concentrate, but I find this one lighter and more flavorful. With it, you can sauce spaghetti, ravioli, potato gnocchi and just about any other kind of pasta you like.

MAKE THE SAUCE:

1   Peel and mince the onion.

2   Heat the oil in a large saucepan over medium-low. Add the onion and sauté with a pinch each of salt and pepper until the onion starts to become translucent, 3 to 4 minutes.

3   Add the tomatoes, stir in the basil and bring the sauce to a boil. Lower the heat and simmer, uncovered, for about ten minutes or the time it takes to cook the pasta.

COOK THE PASTA:

4   Bring at least 5 quarts of water to a boil in a large pot. (It can be the same water used for peeling the tomatoes.)

5   Add a generous pinch of salt to the boiling water, toss in the spaghetti, stir and cover the pot. When the water returns to a boil, cook, uncovered, until the pasta is al dente.

6   Drain and transfer the spaghetti to a serving bowl. Stir in the sauce. Sprinkle in the Pecorino Romano, toss and serve immediately with a bowl of freshly grated Parmigiano-Reggiano and/or Pecorino Romano on the side.

NOTE: Do steps 1–3 and use this sauce to dress a wide variety of dry pasta types (spaghetti and other ribbon pasta, elbows, shells), fresh pasta (fettuccine, *tonnarelli*, ravioli) and potato gnocchi.

Bucatini all'Amatriciana
CLASSIC BUCATINI WITH SPICY AMATRICIANA TOMATO SAUCE

Umpteenth-generation Roman chef Eugenio Velardi, born in a floating trattoria tethered to the banks of the Tiber, started cooking professionally at age fourteen. Since the early 1990s, he's presided over the kitchen of La Matricianella, a much-loved neighborhood restaurant set between the sumptuous aristocratic salons of Palazzo Borghese and the democratic outdoor living room that is the Piazza San Lorenzo in Lucina. An unbending purist, after forty-odd years at the stove he still makes amatriciana sauce—the house specialty—using only guanciale (cured pork jowl or "hog mawl"), canned or bottled tomatoes, red or white wine, olive oil, hot chili pepper and Pecorino Romano cheese. "No garlic or onions!" he growls. "Tomato concentrate? Never!"

Like many cooks from Rome or Amatrice, the mountain town southeast of Rome that gave the sauce its name, Eugenio thinks it's a crime to make amatriciana any other way. But what does "purism" really mean? The cultural affairs office of the city of Amatrice has gone so far as to issue an official amatriciana recipe that calls for spaghetti (not bucatini), guanciale, extra-virgin olive oil, white (never red) wine, either fresh or

canned tomatoes, hot chili pepper, freshly grated Pecorino Romano and salt. This official recipe explicitly states that if the sauce isn't

La Matricianella Restaurant: Chef Eugenio Velardi (left) and assistant chef Giulio Ciccotelli

made with guanciale, it isn't amatriciana. The arbiters of amatriciana may be right, since the use of guanciale constitutes the true substantive difference between amatriciana and the closely related sauce arrabbiata, which is made with pancetta (Italian bacon).

I'm willing to go along with Velardi and the Amatrice culture police. However, for accuracy's sake and because several chefs and home cooks I respect feel very strongly about this vital issue, I have included an amatriciana variant with pancetta (or bacon) and onions. Both versions are delicious and equally easy to make. You decide which you prefer. Whatever you do, though, don't use tomato concentrate—it weighs down the sauce.

4 ounces guanciale (4 ¼-inch-thick slices) (see Sources, page 297)

¼ cup extra-virgin olive oil

1 *peperoncino* (hot chili pepper), shredded, or ¼ teaspoon crushed red pepper flakes

½ cup Italian dry white or red wine

1 (28-ounce) can Italian plum tomatoes, preferably San Marzano

Kosher salt or coarse sea salt

1 pound bucatini, perciatelli, spaghetti or rigatoni

About 1½ cups freshly grated Pecorino Romano

SERVES 4

1 Roughly chop the guanciale. You should have about ¾ cup.

2 Scatter the guanciale around a high-sided heavy frying pan. Add the oil and *peperoncino*. Sauté over high heat for 1 to 2 minutes to melt the guanciale fat, stirring with a wooden spoon or spatula.

3 Once the guanciale colors but before it begins to crisp, pour in the wine and boil to evaporate it, about 1 minute.

4 Pass the tomatoes with their packing juices through a food mill and add them to the frying pan. Lower the heat and simmer until the tomatoes are reduced by half, stirring often, 30 to 40 minutes.

5 Bring at least 5 quarts of water to a boil in a large pot. Add a generous pinch of salt. Drop in the pasta, stir and cover the pot. When the water returns to a boil, remove the lid and cook the pasta, uncovered, until the pasta is barely al dente, about 1 to 2 minutes less than the suggested cooking time on the package.

6 With 2 large forks, tongs or a pasta grabber, transfer the pasta directly from the water to the frying pan. Stir and toss it vigorously to finish cooking it, about 1 minute. Turn off the heat, stir in 4 heaping tablespoons of the Pecorino Romano and toss.

7 Serve immediately with the remaining Pecorino Romano on the side.

NOTE: According to Eugenio Velardi and other stalwarts, for this recipe you should always use thick, long, hollow pasta, preferably bucatini or perciatelli, and you should never drain the pasta in a colander. Transfer the pasta, still dripping, from the pot to the skillet. The hollow tubes in the pasta retain water and help give the sauce the right consistency.

TIP: Use about half of the amatriciana sauce this recipe yields, plus plenty of freshly grated Pecorino Romano, to fill an 8-egg frittata (see page 216). Or mix all the amatriciana sauce this recipe yields with a risotto of farro (see *Arancini di Farro,* page 11, steps 1 to 6).

How to Peel and Seed a Tomato

To peel or not to peel? When using fresh tomatoes that you are going to eat cooked (as opposed to eating them raw in salads or in uncooked salsas), most Italians want them skinless and seedless. The cherry tomato is the only variety that escapes this treatment. I've never been very successful wielding a vegetable peeler on a tomato, especially a ripe one, but if you prefer a peeler by all means use it. Even though the tomatoes are scalded here in the boiling water, and therefore cleaned, I always make a point of rinsing them first because I often use the boiling water in the recipe for other steps: cooking pasta, boiling vegetables and so forth. Also, I don't like to have to clean mud out of my cooking pots, which is what the dirt from farmers' market or garden-picked tomatoes becomes once boiled. Here's the way most Italians peel and seed their ripe fresh tomatoes.

1   Bring 2 quarts or more of water to boil in a large pot.

2   Wash the tomatoes under cold running water to eliminate dirt, dust or pesticides. With a slotted spoon, lower the tomatoes into the boiling water, scalding them for 30 to 60 seconds.

3   Use the slotted spoon to transfer the tomatoes to a colander. Let them sit until cool enough to handle. With a paring knife, make a slit at the top of the tomato where the stem comes in. Carefully slip the skins off with your fingers and the knife.

4   Place the skinned tomatoes on a cutting board and quarter or slice them as required, eliminating the tough core in the middle of the tomato. With a small spoon, such as a teaspoon, remove and discard the seeds.

Amatriciana delle Cinque "P"

FIVE-"P" AMATRICIANA: PASTA, PANCETTA, POMODORO, PEPERONCINO E PECORINO

This "five-P" version of amatriciana features pasta, pancetta, fresh tomatoes (*pomodori*), hot chili pepper (*peperoncino*) and Pecorino Romano, plus onions (no "p" in onion, but then there's no "p" in olive oil or salt, either, and both are essential ingredients). Naturally, few Romans agree whether one of the "Ps" stands for *pepe* (black pepper) or *peperoncino* (hot chili pepper). Since black pepper graced ancient Roman tables, and *peperoncino* was popularized fewer than five hundred years ago, the proponents of the black pepper school win hands down when it comes to history. However they lose, in my opinion, when it comes to taste. Some partisans of the Cinque "P," such as star chef Angelo Troiani at the luxurious Il Convivio restaurant in central Rome, get fancy and, instead of regular onions, use red onions from the town of Tropea, marinated in a sweet-and-sour bath. Troiani also adds a tiny amount of garlic and a 50–50 blend of fresh and canned tomatoes. Agata Parisella, chef-owner of Agata e Romeo, which is widely considered one of Rome's top tables, also likes onions but only to perfume the oil (she briefly sautés, then discards them). My friend Vincenzo Tassielli, a pharmacist-chemist by day and zealous home cook the rest of the time, uses half an onion to flavor his olive oil, and he too discards it. Vincenzo's is about the best updated version of amatriciana sauce I've encountered, so this is his homey recipe, as served at the regular dinner-club evenings he hosts at his apartment in the Casalotti neighborhood, overlooking fields and rolling hills on the western edge of town.

¼ cup extra-virgin olive oil

½ small white onion

4 ounces roughly chopped pancetta, or 2 ounces pancetta and 2 ounces bacon

1 *peperoncino* (hot chili pepper), shredded, or ¼ teaspoon crushed red pepper flakes

½ cup Italian dry white wine, preferably Frascati or Marino

3 cups peeled, seeded and chopped medium-sized fresh Italian plum tomatoes (about 1½ pounds) (see How to Peel and Seed a Tomato, page 93)

Kosher salt or coarse sea salt

1 pound bucatini, perciatelli, spaghetti or rigatoni

About 1½ cups freshly grated Pecorino Romano

SERVES 4

1   Bring at least 5 quarts of water to a boil in a large pot. (It can be the same water used for peeling the tomatoes.)

2   Heat the oil in a very large, high-sided frying pan over medium-low and add the half onion. Sauté for 2 to 3 minutes. With a slotted spatula, remove and discard the onion.

3   Toss the pancetta into the frying pan with the *peperoncino* and sauté until the pork starts to become crisp, 2 to 3 minutes.

4   Pour in the wine and boil to evaporate it, 1 to 2 minutes. Stir in the tomatoes and raise the heat to medium. Continue to sauté while you cook the pasta.

5   Add a generous pinch of salt to the boiling water, throw in the pasta, stir and cover the pot. When the water returns to a boil, cook the pasta, uncovered, until the pasta is barely al dente, about 1 minute less than the suggested cooking time as given on the package.

6   Drain the pasta and toss it into the frying pan, still dripping. Stir in 4 heaping tablespoons of the Pecorino Romano. Turn off the heat and let the pasta sit for 30 to 60 seconds.

7   Serve the pasta with a bowl of the remaining Pecorino Romano on the side.

Carbonara: Where There's Coal, There's Fiery Argument

Spaghetti alla carbonara is one of the most popular recipes in Rome. Theories about its origin range from the sublime to the ridiculous, the most far-fetched being that this is little more than American bacon and eggs mixed with pasta, popularized by GIs stationed in and around Rome during World War II. As improbable as that sounds, at least one major cookbook writer and food historian, the late, great Livio Jannattoni, believed it. And one famous Roman chef I know, Alberto Ciarla, of the highly rated same-name fish restaurant in the Trastevere neighborhood, also subscribes to the GI theory (though he admits that carbonara by other names has been around forever). But Jannattoni, may he rest in peace, also reported that the related recipe *fettuccine alla papalina* (page 101), invented in the 1930s, before the Americans and their wartime bacon and eggs, was described by its inventor as an "ennobled carbonara." Romans I know who are old enough to remember the prewar years also remember *spaghetti alla carbonara,* though they might have known the recipe with a different name, such as *maccheroni a cacio e uova* (noodles with cheese and eggs). My mother is one of those keepers of prewar memories. My father, a GI who fought in Italy and wound up in Rome from 1944 to 1950, has no recollection at all of bacon and eggs with pasta being on the soldiers' menu.

So where did the recipe and the name come from? Some insist carbonara gets its moniker from the large quantities of black pepper in it. The pepper makes it look like it's flecked with carbon (*carbone*). And this leads us to Trattoria La Carbonara on the Campo de' Fiori, whose signature dish is *penne alla Carbonara.* But the link is tenuous. Federico Salomone, who founded the original Carbonara restaurant on Via di Montevecchio back in 1912, was a coal-seller and deliveryman (i.e., a *carbonaro*), and the establishment's first name was Trattoria del Carbonaro. It served *penne alla carbonara* early on, though no one can remember what the dish was called in those pre–World War I days. Federico's daughter, Andreina Salomone, is in her late seventies and she told me that her father adopted but never claimed to have invented the recipe, which is as old as can be.

The most widely held theory is that *spaghetti alla carbonara,* like *spaghetti a cacio e pepe* (see page 82) and *spaghetti alla gricia* (see page 84), are from the Apennine mountain regions northeast and southeast of Rome. These areas were heavily forested, and it was here that nomadic charcoal-makers, called *carbonari,* would set up camp for weeks or months at a time to smolder piles of timber into charcoal. They would carry with them long-lasting ingredients, such as dry pasta, cured pork (guanciale or pancetta), aged Pecorino Romano and eggs, or, more likely still, live chickens to provide them with a regular supply of eggs. They did not have cream, an ingredient that's often misguidedly added to *spaghetti alla carbonara.* Since these charcoal-makers would regularly come into Rome to sell their charcoal, the recipe eventually made it into the urban repertoire. Sound convincing? No doubt denizens of the Eternal City will continue to argue about carbonara as long as the dish maintains its popularity.

Spaghetti alla Carbonara

SPAGHETTI WITH GUANCIALE, GRATED CHEESE AND EGGS

The lunchtime sun pounds down on Campo de' Fiori, casting few shadows around the statue of Giordano Bruno, the luckless reformer standing tall in the center of the market square, past the fruit and vegetable stands, the flower sellers and their displays of blooms and live plants, half of them soaking in a giant birdbath fountain with several centuries' service. Amid the shouts, the flying artichokes and the splashing of the fountains, your waiter appears, weaving among the tables of jovial eaters at Trattoria La Carbonara. Your dish of hot pasta with luscious egg-and-guanciale sauce lands before you flecked with baconlike bits and crowned with a dusting of cheese. You dig in, savoring the rustic flavors, and little can you imagine that this innocent delicacy that gave the trattoria its name, probably the most popular pasta recipe in Rome today, is the subject of fierce, sometimes violent debate. Food historians and passionate amateur etymologists lurk with frying pans held menacingly high as you fork another mouthful of exquisite pasta between your lips.

Carbonara has swept up and down the Italian peninsula, into France, Germany and northern Europe, and across America, where it picked up cream, to become an international favorite. Which explains why, for the last fifty years or more, Romans have been arguing about where the recipe comes from, whether it's Roman or not, and how it should be prepared (see Carbonara: Where There's Coal, There's Fiery Argument, page 96). The only thing all Romans agree upon is that cream has no place in carbonara.

Trattoria La Carbonara makes its signature dish with penne and not spaghetti, and their cooking technique is tricky. They beat the eggs with grated Parmigiano-Reggiano and pepper and cook them with the al dente pasta over a high flame in the pot used to boil the pasta water. This works best with short pasta, which explains their use of penne, and requires a high degree of manual dexterity to avoid making scrambled eggs. Most Romans use the less dramatic but more reliable technique of pouring the scalding-hot spaghetti over the beaten eggs in a warm—not hot—frying pan away from any direct source of heat, and that's what I recommend. For that you'll need a large frying pan or skillet with a lid.

4 ounces pancetta, guanciale or bacon

2 tablespoons extra-virgin olive oil

4 large eggs, at room temperature

2 heaping tablespoons freshly grated Pecorino Romano

Freshly ground black pepper

Kosher salt or coarse sea salt

1 pound spaghetti

About 1 cup freshly grated cheese, half Parmigiano-Reggiano and half Pecorino Romano

SERVES 4

1   Bring at least 5 quarts of water to a boil in a large pot.

2   Roughly chop the pancetta, guanciale or bacon. You should have about ¾ cup.

3   Heat the oil in a very large, high-sided frying pan over medium. Add the pork and stir, sautéing until crisp, 2 to 3 minutes. Turn off the heat under the frying pan and let it cool for 3 minutes.

4   Separate 1 of the eggs. Put the yolk into a small mixing bowl and save the white for other uses. Crack the remaining 3 eggs into the mixing bowl and beat thoroughly, incorporating the 2 heaping tablespoons Pecorino Romano and an extremely generous pinch of pepper. Pour the mixture into the warm frying pan and stir.

5   Add a pinch of salt to the boiling water. Drop in the pasta, stir and cover the pot. When the water returns to a boil, remove the lid and cook, uncovered, until the pasta is barely al dente.

6   Drain the pasta and transfer it immediately to the frying pan with the egg mixture. Stir vigorously until thoroughly coated. Cover the frying pan and let stand for 1 minute.

7   Serve with a peppermill and a bowl of Pecorino Romano and Parmigiano-Reggiano on the side.

NOTE: Use the egg white to make Brutte ma Buone cookies (page 265).

The Herb-and-Spice Man of Campo de' Fiori

$\mathcal{B}$earded, bouncy Mauro Berardi (*below*) was born in the Vicolo del Gallo, an alley connecting Campo de' Fiori to the Piazza Farnese a hundred yards south. He has worked amid the vegetable, fruit and flower stalls at the open market since he was five years old. "I love to cook, and I like experimenting with flavor combinations," he told me one day, scooping up fistfuls of the fragrant herbs and spices he sells to neighborhood regulars, chefs and foreign travelers. All of his concoctions are dried. Some are conceived to be sprinkled directly onto cooked pasta or meat, while others should be sautéed in olive oil or added to basic tomato sauce.

Mauro's most popular Roman blend is carbonara. It's about 80 percent onion, 15 percent chives and 5 percent black pepper. "Vegetarians who don't want guanciale or other pork products in their *spaghetti alla carbonara* love it!" says Mauro. To use his mix, you beat your eggs in a bowl with grated Pecorino Romano, as in a classic carbonara, and sauté the mix in a frying pan in a tablespoon of olive oil or butter, using it as if it were guanciale, pancetta or bacon.

Another of Mauro's Roman favorites is arrabbiata, a palate-bucking blend of garlic, red pepper flakes and parsley in more or less equal proportions that you cook in olive oil or sprinkle on spaghetti dressed with raw olive oil.

Ciociara merges garlic, basil and oregano in equal amounts, with a pinch of red pepper flakes and a few dried zucchini and eggplant slices. You cook it in tomato sauce for a few minutes.

His same-name blend, Pasta Mauro, is a piquant mix of basil, red pepper flakes, oregano, chives and parsley in equal measure, to be sprinkled raw on olive oil–perfumed short pasta. The bruschetta mix, a topping for sliced, toasted bread garnished with olive oil (see page 15), combines lots of garlic with a pinch of red pepper flakes, basil, oregano, parsley and chives, and a tiny bit of salt and black pepper. Naturally, Mauro won't reveal the exact proportions of the ingredients in his ingenious blends. But you can combine them yourself to get the flavor balance you prefer.

Fettuccine alla Papalina

FETTUCCINE WITH PARMA HAM AND A CREAMY EGG-AND-CHEESE SAUCE, "IN THE STYLE OF THE POPE"

The date is sometime in 1935. The place, Ristorante del Colonnato in Via del Mascherino near Saint Peter's and the Vatican City. Chef Cesare Simmi and his crew are winding down the luncheon service. The telephone rings. "This is Cardinal Pacelli," pipes a familiar voice. The cardinal is the Vatican's secretary of state. He regularly calls on chef Simmi to cater dinners at the Vatican's Treasury Dining Room. "We're expecting a rather important guest tonight and wonder if you could supply dinner as usual, with perhaps something a little special for the pasta? I'm counting on you. . . ."

Simmi cradles the telephone and glances at his watch. There isn't much time to come up with anything original. What to do? He knows Cardinal Pacelli, a notorious gourmand, likes *spaghetti alla carbonara* (see page 98). But how to transform that old peasant's dish into something really special? Simmi takes off his toque and puts on his thinking cap. What's nobler than cured pig's jowl, he wonders, pondering the peppery guanciale that goes into classic carbonara. The answer: Parma ham. What's more refined than that salty shepherd's cheese, Pecorino Romano? Obviously, Parmigiano-Reggiano! A little onion sautéed, not in crude olive oil, but in aristocratic butter will give the sauce a touch of unctuous sweetness. And what about using noble fresh fettuccine instead of common dry spaghetti? The color-scheme would be perfect: the yellow and white of the papacy.

That evening Simmi presents Cardinal Pacelli with the dish, dubbing it an "ennobled carbonara," and, needless to add, it is a riotous hit. A few years later, in 1939, the food-loving Cardinal Pacelli becomes Pius XII. Suddenly Cesare Simmi is caterer to the pope. He quickly renames his invention *fettuccine alla papalina*—in the style of the pope—and cashes in.

Many recipes nowadays for *fettuccine alla papalina,* a Roman standard, call for peas and heavy cream. But when I asked Cesare Simmi's septuagenarian son Fausto about this, he clacked his tongue and said, "No, no, no. . . . The cream is superfluous and the

4 ounces Parma ham in
1 thick slice

1 medium-sized white
onion

¼ cup (½ stick) butter

4 large eggs, at room
temperature

About 1½ cups freshly
grated Parmigiano-
Reggiano

Kosher salt or coarse
sea salt

Freshly ground black
pepper

1½ pounds fresh
fettuccine (see *Fettuccine
Fresche all'Uovo,* page 117) or
1½ pounds dry store-
bought fettuccine

SERVES 6

colors are important. The white of the cheese and the
yellow of the fettuccine, those are the colors of the
papacy. Green peas wouldn't have looked right at all."
The color of the ham doesn't seem to matter.

The Simmi family moved from the Ristorante del
Colonnato to La Cisterna restaurant in the Trastevere
neighborhood, Fausto took over from Cesare, and he's
been there ever since, serving his father's *fettuccine alla
papalina* and other house specialties.

1   Bring at least 5 quarts of water to a boil in a large pot.

2   Dice the ham. You should have about ¾ cup. Peel and
    mince the onion.

3   In a large frying pan, melt the butter over medium-low
    heat. Add the ham and onion and sauté until the onion
    becomes translucent, 3 to 4 minutes. Remove the frying
    pan from the heat.

4   Separate 1 of the eggs. Put the yolk into a small mixing
    bowl and save the white for other recipes. Crack the
    remaining 3 eggs into the mixing bowl with the yolk. Add 3 heaping tablespoons of the
    Parmigiano-Reggiano and a pinch each of salt and pepper. Beat until foamy.

5   Add a generous pinch of salt to the boiling water, drop in the fettuccine, stir and cover
    the pot. When the water returns to a boil, remove the lid and cook the pasta, uncovered,
    until the pasta is barely al dente (about 1 minute less than the recommended cooking
    time given on the package of dry fettuccine).

6   Drain the pasta and return it immediately to the pot in which it was boiled. Add the
    sautéed onion and Parma ham. Return the pot to medium-high heat. Stirring quickly,
    pour in the egg-and-cheese mixture. Toss the fettuccine vigorously with the sauce for 30
    to 60 seconds, remove from the heat and transfer immediately to a platter.

7   Serve with a bowl of the remaining Parmigiano-Reggiano on the side.

Fettuccine Alfredo: By Any Other Name It Wouldn't Be the Same

"I'd like awfully to run over to Rome for a few weeks."
"I suppose you see a lot of pictures and music and curios and everything there."
"No, what I really go for is: there's a little trattoria on the Via della Scrofa where you get the best fettuccine in the world."

Sinclair Lewis, *Babbitt* (1922)

Call fettuccine alfredo by its other Roman names—*pasta dei cornuti* (cuckolds' pasta) or *fettuccine con burro e parmigiano* (fettuccine with butter and Parmigiano-Reggiano)—and something vital is lost in the translation. Truth be told, fettuccine with butter and cheese is a nice combination that's been around forever. It's called cuckolds' pasta because, the un-PC story goes, it's so quick to cook and sauce that even an unfaithful spouse can rush home and whip it up for her unsuspecting husband by the time he gets home from the office.

The essential thing that's missing when you leave out the "Alfredo" in the recipe's name is the romance, the aura of authenticity and the family drama of Alfredo Di Lelio and his heirs, a tale almost worthy of being made into a soap opera. There's big money involved, too: Fettuccine Alfredo stars on hundreds of menus worldwide, with multimillion-dollar Alfredo-theme restaurants at Florida's Disney World and in New York's Rockefeller Center.

The recipe is also at the center of Rome's longest-running restaurant rivalry. And that's where the soap opera comes in. In the leading roles are Mario Mozzetti, owner of Alfredo alla Scrofa, and Alfredo Di Lelio III, grandson of the recipe's inventor and owner of l'Originale Alfredo.

Rewind to 1883, when Alfredo Di Lelio I was born to a family of Roman restaurateurs with a simple wine-bar-cum-eatery *osteria* in Piazza Rosa near II Corso, smack in the center of town. In 1908, the young Alfredo invents his fettuccine to induce his wife Ines, who's recently given birth but has no appetite, to start eating again. The fettuccine is so scrumptious that Ines insists he put the dish on the menu. It's a hit, the *osteria* moves up a notch to trattoria, and, in 1914, Alfredo buys a bigger, swankier site in Via della Scrofa. Fast forward to 1925. Prohibition. Rome crawls with thirsty Americans, including Hemingway, Lewis and his fictional hero Babbitt and bevies of Hollywood stars. Alfredo's restaurant is crowded, noisy. Steam and mouthwatering buttery scents waft through the kitchen's swinging doors. VIPs mix with Roman blue bloods, Russian émigrés and brutish Mussolini look-alikes. A small mustachioed man, Alfredo weaves among the tuxedoes and starched tablecloths, wielding a brand-new pair of solid gold serving tools. He bows to kiss the hands of angelic Hollywood starlet Mary Pickford (*Poor Little Rich Girl, Pollyanna*) then embraces her swashbuckling husband Douglas Fairbanks (*Zorro, Robin Hood, The Thief of Baghdad*). Pickford and Fairbanks are on their honeymoon and they've just given Alfredo the golden fork and spoon to thank him for his hospitality and exquisite pasta. The word is out—fettuccine Alfredo is the favorite food of Hollywood idols—and the world's beau monde is knocking down the restaurant's doors.

Fast forward again, this time to 1943, when Alfredo Di Lelio sells the restaurant to his former headwaiter and business partner, a certain Signor Mozzetti. Five years later, with the war over, Alfredo decides to make a comeback and opens an even bigger, swankier place on the Piazza Augusto Imperatore, near the Mausoleum of Augustus Caesar. He calls it l'Originale Alfredo—the Original Alfredo—to distinguish it from, and undercut, the Via della Scrofa joint, now a rival. And the rivalry plays on, and on and on. The golden serving tools are copied, stolen, reappear and disappear. No one is sure who has the originals or the copies. Alfredo dies and is succeeded by his son Alfredo II, who passes the flame to his son, Alfredo III.

Today, l'Originale Alfredo, which isn't the original place at all despite the name, is still in the Di Lelio family's hands, with the amiable Alfredo Di Lelio III at the helm. The Mozzetti family who bought the Via della Scrofa place still own and run it. Both heirs lay claim to the fettuccine Alfredo name and recipe.

The families will doubtless continue feuding as long as the restaurants survive. Recently Mario Mozzetti, in reality an affable young man, ramped up the antagonism by creating an Alfredo web site and launching "Alfredo Restaurant Franchising Ltd." He hopes to open Alfredo theme eateries across America and sell packaged fettuccine Alfredo in supermarkets and specialty food stores, but the legality of the move is hotly contested. Meanwhile Alfredo Di Lelio III has franchised his grandfather's name and recipe to various restaurants in North and South America. The soap is made even bubblier by the fact that Alfredo Di Lelio II, son of the original Alfredo, at some point decades ago sold rights to the family name to a former business partner, Guido Bellanca, who subsequently owned and operated Alfredo's in New York City from 1977 to 1995. And it's Bellanca's son Russell who opened Alfredo of Rome in Rockefeller Center in 2000, hoping to build on the success of his Disney World Alfredo's at EPCOT Center.

Why is everyone arguing over one of the world's most fattening and easy-peasy recipes—pasta, butter and cheese?

Well, the Disney World restaurant generates more than $12 million in annual sales, according to Bellanca's communications officers. And Mario Mozzetti told me his lawyers estimate the fettuccine Alfredo business to be worth $20 million overall per year in the United States alone. Though you can't copyright a recipe, this might explain why everyone wants a serving off old Alfredo's platter—it's his name that still draws customers.

Fettuccine Alfredo al Triplo Burro

FRESH FETTUCCINE WITH PARMIGIANO-REGGIANO AND A TRIPLE DOSE OF BUTTER

Fettuccine Alfredo crops up in various guises on countless restaurant menus nationwide. But few diners know where the recipe comes from, who Alfredo was and how this incredibly simple dish is actually made. In Rome, where fettuccine Alfredo was born almost one hundred years ago, only four ingredients go into the recipe: fettuccine, butter, Parmigiano-Reggiano and a pinch of salt. No cream, no pepper, no parsley, no chives—nothing but massive doses of extravagantly egg-rich pasta (about $1\frac{1}{2}$ eggs per serving), sweet butter and tender, young cheese (aged no more than 16 to 17 months). The trick to making the recipe work, as Alfredo Di Lelio III showed me, is to use top-quality ingredients and to follow the steps laid down by his grandfather Alfred Di Lelio I, the recipe's inventor. Timing and body language are essential. There's a lot of entertainment value in seeing Alfredo and his longtime waiters scooping, turning and flipping fettuccine at table in the landmark building the restaurant has occupied since 1948.

The first time I met Alfredo Di Lelio III it was an emotional encounter. His grandfather and my grandfather, Alessandro Anzi, had fought side by side in World War I and had remained friends for decades afterward. As a child, my mother had eaten many times at Alfredo's first restaurant, Alfredo alla Scrofa, in the 1930s, served by the maestro himself with a solid gold fork and spoon given to Alfredo as a gift in 1925 by Hollywood stars Douglas Fairbanks and Mary Pickford. My grandfather died after World War II, my mother moved to America and somehow, when we lived in Rome in the 1960s, and during my many prolonged visits to the city over the years, I never managed to meet Alfredo III. At long last, my wife and I sat at a starched white tablecloth in the airy, cream-and-white decor, under low-relief sculptures showing four rearing stallions, with Alfredo Di Lelio I as charioteer holding a platter of fettuccine. On another wall, the name "Alfredo" is spelled out with plasterwork fettuccine, and there's a golden fork and spoon and the words "King of Fettuccine." I'd brought some black-and-white photos of our respective grandfathers together during World War I.

Alfredo III told us the history of his family. Then he took us into the kitchen and showed us step by step how to make what must be the world's richest, most luscious and caloric pasta. Later, Alfredo and his headwaiter served us, handing my wife the same solid gold spoon and fork my grandparents and mother had eaten with all those years ago. Delicious? To die for!

Kosher salt or coarse sea salt

1½ pounds *Fettuccine Fresche all'Uovo* (page 117 and note on page 120) or 1½ pounds dry store-bought fettuccine

1 cup (2 sticks) unsalted butter, softened

8 ounces freshly grated tender, young Parmigiano-Reggiano (about 1½ cups)

SERVES 4

1   Bring 5 quarts or more of water to a boil in a large pot.

2   Bring 2 to 3 quarts of water to just under a boil in a wide, shallow pan. Immerse a large serving platter in the water to heat it.

3   Add salt to the boiling water in the large pot, stir vigorously and gently drop in the nested fresh or store-bought fettuccine while the water is still turning.

4   With kitchen gloves or mitts, carefully remove the serving platter from the pan, dry it off with a dishcloth, and place it on a cutting board. Slice the butter into pats and put them on the platter to melt.

5   Reserve about ½ ladle (2 to 3 tablespoons) of the pasta water in a small bowl.

6   Drain the pasta while it is very al dente and transfer it, still dripping, to the platter with the melted butter.

7   Quickly sprinkle the grated cheese on top of the fettuccine and pour the reserved pasta water over it.

8   At the dinner table, toss, flip, stir and sweep the fettuccine in the butter-and-cheese dressing with a large fork and spoon for up to 2 minutes to fully amalgamate the ingredients. Serve immediately.

Cranky Hosts: Rome's *Burberi*

*T*he flimsy flatware wrapped in a paper napkin lands on the Formica tabletop as your host, hands on hips, glares down at you. He's expecting you to set your own place and say "wine and water"—the ritual request you're supposed to make when you settle into a certain kind of Roman *osteria* (wine-eatery) or family-style trattoria.

"Wine and water?" he growls. You nod, then remember to specify "red." Your host shakes his head. "White. No red wine here. Flat water or bubbly?"

Before you can answer, he shuffles away, shouting at someone in the back room, his voice thundering over the ambient chaos. As you arrange your knife and fork, you wonder why he threw them at you, and why he didn't just announce, "White wine" if no red was on tap—literally on tap since the wine he's now drawing for you comes from a spigot on a huge refrigerator. You're feeling pretty uncomfortable until you see your host approaching a table occupied by savvy Romans. They get the same treatment.

Why is this guy so cranky? The answer: He's a *burbero*—a diamond in the rough, a professional grump. He's performing for his guests in the long-standing tradition of Rome's famously gruff, short-tempered tavern-keepers. They perpetuate the kind of earthy Roman scene described by Giuseppe Gioachino Belli in his ribald, roistering anti-papal Roman dialect poetry of the 1830s and 1840s. Historically, among Rome's top *burberi* of the last 100 years is Mario Romagnoli, alias Il Moro, which is also the name of Mario's restaurant. He played the colorful ancient Roman glutton Trimalchio in Fellini's cult movie *Fellini Satyricon*. But the act at Il Moro, now a century old, is tame. The regulars still play cards at "their" table, but there's no cheap, flying flatware or cursing, and the dining room glitters with well-heeled tourists, politicians and journalists whose food is served on fine plates and who sit surrounded by costly original art.

Felice, in the Testaccio neighborhood, is probably the city's most authentic *burbero*-style trattoria today. Felice himself is an unrepentant, crusty character right out of Cinecittà Central Casting. Gaunt and grizzled, with a telegraphic delivery, he smoothes his perfectly ironed white smock and assigns tables by reservation only, at strategic intervals so as not to be overwhelmed. When he feels he has enough customers, he simply locks up and won't let anyone in. If you arrive even a few minutes late, he might not serve you. If you don't order a full meal, he mutters, "You shouldn't come if you're not hungry." Shambling through the wondrously hideous decor, along apricot walls hung with tacky paintings of "old Rome" lit by fluorescent strip lights, Felice watches with feigned dispassion to see if you've cleaned your plate of his prodigious helpings. Leave much *carciofi alla romana, bucatini all'amatriciana* or *cacio e pepe* behind, and you might not expe-

rience the next course: Felice or his fledgling cranky sidekicks will remove your knife and fork. Once, with a table of Roman friends, having shoveled our way through mounds of rib-sticking pasta, one of us ordered an artichoke for a main dish. "*Carciofi* are not a main dish," Felice said deadpan. Our friend never got his artichoke.

Why do Romans keep coming back for abuse to rough-edged places like Felice? "The atmosphere," explained a Roman friend, indicating Felice's dining room and its occupants. "It's so natural, so timeless, so Roman. And the food is just like homemade."

Fontana della Cisterna, Trastevere,
Via della Cisterna

Rigatoni con Asparagi e Ricotta

RIGATONI WITH ASPARAGUS AND RICOTTA

1½ pounds tender young green asparagus

Kosher salt or coarse sea salt

1 pound rigatoni or penne

1½ cup ricotta, preferably Italian ewe's-milk ricotta (about ¾ pound)

2 tablespoons extra-virgin olive oil

3 heaping tablespoons freshly grated Pecorino Romano

Freshly ground black pepper

About 1 cup freshly grated cheese, half Pecorino Romano and half Parmigiano-Reggiano

SERVES 6

You can make this simple Eastertide recipe in the time it takes to boil water and cook pasta. The dish's quick-and-easy nature fits with the Romans' attitude toward asparagus. "Let it be done in less time than it takes to cook an asparagus!" was a common expression during Emperor Augustus Caesar's reign. Apparently the high-strung ruler detested overcooked asparagus as much as rebellious Gauls. The ancients dedicated the asparagus to Venus, goddess of love, and ascribed to it aphrodisiac qualities. Science has yet to prove them. But that doesn't stop modern Romans from believing in this pungent vegetable's prodigious powers of invigoration.

1   Bring at least 5 quarts of water to a boil in a large pot.

2   With a vegetable peeler or paring knife, scrape the asparagus stems and snap off the woody ends, eliminating tough parts and imperfections. Cut the tips to about 1½ inches in length. Chop the stems into roughly 1-inch lengths.

3   Add a generous pinch of salt to the boiling water, drop in the pasta and stir. Wait 1 minute and add the chopped asparagus stems. Cover the pot. When the water returns to a boil, cook the pasta and stems, uncovered, for 3 minutes. Add the asparagus tips, stir and cook until the pasta is al dente, 5 to 8 minutes.

4   While the pasta cooks, scoop the ricotta into a large serving bowl. Ladle in about 2 tablespoons of the pasta water and stir with a wooden spoon or spatula. Add the oil, the 3 heaping tablespoons of Pecorino Romano and a generous pinch of pepper. Stir until smooth and dense.

5   When the pasta and asparagus are al dente, drain and toss them into the serving bowl with the ricotta, stirring and flipping.

6   Serve hot with a bowl of mixed cheeses on the side.

Spaghetti alla Carrettiera

SPAGHETTI WITH TUNA, TOMATO AND PORCINI SAUCE

*T*he trick to getting this straightforward recipe to sing, according to Stefania Porcelli, granddaughter of the famous Checco il Carrettiere, who reputedly invented the dish circa 1935, is to use top-quality ingredients: Italian *ventresca* (from the underbelly) tuna packed in extra-virgin olive oil, Italian dried porcini, San Marzano canned tomatoes. The second secret is to sauce the pasta in the still-hot pot it was boiled in—an unwieldy technique the first time around but quickly mastered. Other cooks might toss in peas or ham, or use fresh mushrooms instead of dried ones, or serve *spaghetti alla carrettiera* topped with grated cheese. Not the Porcelli clan. Tenth-generation Romans, their restaurant has been a Trastevere neighborhood institution for decades. "The simplicity of the process, and the sensibility of the cook, is what makes it great," explains Stefania, an unflagging traditionalist. "Trastevere historically has always had a Jewish connection. This could be a kosher dish. It has no animal fats, pork or dairy products. Adding ham or cheese makes no sense and doesn't improve it. And the flavor of dried as opposed to fresh mushrooms is much more intense."

The name, *alla carrettiera,* derives from the fact that Checco (short for Francesco) was a cart driver, a *carrettière.* In the 1920s and 1930s, he plied the Alban Hills–to–Rome run delivering wine to *osterie.* Spaghetti with canned tuna—then a novelty—was a favorite fast food of such deliverymen. It could be tossed together in the time it took to cook the pasta. Eventually Checco opened his own

1 ounce dried porcini
(about 1 cup)

1 cup warm water

2 cloves garlic

4 to 6 tablespoons
extra-virgin olive oil

1 *peperoncino* (hot chili
pepper), shredded,
or ¼ teaspoon crushed
red pepper flakes

2 (6-ounce) cans Italian
ventresca tuna packed in
extra-virgin olive oil or
tuna packed in water
(about 1½ cups)

Kosher salt or coarse
sea salt

1 (28-ounce) can Italian
plum tomatoes, preferably
San Marzano

1½ pounds spaghetti

SERVES 6

osteria, which became a trattoria, then a restaurant. Checco's improvement to the original recipe was to add mushrooms and tomatoes. His brainchild has been popular (and imitated) ever since, and his family's restaurant continues to thrive.

1 Soak the mushrooms in a small bowl in the water for 15 to 20 minutes. When the mushrooms are tender, use a slotted spoon to remove them from the bowl. Wipe them carefully with paper towels to absorb excess liquid. With your fingers, clean off any remaining soil. Cut away and discard any tough parts or imperfections. Filter the soaking water through a fine-mesh sieve or strainer lined with a paper towel or a paper coffee filter. Reserve ½ cup of the mushroom water for step 6 and reserve the rest for other recipes. Cut the mushrooms into rough ¼- to ½-inch pieces.

2 With the heel of your hand or the flat part of a wide-bladed knife, crush the garlic on a cutting board. Spread the cloves open with your fingers. Discard the skins and green shoots.

3 Heat 4 tablespoons of the oil in a heavy frying pan over medium-low heat. Add the garlic to the oil, sauté for about 1 minute and discard it. Add the *peperoncino* and stir with a wooden spoon or spatula until thoroughly distributed.

4 Add the mushrooms to the frying pan and stir.

5 With the tines of a fork, flake the tuna into the frying pan with its extra-virgin packing oil. Stir while adding a pinch of salt. If you are using water-packed tuna, drain the water and add the tuna with the remaining 2 tablespoons oil.

6 Raise the heat to medium. Sauté for 2 to 3 minutes while incorporating and reducing the reserved ½ cup of filtered mushroom water, 1 tablespoon at a time.

7 Pour the tomatoes and packing juices into the sauce and crush while stirring with a fork or wooden spoon. Lower the heat and simmer, uncovered, for 20 minutes.

8 While the sauce simmers, bring at least 5 quarts of water to a boil in a large pot. When the water comes to a boil, add a generous pinch of salt, drop in the spaghetti and stir. Cover the pot. When the water returns to a boil, cook the pasta, uncovered, until barely al dente. Drain the spaghetti and toss it back into the pot in which it was boiled. Top immediately with the sauce. Away from direct heat, stir vigorously for 1 minute.

9 Transfer the spaghetti to a deep serving bowl, toss and serve immediately.

Spaghetti con Fave, Lattuga e Pancetta

SPAGHETTI WITH FRESH FAVAS, LETTUCE HEARTS AND PANCETTA

3½ pounds fresh young fava beans in their pods (about 12 ounces shelled)

1 medium-sized yellow or white onion

4 ounces pancetta or bacon strips

1 head lettuce, preferably escarole or butter lettuce

¼ cup extra-virgin olive oil

Kosher salt or coarse sea salt

1 pound spaghetti, *spaghettoni, bavette, trenette* or linguine

½ cup freshly grated Pecorino Romano cheese

Freshly ground black pepper

1 heaping tablespoon minced fresh spearmint

About 1 cup freshly grated Parmigiano-Reggiano and/or Pecorino Romano

SERVES 6

*F*resh favas are a springtime treat in Rome. No paschal table is complete without them. This medley of fresh beans, tender lettuce hearts and pancetta, also called *spaghetti con la scafata,* has long been one of our friend Verdella Caracciolo's favorites. A mother of three young children, Verdella lives on the edge of the former Ghetto in a Renaissance palazzo overlooking the celebrated Fontana delle Tartarughe (Fountain of the Turtles). The Campo de' Fiori and its produce stands are a 10-minute walk from there, so over the years Verdella has become a master at making dozens of fresh vegetable-based dishes, especially pasta dishes that her kids love, like this one. The lettuce in this recipe counterbalances any slight bitterness the beans might have at the end of the growing season, Verdella explains. Once shelled, if the favas are bigger than your thumbnail, you should blanch them for a minute or so and remove the tough translucent skin to reveal the sweet, deep-green heart beneath.

1   Bring at least 5 quarts of water to a boil in a large pot.

2   Shell the favas by cracking open the pods and running your index finger along inside. You should have 2½ cups. Blanch for 1 to 2 minutes and remove with a skimmer. If the beans are still tough or bitter, eliminate the skins by rinsing the favas in a strainer under cold water and gently pinching with thumb and forefinger. Keep the water boiling for the pasta.

3   Peel and thinly slice the onion. Slice or tear the pancetta into rough 1-inch squares. You
    should have about ¾ cup. Rinse the lettuce, discarding tough outer leaves. Tear the
    tender inner leaves into rough 2-inch ribbons.

4   Heat the oil in a very large, high-sided frying pan over medium-low. Add the onion,
    pancetta and a small pinch of salt. Sauté, stirring frequently, until the onion softens and
    the pancetta begins to brown, 6 to 7 minutes.

5   Add a generous pinch of salt to the boiling water. Cover the pot and bring it back to a
    boil. Toss in the pasta and stir. Cover the pot, bring it back to a boil, uncover and cook
    while finishing the sauce. Reserve ¼ cup of the pasta water.

6   Add the lettuce and blanched favas to the frying pan and sauté until the favas are al
    dente, about 4 minutes.

7   Drain the pasta when barely al dente, about 2 minutes less than the recommended cooking time given on the package, and toss it into the frying pan. Sauté, stirring while sprinkling in the Pecorino Romano, the reserved pasta water and a pinch each of salt and pepper. Remove the skillet from the heat and let it sit for 1 minute.

8   Transfer the pasta to a serving dish and garnish it with the mint. Serve hot with a bowl of Parmigiano-Reggiano and/or Pecorino Romano on the side.

TIP: By blanching the favas and cooking the pasta in the same water, then adding the pasta and reserved water to the fava mixture in the skillet, you amalgamate the ingredients, binding and imparting extra flavor, a sauté technique called *saltare in padella* or *passare in padella* (sautéing in the frying pan). When you also toss cheese into the pan, the technique is known as *mantecare,* to mix and meld.

VARIATION: This vegetable preparation makes an excellent side dish or appetizer. Leave out the mint (and the pasta) and add 1 *peperoncino* (hot chili pepper) or ¼ teaspoon crushed red pepper flakes. Depending on where you come from in or around Rome, the variation is called *la scafata* or *fave col guanciale.*

Fettuccine Fresche all'Uovo

FRESH EGG FETTUCCINE

Fettuccine is among the oldest and probably the most popular fresh pasta in Rome—think of *fettuccine Alfredo* (see page 106) or *fettuccine alla Romana* (see page 122). They've been around for centuries. Handmade fettuccine—meaning fettuccine kneaded, rolled out and cut by hand, a straightforward but time-consuming job—is a rarity lovingly produced by a clutch of stalwarts. They include our Roman friend Daniela Maggioni and my mother, when she's feeling energetic.

There's a good reason for preferring totally handmade pasta beyond simple nostalgia for grandma's cooking. Handmade fettuccine is springier and more porous than its perfect, store-bought counterpart because metal rollers haven't compressed the delicate ribbons into leathery strips. When cut by hand with a sharp knife or pasta wheel, the fettuccine come out irregularly shaped. A mass of springy, porous irregular fettuccine absorbs sauce better than compact, regular fettuccine.

The golden rule of Roman fettuccine-makers says that for each generous serving, you need 100 grams (about 1 cup or 4 ounces) flour, 1 large egg and 1 tablespoon water. If you're making extra rich pasta, you can use olive oil and/or wine instead of water, or whole eggs (for *fettuccine Alfredo*), or egg yolks only (3 large egg yolks equal 1 large egg). Since homemade, handmade pasta that is composed entirely of all-purpose flour—the closest thing you can get in America to Italian "00" flour—is too tender for most Roman palates and my own, the ideal flour mix in the Eternal City is half all-purpose flour and half durum wheat flour (for *fettuccine Alfredo,* it should be 100 percent durum wheat). Don't worry: The durum wheat doesn't make the pasta slick or in any way impede its ability to absorb luscious buttery sauces—which is what fresh egg noodles are designed to do. Italian law currently requires all commercial fresh pasta makers to use at least 50 percent durum wheat. Almost every supermarket and bakery in Italy sells 500-gram (1-pound) bags of durum wheat flour especially for home pasta-makers, the same kind sold at many Italian food shops or by mail order in the United States (see Sources, page 297).

2 cups all-purpose flour

2 cups durum wheat flour, plus 3 to 4 heaping tablespoons for dusting

4 large eggs

About 4 tablespoons warm water, or more as needed

½ teaspoon fine salt

SERVES 6 TO 8
(ABOUT 1½ POUNDS)

The only real competition to fettuccine comes from *tonnarelli,* and to a much lesser degree, from *pappardelle* (in essence, double-wide fettuccine). Once upon a time, *tonnarelli* looked like thick spaghetti (the name comes from *tondo,* round). Now they're square-shaped and more akin to the Abruzzi region's *maccheroni alla chitarra* (literally "guitar macaroni," because they're cut with a stringed-tool resembling a guitar). With this recipe you can make either fettuccine or *tonnarelli,* provided you have the right kind of square *tonnarelli*-cutting attachment or stringed tool for hand-cutting.

As concerns automatic pasta extruders, I don't believe in them for one simple reason: The quality of the pasta is never the best. I urge you to give handmade a try. At the least, making this recipe is a good workout even if you can't pull it off perfectly the first time around. Once you've mastered homemade, handmade pasta, the satisfaction that will engulf you will numb you to the effort, like a marathoner with runner's high. You'll never want "fresh" store-bought pasta again.

The recipe yields about 1½ pounds of pasta, enough for 4 to 6 generous Roman-style heaping-mound servings, though I think 6 to 8 normal servings is a more accurate estimate, especially if you're going to follow it with a main course. Use this fettuccine recipe when you make the robust *Fettuccine alla Romana* (page 122) or *Garofolato e Sugo d'Umido* (page 146). Or dress the fettuccine with the sauce made for *Spaghetti col Sugo Finto* (page 89) or the butter and sage sauce for *Ravioli Quaresimali con Burro e Salvia* (page 72). Because of its soft texture and absorbency, fettuccine (and other fresh egg pasta) isn't ideal for seafood sauces or recipes with lots of olive oil to soak up.

HAND-MIXING METHOD:

1   To make the fettuccine entirely by hand, you'll need a pasta board or food-safe countertop or tabletop. Pour the all-purpose and durum wheat flour into a large bowl and stir them together with a fork until thoroughly mixed. With your fingers or a wooden spoon, dig a well in the flour, crack in the eggs, dribble in the water and sprinkle in the salt.

2   With a wooden spoon, break up the egg yolks and stir slowly clockwise until the flour absorbs the eggs and water. Squeeze and knead the dough with your fingers until it is very stiff and uniform, about 10 to 12 minutes. Transfer the dough to a large wooden cutting board or marble slab and let it sit for 30 minutes.

STANDING-MIXER OR FOOD-PROCESSOR METHOD:

1   Combine the all-purpose and durum wheat flours in the bowl of a standing mixer fitted with a dough hook or paddle attachment, or in a food processor fitted with a wide blade. Mix or process at low speed for about 15 seconds. Crack in the eggs and add the water and salt. Mix or process at low speed until the dough becomes hard and granular in consistency.

2   With about 1 tablespoon of the remaining durum wheat flour, dust a large wooden cutting board or marble slab and turn out the grainy dough onto the work surface. Flour your hands with the durum wheat flour and squeeze and knead the dough until uniform and very stiff, adding a tablespoon or so of warm water as needed. Let the dough sit for 30 minutes.

ROLLING OUT AND CUTTING THE FETTUCCINE:

1   With a rolling pin, roll out the dough to make a stiff but elastic sheet of pasta no more than $1/8$ inch thick. With a sharp knife, slice the sheet in half. Dust each sheet with durum wheat flour on both sides, lifting with your fingers as you work. Put one sheet out of the way on the edge of the work surface or on a flour-dusted platter.

2   Flatten the first sheet until almost translucent, rolling firmly outward from a central point in all directions, gently lifting and turning the dough a quarter turn at a time, to form a rough disk. Carefully put the pasta sheet to the side on a cutting board or platter. Trim the edges of the sheet with a sharp knife, making a rectangle. With the knife or a pasta wheel, start cutting the first sheet vertically from the right side to the left, slicing off ribbons about $1/8$ inch wide until the sheet has been wholly sliced.

3   With your fingers, separate the fettuccine by $1/8$ inch or so. Sprinkle several generous pinches of durum wheat flour over them and rub some along the surface of the rolling pin. Use it to gently flatten the fettuccine again, making sure not to break them or allow them to stick to the rolling pin.

4   Dust a platter with durum wheat flour. With the fingers of one hand, lift the fettuccine 5 or 6 ribbons at a time, coil them loosely around the palm of the same hand and nest them on the platter. Sprinkle each nest with durum wheat flour. Continue to coil and nest the fettuccine, transferring them to the platter, until you've finished the first sheet of dough.

5   Stretch the second sheet on the floured cutting board or marble slab. Roll it out, cut and flatten it and nest the fettuccine on the platter, repeating the operations as with the first sheet.

6   Let the fettuccine sit for 30 minutes before cooking. To store, sprinkle durum wheat flour, coarse semolina or cornmeal in the bottom of a ceramic, glass or plastic container, place the fettuccine inside, sprinkle with more flour, wrap the container with a clean dishcloth and refrigerate it for up to 24 hours. Don't cover the fettuccine with plastic wrap or they'll become mushy.

NOTE: If you are using a pasta-making machine, combine the ingredients following the manufacturer's instructions for making fettuccine. For *fettuccine Alfredo*, use only durum wheat flour (4 cups), 6 large eggs and 1 to 2 tablespoons warm water, as needed. To roll and cut the pasta with a machine, see How to Use a Home-Style Pasta-Rolling Machine, page 121.

How to Use a Home-Style Pasta-Rolling Machine

If you don't need the challenge of rolling out fresh egg pasta by hand, use a hand-cranked or electric machine with rollers instead. Make the pasta dough and let it sit for about 30 minutes before feeding it through the machine. Divide it into six equal pats about the size of a stick of butter, one pat per serving. Lightly flour a wooden board with durum wheat flour, coarse semolina or cornmeal. Working one at a time, with a rolling pin, roll out each pat into a rectangle just smaller than the width of the machine's rollers. Make sure you've flattened the dough enough to get it through the machine's widest roller setting. Start with the widest setting, crank the sheet of dough through, fold it like a hand towel into thirds and run it through the rollers two more times without folding it over. Fold it into thirds again and run it through once more. Adjust the machine one setting tighter and continue to roll the sheet of dough through, repeating the operation while tightening the rollers one setting at a time, until you've run the dough through on the third-narrowest setting for *tonnarelli,* the second-narrowest setting for ravioli and the narrowest setting for fettuccine. Never make the pasta at the thinnest setting for ravioli or they might tear while you're filling or cooking them.

To hand-cut the pasta, follow the recipe for *Fettuccine Fresche all'Uovo* (page 117) or *Ravioli Quaresimali* (page 72), or use the pasta machine's fettuccine or *tonnarelli* cutter attachment.

Fettuccine alla Romana

FETTUCCINE WITH A SAUSAGE, SHORT RIB, BEEF AND TOMATO SAUCE

2 ounces dried porcini (about 2 cups)

1 cup warm water

2 cloves garlic

1 large onion

2 carrots

3 stalks celery

3 tablespoons extra-virgin olive oil

2 *peperoncini* (hot chili peppers), shredded, or ¹/₂ teaspoon crushed red pepper flakes

12 ounces mild Italian sausage

1 pound short ribs

8 ounces chicken livers

8 ounces ground pork

8 ounces ground beef

1¹/₂ cups Italian dry red wine

2 (28-ounce) cans Italian plum tomatoes, preferably San Marzano

Kosher salt or coarse sea salt

*T*he recipe's name says all: This is *the* way to make fettuccine in Rome. When Romans want to indulge in serious feasting—for the holidays, a birthday or an anniversary, for example—*fettuccine alla romana* is the number-one pasta choice. The recipe has been around for centuries. The late, great cookbook writer Ada Boni considered it on a par with *tagliatelle alla bolognese* and *lasagne genovesi* as among the great classics of Italian cooking.

Once upon a time, the main ingredient for the sauce was chicken giblets, now largely replaced by mixed ground meats and short ribs. The signature dish of umpteen restaurants in the early 1900s, you'll rarely see it today on a menu. It's too time-consuming. But it's worth it. This is one of my personal favorites. Most of our Roman friends make *fettuccine alla romana* at Eastertide, specifically on Easter Sunday (Pasqua) or the following day, *Lunedì dell'Angelo* (the Angel's Monday), also called *Pasquetta* (little Easter).

1 Soak the dried mushrooms in a small bowl in the water for 15 to 20 minutes. When the mushrooms are tender, use a slotted spoon to remove them from the bowl. Wipe them carefully with paper towels to absorb excess liquid. With your fingers, clean off any remaining soil. Cut away and discard any tough parts or imperfections. Filter the soaking water through a fine-mesh sieve or strainer lined with a paper towel or a paper coffee filter. Set aside.

Freshly ground black
pepper

1½ pounds *Fettucine Fresche
all'Uovo* (page 117) or
1½ pounds dry store-
bought fettuccine

½ cup freshly grated
Parmigiano-Reggiano

½ cup freshly grated
Pecorino Romano

1 cup freshly grated cheese,
half Pecorino Romano and
half Parmigiano-Reggiano

SERVES 8

2   Peel and mince the garlic, onion and carrots, discarding
the garlic's green shoots. Rinse the celery, remove the
stringy parts and mince it.

3   Heat the oil in a very large saucepan over medium-high
heat. Add the *peperoncini,* garlic, onion, carrots and
celery. Sauté until tender, stirring frequently with a
wooden spoon or spatula, 8 to 10 minutes.

4   Remove the casings and break up the sausage meat into
roughly 1-inch chunks. Stir them into the vegetables
and increase the heat to high. With a paring knife,
remove the meat from the short rib bones, dice the
meat and add it to the saucepan, browning for 3 to 4
minutes. Discard the bones.

5   Rinse and finely chop the chicken livers. Add to the
saucepan along with the ground pork and ground beef.
Stir and flip with a wooden spoon or spatula, browning
the ingredients, about 20 minutes.

6   Pour in the wine and boil to evaporate it, 2 to 3 minutes.

7   Drain the canned tomatoes, saving their juices. Add the tomatoes to the sauce, crushing
with a wooden spoon or spatula. Add the mushrooms and the filtered mushroom water.
Lower the heat to a minimum and simmer, partly covered, for 45 minutes. Remove the lid
and simmer, uncovered, for 45 minutes more, adding the tomato juices, 1 tablespoon at a
time, as needed to keep the sauce from excessive thickening. Season with salt and pepper.

8   Bring at least 5 quarts of water to a boil in a large pot. Add a generous pinch of salt to the
water, carefully drop in the fettuccine, stir and cover the pot. When the water returns to
a boil, cook the pasta, uncovered, until it is barely al dente. Drain the pasta and toss it,
still dripping, into the saucepan. Add the ½ cup Parmigiano-Reggiano and ½ cup
Pecorino Romano. Toss vigorously and remove the pan from the heat immediately.

9   Transfer the pasta to a large platter and serve immediately, with a bowl of mixed
Parmigiano-Reggiano and Pecorino Romano on the side.

Bavette con Mazzancolle in Acqua di Rucola

RIBBON PASTA WITH SHRIMP, ARUGULA AND FRESH TOMATOES

1 pound ripe cherry tomatoes (about 2 cups)

4 ounces arugula (about 4 cups loosely packed)

1 pound large fresh shelled shrimp or prawns

2 cloves garlic

¼ cup extra-virgin olive oil

Kosher salt or coarse sea salt

1 *peperoncino* (hot chili pepper), shredded, or ¼ teaspoon crushed red pepper flakes

1 pound *bavette, trenette,* linguine or other dry ribbon pasta

Freshly ground black pepper

SERVES 4

Roman home cooks often get their inspiration and recipes from the city's outdoor markets. Greengrocer Claudio Zampa, whose stand at Campo de' Fiori is jokingly referred to as Cartier because it carries top produce at high prices, is a precious source of information to hundreds of center-city homemakers. Our friend Verdella Caracciolo lives a few minutes' walk from the market square and learned this recipe from Claudio. She taught us how to make it. Verdella's three children love it. That's in part because the *rucola* or *rughetta* (varieties of arugula), the peppery salad green Romans worship, is cooked in the pasta water, becoming milder while imparting its distinct piquancy to the strands of pasta. Several distinct advantages in using cherry over plum tomatoes are that there's no need to peel or seed them and they're often sweeter and lower in acidity than other kinds of tomatoes any time of year. The shrimp or prawns—a large Mediterranean variety called *mazzancolle* in Rome—merge deliciously with the recipe's other ingredients.

1 Bring at least 5 quarts of water to a boil in a large pot.

2 Rinse the tomatoes and let them drip dry in a colander. Rinse, spin dry and roughly chop the arugula. Rinse the shrimp or prawns, leaving them whole. Peel the garlic with a paring knife, removing any imperfections, including the green shoots, and mince.

3   Heat the oil in a large frying pan over medium. Add a pinch of salt, the garlic and *peperoncino*. Add the shrimp and sauté for 2 to 3 minutes. Add the tomatoes and barely cook them, stirring gently, for 2 to 3 minutes. Remove the frying pan from the heat.

4   Add a generous pinch of salt to the boiling water. Toss in the pasta and about half the arugula, stir and cover the pot. When the water returns to a boil, cook, uncovered, until the pasta is al dente. Drain the pasta and arugula.

5   Transfer the pasta and cooked arugula to a serving dish and top with the tomato-and-shrimp sauce. Add several turns of the peppermill, toss and top with the remaining fresh arugula. Serve immediately.

Claudio Zampa with Lina Clemente

Tonnarelli alla Ciociara

Fresh Tonnarelli with Mushrooms, Peas and Pancetta

*L*uigi del Grosso, better known as Gino *(below)*, started running restaurants in Rome in 1954. In the forty-odd years since he invented it, his *tonnarelli alla ciociara* has become a classic. Lots of fanciful tales have cropped up to explain the name. One claims that in Ciociaria, a farming district south of Rome, this dish was a favorite of pea growers who would gather mushrooms in the nearby woods and use homemade pancetta to flavor the sauce. But Ciociaria isn't pea country and most locals don't make *tonnarelli* pasta. Fresh mushrooms, while not unknown thereabouts, aren't exactly staples.

"I had a waiter back in the early fifties," Gino explains, amused. "He was from Ciociaria. We devised this dish with ingredients the Romans know and like and instead of calling it *alla Gino* I named it *alla Ciociara* in his honor. Those stories are pure silliness," he chuckles.

Two tricks make this simple pasta recipe sing. First, use fresh, top-quality peas, mushrooms and pancetta, and cook them separately, assembling them at the last minute. Second, finish cooking the pasta in the frying pan with plenty of grated cheese. Timing is important. When you toss the pasta into the boiling water, you should have the peas and mushrooms cooked, standing by, and be ready to crisp up the pancetta in a matter of minutes. You'll need a high-sided frying pan big enough to hold all the ingredients at once with room to toss and turn them.

8 ounces fresh, small porcini, cremini, portobello or a mixture of mushrooms

2 tablespoons extra-virgin olive oil

1 clove garlic

Kosher salt or coarse sea salt

Warm water (optional)

2 pounds fresh, tender young peas in their pods, or 1 (10-ounce) package of top-quality frozen peas

1 small white onion

8 ounces pancetta or bacon strips

2 tablespoons butter (optional)

$\frac{1}{4}$ cup dry Italian white wine, preferably Frascati or Marino

1 pound fresh *tonnarelli* (or fresh or dry fettuccine, linguine or other ribbon pasta, including *Fettuccine Fresche all' Uove,* page 117)

2 to 3 heaping tablespoons freshly grated Parmigiano-Reggiano

2 to 3 heaping tablespoons freshly grated Pecorino Romano

Freshly ground black pepper

About 1 cup freshly grated cheese, half Pecorino Romano and half Parmigiano-Reggiano

SERVES 4

1   Clean the mushrooms carefully with moistened paper towels. With a paring knife, cut off the bases of the stems. Thinly slice the mushrooms and attached stems. You should have about $2\frac{1}{2}$ cups.

2   Heat the oil in a large frying pan over medium-low. Peel the garlic and drop in the clove whole with a pinch of salt. Sauté the garlic for 1 to 2 minutes, then discard it.

3   Add the mushrooms and cook, covered, for 3 minutes. Remove the lid and sauté, uncovered, for 2 to 3 minutes. If the mushrooms seem dry, add several tablespoons of warm water. Remove the frying pan from the heat and spoon the mushrooms and their juices into a bowl.

4   If you are using fresh peas, shell the peas by cracking open the pods and running your index finger along inside. You should have 1 $\frac{3}{4}$ cups. Put them in a small pot and cover with cold water. Peel the onion, add it whole, and bring the water to a boil. Lower the heat and simmer for 2 to 3 minutes, until the peas are barely al dente. (If you are using frozen peas, add them directly to the frying pan in step 7.) Place a colander over a large pot and drain the peas in it, capturing the cooking water. Discard the onion. Transfer the peas to the bowl with the mushrooms.

5   Add 5 quarts of water to the pea cooking water and bring the water to a boil. Add a generous pinch of salt.

6   Dice the pancetta. You should have ¾ cup. Add the pancetta to the frying pan previously used for cooking the mushrooms. Heat over medium-high heat until the pancetta begins to crisp. If the pancetta is lean, add 1 tablespoon of the butter; if it is fatty, drain off some of the fat and forgo the butter. Sauté, turning, scraping and flipping with a wooden spoon or spatula, 2 to 3 minutes.

7   Pour in the wine and boil to evaporate it, 1 to 2 minutes. Add the remaining 1 tablespoon butter, if using, lifting and tipping the frying pan to distribute it. Add the mushrooms and peas and stir. Lower the heat to minimum and keep the frying pan hot.

8   Add a generous pinch of salt to the boiling water, carefully drop in the pasta, stir and cover the pot. When the water returns to a boil, cook the pasta, uncovered, until the pasta is barely al dente, about 2 minutes less than the recommended cooking time given on the package.

9   Drain the pasta and transfer it, still dripping, to the frying pan with the mushrooms, peas and pancetta. Sauté for 1 minute, tossing vigorously. Sprinkle in the Parmigiano-Reggiano and Pecorino Romano while tossing. Add several turns of the peppermill. Remove the skillet from the heat and let it sit for 30 seconds.

10   Serve the pasta with a bowl of freshly grated cheeses on the side.

Risotto con l'Indivia

CURLY ENDIVE RISOTTO

4 cups chicken broth
(see page 62)

1 large head curly endive

2 cloves garlic

3 tablespoons extra-virgin
olive oil

Kosher salt or coarse
sea salt

1 cup risotto rice,
preferably carnaroli,
arborio, vialone nano or
other high-quality Italian
risotto rice

About 1½ cups freshly
grated Pecorino Romano

Freshly ground black
pepper

SERVES 4

This is a tasty, classic Roman-Jewish risotto. My
mother makes it in the traditional way with tart, curly
endive. But my father, who objects to even slightly bitter
greens, usually asks her to use spinach instead, add butter
and double or triple the amount of cheese, favoring
Parmigiano-Reggiano over Pecorino Romano. Ada Boni,
the famous Italian cookbook writer, and other Roman
gastronomes such as Livio Jannattoni, author
of numerous books on Roman food, give a non-Jewish
version of this risotto, calling it *riso e indivia* (rice and
endive). Their recipe calls for pancetta or guanciale.
I prefer the traditional version; it's simpler and the green
flavor of the endive is unmediated. This is a low-fat
risotto made without butter; it lets the starchy goodness
of the rice shine through.

1   Heat the chicken broth over medium-low to just under
    a boil.

2   Destem, rinse and spin dry the curly endive, discarding
    any woody or spoiled sections. Chop it medium-fine.
    You should have about 8 cups, tightly packed.

3   Peel and halve the garlic with a paring knife, removing any imperfections, including the green shoots.

4   Heat the oil in a large saucepan over medium-low. Add the garlic and a generous pinch of salt and sauté, stirring, for 1 to 2 minutes, until the garlic begins to color. Discard the garlic, raise the heat to medium-high and add the chopped endive. Sauté for about 2 minutes stirring vigorously, until the endive expels its juice.

5   Add the rice, stir and sauté for 1 minute. Lower the heat to medium-low, ladle in enough hot chicken broth to cover the rice and continue to stir until the broth has thickened, 1 to 2 minutes. Add more broth, one ladle at a time, every 5 minutes or so, stirring occasionally, until the rice is al dente and the risotto is dense, about 30 minutes total.

6   Remove the risotto from the heat, stir in 4 heaping tablespoons of the Pecorino Romano and 3 to 4 turns of the peppermill. Mix thoroughly and cover. Let the risotto sit for 3 minutes.

7   Serve at once, with a bowl of the remaining Pecorino Romano on the side.

Risotto di Seppie al Forno

BAKED RISOTTO WITH LEMONY RISOTTO-STUFFED SQUID

1½ pounds large fresh squid, cleaned and prepped (or other large fresh or frozen cuttlefish) (see page 133)

8 cups cold water

Kosher salt or coarse sea salt

2 tablespoons minced fresh flat-leaf parsley, plus several sprigs for the stock

2 small white onions

1 stalk celery, halved

1 carrot, halved

5 tablespoons extra-virgin olive oil

2 cups risotto rice, preferably carnaroli, arborio, vialone nano or other high-quality Italian risotto rice

¾ cup Italian dry white wine, preferably Frascati or Marino

Minced or grated zest of 1 lemon

Freshly ground black pepper

SERVES 6

*F*ishmonger Anna Elisa Scipioni (*below*) makes this simple, delicious recipe on Tuesdays and Fridays, the traditional fish and seafood days in Rome. It's really two dishes in one: risotto with squid and baked squid stuffed with risotto. The double cooking redoubles the flavor.

Risotto is always a challenge as a party dish because you have to keep stirring and coddling it to the last moment. That's another great thing about this recipe: You make the risotto first, stuff the squid and bake, so there's no last-minute rush.

1   Mince one squid and place it in a medium saucepan. Reserve the remaining squid in a separate bowl.

2   Make the squid stock by pouring the water into the saucepan with the minced squid. Add a generous pinch of salt and several whole sprigs of parsley.

3   Peel the onions, halve 1 and mince the other. Put the minced onion in a small bowl and set aside. Put the halved onion in the saucepan with the minced squid.

Add the celery and carrot to the saucepan. Bring the stock to a boil and boil for 5 to 6 minutes. Lower the heat and let simmer.

4   To prepare the squid tentacles, remove and discard the bulblike beak at the base, pushing it out with your fingers. Thoroughly rinse under cold running water to remove any remaining sand. Mince and return the tentacles to the bowl.

5   Heat 3 tablespoons of the oil in a large pot over medium. Add the minced onion and parsley and sauté until the onion becomes translucent, 2 to 3 minutes. Stir in the minced tentacles and sauté for 2 to 3 minutes. Add the rice, raise the heat to medium-high, stir and sauté for 1 minute.

6   Pour in the wine and boil to evaporate it, 1 to 2 minutes. Lower the heat to medium-low and ladle in enough squid stock to barely cover the rice. Simmer while preparing the lemon.

7   Add the zest and 1 tablespoon of lemon juice to the rice. Cook, uncovered, stirring constantly, until thickened, 1 to 2 minutes.

8   Ladle in more stock every 2 to 3 minutes, stirring frequently, until the rice is barely al dente and the risotto dense, about 25 minutes. Adjust the salt, add several turns of the peppermill and remove the risotto from the heat. Let it cool for 5 to 6 minutes, until easy to handle.

9   Preheat the oven to 375°F. Grease a 7-by-12-inch baking pan or ovenproof casserole, using 1 tablespoon of the oil.

10   With a small spoon and your fingers, stuff the risotto into each of the cleaned squid bodies to about two-thirds full. Put the stuffed squid in the baking pan and distribute the remaining risotto around and on top of them. Moisten the risotto with a few tablespoons of the remaining squid stock and the remaining 1 tablespoon oil. Cover with aluminum foil.

11   Bake for 20 minutes, remove the foil and bake until the risotto is crispy on top and the squid is tender, 8 to 10 minutes.

12   Serve hot.

How to Clean Squid, Cuttlefish and Calamari

If you are using frozen precleaned squid, cuttlefish or calamari, thaw and rinse them following the instructions on the package. If you are using them fresh, rinse thoroughly under cold running water. Holding one at a time in your left hand, use your right thumb and index finger to detach the head and tentacles with a neat jerk. The intestines should come free in a single piece. Peel off the skin with your fingers. Use a paring knife on a cutting board to cut off the tentacles just forward of the eyes. Rinse and reserve the tentacles. Discard the head and intestines. Cut away the hard, sandy evacuation tube in the center of the tail. With your index finger and thumb, pull out the cartilage and any remaining material inside and rinse thoroughly.

To prepare tentacles, push out the bulblike beak at the base with your fingers and discard. Thoroughly rinse under cold running water to remove any remaining sand.

Shepherd with flock in Rome's Caffarella parklands

SEGONDI

MEAT, POULTRY, FISH AND EGGS

ROMANS ARE KNOWN THROUGHOUT ITALY as insatiable meat and poultry eaters, with a preference for long-cooked stews and herb-infused roasts. Lamb and pork vie for supremacy on their tables; both meats have been staples for most central Italians—from Lazio, Tuscany and Abruzzi—since earliest recorded history. Roman suckling lamb—*abbacchio*—is renowned as some of the finest anywhere. Lambs are slaughtered when they are less than 2 months old and weigh 15 to 20 pounds. In line with a tradition ridiculed by the satirical poet Juvenal nearly two thousand years ago, true *abbacchio* must be entirely milk-fed. Juvenal's jibes were aimed at extravagant Imperial-era entertainers, but he recognized that suckling lamb is enormously different in flavor and texture—it's sweeter, milder and meltingly tender—from even very young lamb that has fed on grass. Romans differentiate between the two by calling milk-fed lamb *abbacchio* and all other lamb *agnello*. In the rest of Italy, *abbacchio* is known as *agnello da latte*. Suckling lamb is hard to come by in America, but it is available from a handful of farmers and butchers, usually by mail order (see Sources, page 297). Top-quality young domestic lamb is a fine substitute, but mutton is not appropriate for these recipes.

You can see shepherds and swineherds with their flocks of sheep and their pigs roaming the rolling hills of Lazio year-round. Pigs are also raised on an industrial scale to satisfy the capital's enormous demand for fresh pork and cured pork products. They come not only from Lazio, but also from Tuscany and especially Umbria. The Romans have a special predilection for pork that goes back to before the she-wolf, *la Lupa,* became the symbol of the city. Before the wolf, there was the sow, *la Scrofa.* According to Roman tradition, the sow showed Aeneas and the Trojans, the ancestors of the city's founders, where to find fresh water and build their settlement at Lavinio, south of the Tiber's mouth, after they fled the fall of Troy. In thanks, the Trojans slaughtered the sow and her thirty piglets, roasted them and feasted in thanksgiving. This may have been the first recorded example of *porchetta*—spit-roasted pig stuffed with wild herbs—a Roman favorite to this day. The *Scrofa* was really a boar, as ancient sculptures attest, and Romans still eat boar, not roasted but in stews (see *Cinghiale in Agrodolce,* page 174). Pliny the Elder claimed to be able to find fifty different flavors in pork, which was long judged the most versatile of meats. The Romans' favorite cut of pork for braising in milk (see *Maiale in Tegame al Latte,* page 166) is the neck and shoulder or *il collo* (plate or butt, in English). This cut is marbled with fat and especially flavorful. Other preferred cuts are the loin and saddle—easier to find than neck in supermarkets in the United States.

As a food, beef is a relative newcomer to Rome. Tough old oxen and milk cows, butchered when no longer productive then turned into stews, were considered good enough only for the poor. Beef cattle raised specifically for their meat became popular only in the nineteenth century and were reserved for the middle and upper classes (working-class Romans bought cheap organ meats instead). One of Rome's most popular recipes, *saltimbocca alla romana* (veal rolls with cured pork and sage, see page 138), comes out of the nineteenth century. The older version, *involtini di manzo coi piselli* (see page 144), employed scraps of beef rolled around carrots and celery. I give both recipes because they're very different in texture and taste but equally delicious.

Romans think of poultry as the prime ingredient for a variety of festive meals. Stuffed roasted chicken, capon or turkey is served on Christmas and holidays and occasionally for a big Sunday lunch. Chicken stewed with sweet peppers is the official dish of ferragosto, the mid-August national holiday that's been in effect since Augustus Caesar's day (it's named after him). There are plenty of everyday, simple poultry recipes, too, like chicken sautéed with herbs (see *Pollo in Padella,* page 177) and spicy grilled chicken with red chili peppers (see *Galletto alla Diavola,* page 188).

Eggs are an important part of the Roman diet, matched with everything from vegetables to meat. Frittata is the Italian answer to omelet and Romans make their frittatas with zucchini, sweet peppers, bacon and cheese, and even spicy amatriciana pasta sauce (see page 90).

In Rome, aged cheeses like Parmigiano-Reggiano or pecorino (of various kinds and origins) are sometimes served as is in big chunks as a simple main course, while scamorza, caciocavallo or provola—three pear-shaped cheeses found throughout central-southern Italy—are also grilled and eaten hot.

Rome is only about 10 miles from the Mediterranean, and the coast of Lazio stretching from Campania in the south to Tuscany in the north is dotted with fishing ports. Romans have been eating fish for a lot longer than anyone can remember. In its original form, Marcus Gavius Apicius's first-century recipe collection filled ten separate books, two of them entirely on fish. Emperor Domitian (A.D. 51–96) is famous among other things for having called the Senate to special session to decide how best to cook a giant turbot he'd received as a gift. However, since Rome's cooking today is derived primarily from the last few centuries' so-called *cucina povera*—poor folks' cooking—many Roman recipes call for types of fish or seafood that were formerly cheap. That's why the most popular fish in Rome are still anchovies (either fresh or preserved), salt cod, mollusks of all kinds, red mullet, shark or dogfish, eel, skate, monkfish, scorpion fish, squid, octopus and, to a lesser degree, river or lake fish, such as perch, pike and trout. Tiny freshwater fingerlings called *lattarini* found exclusively in Lake Bolsena north of Rome are eaten whole, usually after frying and pickling. Everywhere in Italy and the United States, fish of all kinds are a costly delicacy nowadays, yet Romans consume great quantities of them, including what they consider "new" species, such as farmed bream, porgy and bass, popularized in the last fifty years. Some Mediterranean varieties prized in Rome are tough to find in America, especially fresh anchovies, so use sardines instead of anchovies, domestic sea bass instead of gilthead, rockfish or snapper instead of red mullet, and shark steaks instead of dogfish. Atlantic or Pacific squid and sole are all fine substitutes for their Mediterranean cousins.

Saltimbocca alla Romana

VEAL ROLLS WITH PARMA HAM AND FRESH SAGE

1½ pounds thin veal scallops (12 to 14 scallops)

12 to 14 fresh sage leaves

12 to 14 translucent strips prosciuttto crudo (Parma ham) (about 4 ounces)

Kosher salt or coarse sea salt and freshly ground black pepper

2 tablespoons extra-virgin olive oil

¾ cup Italian dry white wine, preferably Frascati or Marino

SERVES 6

The name means "jump in your mouth" because these sage-perfumed veal rolls are so good they just seem to leap into the jaws of diners. The recipe is famous the world over and needs little introduction. Oddly enough, you rarely see saltimbocca on Roman menus these days. Victims of their own celebrity? Perhaps, but they're as popular as ever at home. The original recipe calls for veal scallops, pancetta, sage, butter and sweet Marsala wine. Lightened versions, like this one, use olive oil instead of butter, Parma ham instead of pancetta, and dry white wine intead of Marsala. A lot of people now make saltimbocca with flattened chicken or turkey breast instead of veal. This is the recipe my mother has been making for the last fifty years or so, and it has never let her or me down. If you want to make the recipe as it was made one hundred years ago, use butter, pancetta and Marsala instead, in the same proportions.

1. Stretch the veal scallops on a cutting board between two sheets of waxed paper and, with a mallet or rolling pin, hit and flatten them until nearly translucent. Brush off or rinse and pat dry the sage leaves.

2. Place 1 strip of ham atop each veal scallop and 1 sage leaf atop each slice of ham. Roll up the scallops like jellyrolls and pin each with a toothpick. Repeat the operation until the veal, ham and sage are used up. Sprinkle the rolls with a pinch each of salt and pepper.

3. Heat the oil in a large frying pan over medium heat. Add the veal rolls and brown thoroughly, flipping and turning with a wooden spatula, for 4 to 5 minutes.

4. Pour in the wine and boil to evaporate it, 1 to 2 minutes. Lower the heat to minimum and simmer for 3 to 4 minutes.

5. Transfer the rolls to a serving platter, remove the toothpicks, drizzle with pan juices and serve immediately

Coda alla Vaccinara

ROMAN OXTAIL STEW

For several thousand years, right up to the Second World War, teams of oxen plowed fields and pulled loads around Rome. The great oxen retirement home was the slaughterhouse, where their skins became leather, their horns a variety of accessories and their meat stews. The women and men whose job was to slaughter, butcher and skin the oxen were called *vaccinari,* from the word *vacca,* meaning cow. They were paid in kind with skins, unwanted organ meats and oxtails. This engendered a style of cooking associated with the neighborhood where the slaughterhouse and tanneries were located, Testaccio. It flanks the Tiber on the southern end of central Rome (see Simply Offal: Rome's Gutsy *Quinto-Quarto* Cooking, page 152). In Italy and elsewhere in Europe, the custom of raising beef for meat, as opposed to raising oxen for plowing and transportation, is relatively recent, dating back to the 1800s. That's why, in English, we still refer to "oxtails" and not to "beef tails," though there are practically no true oxen left anywhere in the Western world. Most butcher shops and supermarkets in America actually sell the cut as "beef oxtails." Go figure.

This and the related recipe *Garofolato* (see page 146) are considered the archetypal Roman beef stews. *Coda alla vaccinara* is made from humble ingredients, but comes out heavenly nonetheless: rich, tender and redolent of cloves and slow-cooked vegetables. Every family has its own version of *coda,* as it's called for short, and a handful of trattorias and restaurants in Rome still offer it on the menu, especially in the ex-slaughterhouse neighborhood, Testaccio. Some cooks add a tablespoon of bittersweet chocolate before serving the stew. Others use pine nuts, cinnamon, nutmeg, raisins or candied fruit to achieve sweet-and-sour piquancy. Our Roman friend Carla Bertini makes the best *coda alla vaccinara* I've ever eaten. Her family has been stewing up oxtails this way since before anyone can remember. A professional photography researcher and home cook by election, Carla combines cloves, bay leaf and black pepper to impart an earthy tang to her *coda*. She hates the fuss of removing the cloves, though, so ties them up in gauze, as in a tea bag, and reels the bag in before serving the stew. "The longer it stews the better," she says, recalling the days of her grandmother's coal-fired stoves and slow-cooked meals. "I make it a day or two ahead, because it's best of all when reheated."

1 beef oxtail (2½ to 3 pounds)

12 celery stalks

1 clove garlic

1 carrot

1 medium-sized white onion

4 ounces pancetta

2 heaping tablespoons minced fresh flat-leaf parsley

4 tablespoons extra-virgin olive oil

Kosher salt or coarse sea salt and freshly ground black pepper

1 cup Italian dry red wine

1 tablespoon tomato concentrate

2 (28-ounce) cans Italian plum tomatoes, preferably San Marzano

6 to 8 cups boiling water

5 cloves

1 bay leaf

SERVES 6

1   Rinse the oxtail under warm running water and eliminate any fat or gristle with a paring knife and your fingers. Chop it into sections along the vertebrae. Pat them dry with paper towels.

2   Remove the stringy parts of the celery. Mince 1 stalk and reserve the rest. Peel and halve the garlic with a paring knife, removing any imperfections, including the green shoot. Mince the garlic with the carrot and onion. Mince the pancetta; you should have ¾ cup. Combine the minced vegetables and pancetta with 1 heaping tablespoon of the parsley.

3   Heat the oil in a large pot over medium-high. Add the minced vegetable-and-pancetta mixture and sauté, stirring with a wooden spoon or spatula until the onion becomes translucent, 4 to 5 minutes.

4   Add the oxtail, a generous pinch of salt and several turns of the peppermill. Brown thoroughly, stirring, flipping and scraping, for about 15 minutes.

5   Pour in the wine and boil to evaporate it, 1 to 2 minutes. Stir in the tomato concentrate. Add the tomatoes and their packing juices, crushing and stirring. Add just enough of the water to completely submerge the oxtail bones.

6   Wrap the cloves in a beggar's purse of gauze and tie it closed with kitchen string, leaving about 1 foot of string attached. Lower the purse into the stew and secure the string to a pot handle. Drop in the bay leaf and stir.

7   Lower the heat to minimum and simmer, partially covered, for 2 hours.

8   Slice the remaining 11 celery stalks into sticks the size of an index finger. Add them to the stew and simmer, covered, for 40 minutes.

9   Remove and discard the purse of cloves and the bay leaf. Stir in the remaining 1 heaping tablespoon parsley. Serve hot in soup bowls.

NOTE: Save any leftover oxtail meat and sauce to dress fettuccine or other pasta.

Er gargarozzo e'stretto, ma cce cape la casa co'tutt'er tetto.
(Your throat may be narrow but [if you chew and chomp]
you can get a whole house down it, including the roof.)

—Old Roman saying

The Vatican's Unlikely Wine Cellars

*W*ould you store your finest vintages in a dump? That's what popes and cardinals did for centuries, and the tradition is carried on today by one of Rome's top restaurants, Checchino dal 1887. Checchino is wedged into a grotto carved from the flank of a hill once known in Latin as the *Mons Testaceus,* Monte Testaccio in modern Italian. It rises in the middle of the Testaccio neighborhood near the Tiber River in southeastern central Rome. Testaccio gets its name from the broken amphorae—the no-deposit, no-return bottles of antiquity—dismantled and piled there from the fifth century B.C. until the fall of the Empire, about eight hundred years' worth of junk. The amphorae were called *testae,* because they looked like human heads (*testa* means head), possibly the origin of our insult "jug head." Being formidable neatniks, the Romans issued hammers and assigned thousands of slaves to carefully knock apart each arriving terra-cotta jug and stack its components in a specified section of the Imperial garbage dump. The piles of jug handles, jug sides, jug necks and jug bottoms eventually formed a mountain 160 feet tall and a quarter mile around. In the Middle Ages, hundreds of years after the mound had been abandoned and overgrown, people dug into the shards seeking shelter amid the ruins. They found it oddly bone-chilling. Word of the mound's miraculous coolness reached the Vatican, and someone in charge, presumably a medieval pope, ordered the grottoes to be excavated. In so doing, the world's first perfect wine cellars were created, with aerated tunnels of terra-cotta with a constant 53° to 57°F. Today there's no trace of trash on Monte Testaccio. You can visit the archeological site atop the mound by appointment or, more entertainingly, dine at Checchino dal 1887 and ask for a special tour of the Roman jug cellars.

Involtini di Manzo coi Piselli

Beef Scallops Rolled with Carrot and Celery and Stewed with Peas

12 thin slices beef, preferably London broil (about 3 pounds)

12 thin slices Parma ham

2 celery stalks

2 carrots, peeled

2 heaping tablespoons all-purpose flour

1 small white or red onion

1 clove garlic

2 tablespoons extra-virgin olive oil

1 bay leaf

1 clove

½ cup Italian dry white wine, preferably Frascati or Marino

3 cups peeled, seeded and quartered medium-sized fresh Italian plum tomatoes (about 1½ pounds) (see How to Peel and Seed a Tomato, page 93)

Kosher salt or coarse sea salt and freshly ground black pepper

Pinch of nutmeg

3 pounds fresh, tender young peas in their pods, or 1 (1-pound) package frozen peas

Serves 6

*S*weet carrots and fresh peas transform these simple beef rolls into mouthwateringly tender delicacies. The recipe comes from chef Adriana Montellanico of La Briciola restaurant in Grottaferrata south of Rome. Adriana loves food history and lore, calling this one of the easiest and oldest recipes in the *cucina povera* (poor folks' cooking) repertoire. The origin of *involtini di manzo* is straightforward: The cut of meat favored in the original recipe is called *panicolo,* the raggedy bits clinging to the beef bones. The poor would buy the bones, detach the scraps and roll them with carrots and celery. In springtime, the rolls are stewed with fresh peas, another formerly cheap ingredient. You can make the recipe with just about any cut of beef, provided you can flatten it into scallops. I find very thin slices of London broil work best.

1   Place the sliced beef between two sheets of waxed paper on a cutting board. With a mallet or rolling pin, pound the meat into thin scallops.

2   Remove the fat from around the edges of the Parma ham and reserve. Place 1 slice of ham on each of the 12 scallops.

3   Remove the stringy parts from the celery. Slice the celery and carrots into sticks about 4 inches long and ½ inch wide. Place 1 carrot stick and 1 celery stick on each scallop atop the ham, reserving leftover sticks. Roll up and pin the scallops with toothpicks.

4   In a shallow bowl, roll the beef rolls lightly in the flour, transferring them to a platter as you work.

5   Peel and halve the onion and garlic with a paring knife, discarding the garlic's green shoot. Mince any leftover carrot and celery sticks with the Parma ham fat, onion and garlic.

6   Heat the oil in a large frying pan over medium-low. Add the minced vegetables and ham fat and sauté for about 2 minutes, stirring with a wooden spoon or spatula. Stir in the bay leaf and the clove. Add the beef rolls and brown them thoroughly, stirring, turning and scraping, for 4 to 5 minutes. Pour in the wine and boil to evaporate it, 1 to 2 minutes.

7   Add the tomatoes and a pinch each of salt, pepper and nutmeg. Lower the heat to minimum and simmer, covered, for 45 minutes.

8   If you are using fresh peas, shell them by running your index finger along the inside of the pods. You should have 2⅔ cups. Stir the fresh or frozen peas into the frying pan, cover and simmer for 10 to 12 minutes for fresh peas, 1 minute for frozen peas. Remove the lid and simmer for another 3 to 5 minutes.

9   Remove the bay leaf, clove and toothpicks. Serve immediately.

Garofolato e Sugo d'Umido

SLOW-COOKED RUMP ROAST WITH CLOVES AND BACON THAT DOUBLES AS PASTA SAUCE

5 pounds rump roast or similar cut of stewing beef

12 to 14 small sprigs fresh marjoram

4 cloves garlic

4 ounces bacon (4 to 6 strips)

6 cloves

Kosher salt or coarse sea salt and freshly ground black pepper

1 stalk celery

1 large white onion

1 carrot

4 heaping tablespoons minced fresh flat-leaf parsley

3 tablespoons extra-virgin olive oil

1 cup dry Italian red wine

2 heaping tablespoons tomato paste

Hot water

SERVES 6 TO 8 AS A MAIN COURSE; SERVES 8 TO 10 AS PASTA SAUCE

Garofolo means clove in Italian. Clove is the primary seasoning in this long-cooked stew that doubles as a pasta sauce. The longer it cooks, the better it is. You can make *garofolato* a day or more ahead and reheat it. It's similar to *coda alla vaccinara* (see page 140) but includes bacon and marjoram and uses a beef roast instead of oxtails. Serve it as a pot roast, or use it to top fresh fettuccine (see *Fettuccine Fresche all' Uovo,* page 117), potato gnocchi (see *Gnocchi di Patate,* page 70) or ravioli (see *Ravioli Quaresimali con Burro e Salvia,* page 72).

1   Pat the roast dry with paper towels and set it on a cutting board. With a sharp knife, make eight incisions, about 2 inches deep, at regular intervals along its length between the strings binding it. Flip the roast over and make eight comparable incisions. Rinse the marjoram sprigs, pat them dry with a paper towel and break them into short sections. With a paring knife, peel and quarter the garlic, discarding the green shoots. Slice the bacon into strips about 1/4 inch wide and 1 inch long. With your fingers, push 1 section of marjoram sprig, 1 section of garlic and 1 strip of bacon to the bottom of each incision. Flip the roast over and repeat the operation on the other side. Make two more incisions per side and slip 1 clove into each. Sprinkle the roast with a very generous pinch each of salt and pepper. With your fingertips, rub the seasonings over the meat and into the incisions.

2   Remove the stringy parts of the celery. Peel the onion and carrot. Roughly chop the celery, onion and carrot. Combine the vegetables with the minced parsley.

3   Heat the oil in a heavy-bottomed pot big enough to easily hold the roast over medium heat. Brown the roast on all sides and both ends, flipping and turning with a cooking fork and steel spatula, about 10 minutes.

4   Add the chopped vegetables and parsley and any leftover bacon and marjoram and brown them, stirring vigorously, for 4 to 5 minutes.

5   Pour in the wine and boil to evaporate it, 2 to 3 minutes.

6   Put the tomato concentrate in a ladle, fill the ladle with hot water and stir until the concentrate dissolves. Pour the mixture into the pot. Add the remaining 2 cloves, stirring and scraping with a wooden spoon or spatula. Ladle in enough hot water to almost cover the roast. Bring the liquid to a boil.

7   Lower the heat to minimum and simmer, covered, for 1½ to 2 hours, until the meat is extremely tender, flaking apart at the flick of a fork. Remove the lid and reduce the juices for 10 minutes.

8   Transfer the roast to a cutting board, slice it thinly, place the slices on a platter and top them with the pan juices, discarding the cloves. Alternatively, to make a pasta sauce, slice the meat and process it in a food processor with its pan juices for 30 to 45 seconds and use it to dress the pasta.

The Untouchables:
Delicious and Authentic But You
Probably Wouldn't Eat Them

Romans are famed throughout Italy as *ghiottóni* (gluttons) for the gusto with which they eat and the gutsy character of many of their traditional dishes. Here's a short list of Roman favorites only stalwarts still make. For obvious reasons, few feature on the menus of Roman trattorias and restaurants nowadays. My mother loved several of these recipes and couldn't understand why her American children and their friends ran in the other direction when she offered a taste. A few are truly delicious: I've come to enjoy them with something approaching my mother's Roman relish. But they aren't in this cookbook because you won't find most of the ingredients and even if you did you probably wouldn't eat them:

Battered and fried brains

Hearts and lungs of lamb with slivered artichokes

Sautéed lamb head

Grilled milk-filled lamb or calf intestines

Braised pig's trotters

Snails in tomato sauce

Vinegar-pickled tiny fried *lattaríni* (lake fish)

Tomato sauce with cocks' crests

Chicken intestine stew

Fried chicken blood

Chicken gizzards and meat sauce

Beef spleen in tomato sauce

Pan-fried bull testicles with lungs and various glands

Kid's hooves with fava beans

Poached fish heads

Frog soup

Sautéed songbirds

Trippa alla Romana

Tripe in a Spicy Tomato Sauce with Mint and Pecorino Romano

The first time I witnessed my mother preparing tripe, I thought she was washing the fleece we used to dry the family car. I watched in mild amusement as she rinsed and picked at the frizzy, hairy white strips, which I soon realized weren't fleece but flesh. The process seemed to take forever. That day I must have been sick and stayed home from school. My mother would never cook "funny food" when my father or sisters and brothers were around to see. Eventually, she put the tripe in a big stockpot, filled it with water, and added an onion spiked with cloves that looked like a medieval mace, a carrot and some celery. I drifted in and out of the kitchen and several hours later, around lunchtime, saw that the tripe was still boiling. I said nothing, used to my mother cooking things for hours at a time, often in secret. We were a large family, and for years we also fed several informally adopted friends. That meant planning out meals ahead and cooking huge quantities, most often pots of stew or vats of pasta sauce. That afternoon my mother made her usual Wednesday vat of tomato-and-beef ragù. When it had bubbled for several hours, she renewed her attention to the fleece, slicing it until you couldn't tell what it was. Then she added it to a pot of ragù she'd subtracted from the vat. I honestly don't recall the many other steps involved in transforming the fuzzy white pelt into a stew perfumed with fresh mint from the garden, with mounds of grated cheese on top. "What is it?" I finally asked her. "*Trippa*," she answered, shooing me out of the kitchen. "It's beef. You eat it all the time and don't know it. Call everyone and sit down. Dinner's ready."

As we settled in around the dinner table—eight or more of us—my siblings and father began tucking in with the usual sounds of contentment.

"But what kind of beef is *trippa*?" I asked my mother, gobbling the delicious stew.

She went pale. My father dropped his fork. He'd lived in Rome for six years and understood Italian, though he rarely spoke it. He lifted his nearly empty plate and politely asked my mother to step into the kitchen. There was a clashing of pans and a

2½ pounds honeycomb tripe

1 celery stalk

1 carrot

1 large onion

2 tablespoons extra-virgin olive oil

1 *peperoncino* (hot chili pepper), shredded, or ¼ teaspoon crushed red pepper flakes

1 bay leaf

½ cup Italian dry white wine, preferably Frascati or Marino

3 cups peeled, seeded and chopped medium-sized fresh Italian plum tomatoes (about 1½ pounds) (see How to Peel and Seed a Tomato, page 93)

Kosher salt or coarse sea salt and freshly ground black pepper

3 heaping tablespoons minced fresh spearmint

About 1½ cups freshly grated Pecorino Romano

SERVES 6

rushing of water. My brothers and our adopted friends didn't seem to notice, and the volume around the table rose in the absence of paterfamilias. The garbage disposal unit built into the kitchen sink, with the unforgettable manufacturer's name Insinkerator, roared into life, momentarily silencing us. Soon my father was back at his place at the head of the table, happily spinning strands of spaghetti with tomato-and-meat sauce onto his fork. We never ate *trippa* again as a family, or, if we did, never realized it. Even when I discovered exactly what tripe was—the lining of the stomach—I still enjoyed it.

Times have changed in America. Nowadays, tripe is sold in just about every supermarket in the land, a fact that has encouraged me to include this recipe. *Trippa alla romana* is one of those iconic Roman dishes that's been around for centuries and is still going strong, a regular feature, usually served on Saturdays, in every trattoria with "*cucina romana*" on the shingle, and a must in every Roman home. What makes it stand out from all other Italian tripe recipes is the punchy duo of fresh mint and Pecorino Romano.

1 Place the tripe in a colander and thoroughly wash it under cold running water for at least 5 minutes, removing any fat with a paring knife.

2 Bring a large pot of water to a boil, add the tripe and boil for 1 hour.

3 Drain the tripe in the colander and transfer it to a cutting board. Slice it into strips the size and shape of an index finger.

4   Remove the stringy parts from the celery and mince it, along with the carrot and onion.

5   Heat the oil in a large pot over medium heat. Add the minced vegetables and *peperoncino* and sauté, stirring regularly. Immediately stir in the tripe and add the bay leaf. Sauté for 2 to 3 minutes, until the vegetables begin to brown. Pour in the wine and boil to evaporate it, 1 to 2 minutes. Lower the heat to minimum and simmer.

6   Stir the tomatoes into the tripe with a generous pinch each of salt and pepper.

7   Raise the heat to high and bring the stew to a boil. Lower the heat and simmer, covered, for 30 minutes.

8   Stir the mint into the tripe and turn off the heat. Remove and discard the bay leaf. Sprinkle in 4 heaping tablespoons of the Pecorino Romano, stir and let the pot sit for 2 minutes.

9   Serve with a bowl of the remaining Pecorino Romano on the side.

Pecorino Romano (left) and Parmigiano-Reggiano (right)

Simply Offal: Rome's Gutsy
Quinto-Quarto Cooking

Er monno è una trippetta, e l'omo è un gatto
Che je tocca aspettà la su' porzione.
The world is a piece of tripe and humankind is a cat
Who has to wait for his ration of it.

—Giuseppe Gioachino Belli

In the beginning, that is to say sometime back in the eighth century B.C., while the contractors were still building Rome's foundations, Remus, Romulus's problematic twin, graduated from she-wolf milk to fresh innards. Against the advice of elders and the gods, young Remus ate the intestines of a goat that had been sacrificed to Faun, a lively local deity. Faun protested loudly at this brazen act of impiety. It gave rise to the annual Lupercalia feast and footrace in which participants behaved madly, like the wolves that tore sheep limb from limb and ate their innards (*lupus* is Latin for wolf, hence *Lupercalia*). The maverick Remus later broke another fundamental law of early Rome by scaling the new city walls into his brother's compound, an offense punishable by death at the hands of the city's ruler, who just happened to be Romulus. That's why it's said that Rome was born in a fratricidal bloodbath.

When it comes to cooking, the offal element lives on. I can't help wondering if wolfish old Remus should get the credit for the Roman obsession with organ meats in all their shapes, sizes and functions.

For the last two hundred years or so, Rome's offal cuisine has been known as *Quinto-Quarto,* because its components—inner organs, hooves, heads, tails, glands, brains, sweetbreads, testicles—weigh about one-quarter (*un quarto*) of the slaughtered animal's total weight. It's the quarter no one wanted to buy, hence the "fifth," meaning useless or worthless, as in "the economy's fifth wheel."

Some years ago, I met a legendary Testaccio restaurateur, the late Ninetta Ceccacci Mariani, whose family still owns and operates Checchino dal 1887 facing the Testaccio neighborhood's former slaughterhouse. Ninetta explained to me the origins of *Quinto-Quarto* cooking, still the backbone of the restaurant's menu. In the days before refrigeration, said Ninetta, organ meats were difficult to keep. They're the first things to spoil—and that's why slaughterhouse workers received them as partial in-kind payment, like it or not. This gave rise to scores of recipes, most for beef parts, since the Testaccio slaughterhouse handled beef and veal. Roman oxtail stew (see *Coda alla Vaccinara,* page 140) and tripe in tomato sauce (see *Trippa alla Romana,* page 149) are the most famous two. There are dozens of others, including panfried spleen, liver-and-onions, and chilled veal tongue served with pepper sauce.

Though some *Quinto-Quarto* dishes are available year-round in Rome, especially in Testaccio's many eateries, spring is the best time for innards aficionados. That's because, in addition to beef parts, you find suckling lamb or kid offal on the menu, too, from hoofs to horns. As cooked up by most Testaccio *trattorie,* delicacies such as *pajata* (Remus's much-loved suckling kid, lamb or veal intestines, still full of milk), *coratella* (heart, lung and esophagus of lamb or kid sautéed with artichokes) and *testarelle* (whole roasted lamb's or kid's head—my maternal grandfather's favorite food) couldn't be gutsier. You'll have to take a trip to Rome to taste them; those recipes are not in this book.

Testaccio, detail of entrance to ex-slaughterhouse

Agnello alla Cacciatora in Bianco Disossato

Spicy Boned Lamb Leg Sautéed with Rosemary, Wine and Vinegar

3-pound boneless leg of lamb

1 large white onion

2 cloves garlic

5 tablespoons extra-virgin olive oil

1 *peperoncino* (hot chili pepper), shredded, or ¼ teaspoon crushed red pepper flakes

1 cup Italian dry white wine, preferably Frascati or Marino

1 cup white wine vinegar

1 teaspoon balsamic vinegar

2 heaping tablespoons fresh whole rosemary leaves

Kosher salt or coarse sea salt and freshly ground black pepper

SERVES 6

This recipe has an alluring sweet-and-sour quality that comes from mixing wine and vinegar with stewed lamb juices, a technique used in Rome since antiquity. The dish is a favorite in the Alban Hills south of Rome. I learned how to make one version of it from exuberant chef Adriana Montellanico, owner of La Briciola restaurant in Grottaferrata. Instead of using the gristly or bony cuts and tomatoes called for in traditional *agnello alla cacciatora* recipes, Adriana prefers small chunks of boneless lamb leg prepared *in bianco* (without tomatoes). She also adds a teaspoon of balsamic vinegar to enhance sweetness.

1   Rinse the lamb and pat it dry with paper towels. Cut it with a carving knife into kebab-style 1-inch cubes.

2   Mince the onion. With the heel of your hand or the flat part of a wide-bladed knife, crush the garlic on a cutting board. Spread the cloves open with your fingers. Discard the skins and green shoots.

3   Heat the oil in a large nonreactive pot over medium-high heat. Add the lamb and brown for 3 to 4 minutes, stirring, flipping and scraping with a wooden spoon or spatula.. Stir in the onion. Add the garlic, sautéing for 2 to 3 minutes, and discard it.

4   Add the *peperoncino*. Slowly pour in the wine. Add the balsamic and white wine vinegars. Boil to evaporate the liquids, stirring for 2 to 3 minutes. Sprinkle in the rosemary. Lower the heat to minimum and simmer uncovered until the meat is tender, 30 to 40 minutes.

5   With a ladle and a slotted spoon, transfer the juices, onion and herbs to a food processor. Add a pinch each of salt and pepper and process until smooth. Alternatively, pass them through a food mill and season them with salt and pepper. Return the puréed juices to the pot, increase the heat to high, and reduce uncovered, stirring for 1 to 2 minutes.

6   Serve immediately.

On the Lamb:
Rome's Suckling *Abbacchio*

*L*ike suckling pig, suckling lamb—called *abbacchio* in Rome—has been the object of a Roman culinary cult ever since Aeneas and his band of defeated vets, fleeing the Fall of Troy, washed ashore south of Rome circa 1200 B.C. Or so the legend goes. Witness the sheer number of lamb recipes recorded by the gluttonous first-century gastronome Apicius, and the even greater variety of them around today. The wisecracking poet Juvenal (A.D. 60 to ca. A.D. 127), ridiculing Imperial Rome's various eating disorders, wrote of suckling lamb as "The tenderest of the flock, with more milk than blood, that has not lost its virginity by eating grass."

Juvenalia aside, suckling lamb is very different from lamb that has switched from milk to normal feed. It's pale, buttery soft and sweet, with no hint of the sheep or mutton the animal would become if allowed to grow. Roman lamb is slaughtered when 1 to 2 months old, at 15 to 20 pounds. It has burned off most of its baby fat but hasn't had time to become tough. Every ounce of the animal is consumed with relish, from legs to ribs, organ meats to intestines and brains.

Nowadays Romans and visitors alike demand milk-fed lamb year-round. But once upon a time, *abbacchio* was strictly a springtime treat. In those forgotten pre-Roman days, when Italic shepherds roamed free, sheep were the basic monetary unit, called a *pecus.* Their skins and wool provided clothing. Their milk, cheese and meat were a major source of protein. The early Romans worshipped the she-wolf that suckled Romulus and Remus, but, recognizing a good thing, they donned shepherd's clothing and went *pecus*-wild. In Roman law, *peculium,* derived from *pecus,* came to mean the property a son, wife or slave could own. And that's how we get our word "pecuniary." The Divino Amore district between the Alban Hills and central Rome was a favorite pasturage in classical times. For the last one thousand years or so, it's been named after the sanctuary to the Madonna del Divino Amore, and connoisseurs swear that sheep ranchers still raise the best *abbacchio* in the world there.

Some people are squeamish about eating milk-fed lamb, but the dispassionate economic rationale is nonetheless clear. Sheep are not entirely environmentally friendly; they nibble everything in sight and cause soil erosion and compaction. Each dairy ewe lives about a decade, producing two *abbacchi* a year, sometimes more. When there are too many lambs for a given pasturage to support, ranchers whisk them to the slaughterhouse, the earlier the better.

"Lamb and organ meats"

The term *abbacchio* arises from this harsh reality: The Italian verb *abbacchiare* means to beat down (and by extension to demoralize). It in turn derives from *bacchiare,* to beat fruit from trees with a *bacchio,* a long stick called *baculum* by the ancients. Suckling lambs were carried to market with their hooves twined over the *baculum,* and possibly also slaughtered with it, and that's why they were labeled *abbacchiati* or *abbacchi.* The verb also means to sell at bargain-basement prices, "to dump" on the market, reflecting the overabundance of spring lambs that drove down prices. In the early Christian era, shepherds and butchers were clever in their marketing, using religious festivities to hike up prices; everyone in Rome is expected to eat *abbacchio* at Easter, so demand keeps up with supply.

Nowadays, the expression *sentirsi abbacchiato,* literally to feel downbeat or demoralized, is common enough even in joyful Rome, but the locals and foreigners I've seen at table sure don't seem *abbacchiati* as they dig into their delicious little lambs. Once, several years ago in springtime, I lunched at a neighborhood trattoria near Campo de' Fiori and asked my waiter how many Roman lamb dishes he could think of and how each was made. He began a mouthwatering recitation that ran on for several minutes. Stuff or spike baby lamb with minced rosemary and garlic, he said, roast it with new potatoes, and that's called *abbacchio al forno con le patate* (see page 162), the centerpiece at Easter lunch or dinner. Braise the lamb in broth with white wine and scrambled egg yolks and it's called *abbacchio brodettato* (see page 158), an Easter Monday specialty. Cleave it into dainty chops, sprinkle them with rosemary and grill them and you get *abbacchio scottadito,* so named because the chops burn (*scottare*) your fingertips (*dito* is a finger) when you pick them up. If you sauté the lamb's internal organs instead, adding tender slivered artichoke hearts, you get *coratella con carciofi.* That's a hearty dish to eat on Easter morning around 10 A.M. if you've fasted on Saturday, or at lunch if, like most Romans, you haven't fasted at all. The waiter's list went on. Skewer bite-sized *abbacchio* chunks with bread and herbs and barbecue them and you get *crostini d'abbacchio* (see page 164). Tie the baby lamb's tiny milk-filled intestines into loops and sauté them with tomatoes and you have *pajata d'abbacchio,* served with rigatoni or grilled and eaten as a second course. Batter the poor beast's brains and deep-fry them, again with sliced artichokes, and you get *cervelli fritti.* Whole, oven-roasted lamb's head, split open, sprinkled with salt, pepper and rosemary, becomes *testarelle d'abbacchio.* Every part of the animal is used, confirmed the waiter. The lamb does not die in vain.

Abbacchio Brodettato

SUCKLING LAMB IN A HERBED LEMON, EGG AND CHEESE SAUCE

2 pounds boneless lamb
(preferably shoulder or leg of
suckling lamb)

1 stalk celery

1 carrot, peeled

Water

4 tablespoons extra-virgin
olive oil

Kosher salt or coarse sea salt
and freshly ground black pepper

1 large shallot, peeled and minced

1 heaping teaspoon fresh thyme

2 whole bay leaves

4 whole fresh mint leaves

1 teaspoon fresh rosemary leaves

1 cup Italian dry white wine,
preferably Frascati or Marino

3 large egg yolks, at room
temperature

2 heaping tablespoons freshly
grated Parmigiano-Reggiano or
Pecorino Romano

2 heaping tablespoons minced
fresh flat-leaf parsley

1 lemon

SERVES 4

Over the years I've eaten excellent *abbacchio brodettato*—chunks of suckling lamb in a lemony egg sauce—at a dozen trattorias, restaurants and homes in and around Rome. This is my favorite way to prepare it, merging elements from the Mariani family's recipe at their historic Testaccio restaurant, Checchino dal 1887, and from Sora Lella, Aldo Trabalzi's upscale trattoria on the Tiber Island. Trabalzi's innovation is the addition of freshly grated Parmigiano-Reggiano, extra herbs, and shallots instead of garlic. My gourmet friend Alessandro Bocchetti, originally from the mountainous Abruzzi bordering Rome's region, Latium, also makes his lamb with cheese, but uses Pecorino Romano instead. He calls it *agnello cacio e uova* (lamb with cheese and eggs).

In any of its many mouthwatering incarnations, this delicacy was probably invented by mountain folk from the Apennines. It's still favored in areas with lots of sheep and wild herbs for the taking. *Abbacchio brodettato* features on menus and family tables year-round, but it's especially delicious in spring, when the milk-fed local lamb is at its best.

1   Rinse the lamb, pat it dry with paper towels and cut it into kebab-style 2-inch cubes.

2   Make the lamb stock. Remove the stringy parts of the celery. Combine 2 lamb cubes and any lamb bones, the whole carrot and celery in a medium-sized saucepan. Fill the saucepan with 8 cups cold water and boil it for about 10 minutes. Lower the heat to minimum and simmer.

3   Heat 3 tablespoons of the oil in a large, high-sided heavy frying pan over medium-high. Add the remaining lamb cubes and a generous pinch each of salt and pepper. Brown the lamb on all sides, flipping, turning and scraping with a wooden spoon or spatula, 5 to 7 minutes. Lower the heat to minimum. Remove the lamb to a warm platter and cover it.

4   Peel and mince the shallot. Pour the remaining 1 tablespoon oil into the frying pan, increase the heat to medium and add the shallot, stirring with a wooden spoon or spatula. Stir in the thyme, bay, mint and rosemary. Return the lamb to the pan and increase the heat to medium-high.

5   Pour in the wine and boil to evaporate it, stirring vigorously, 2 to 3 minutes.

6   If the lamb seems dry, ladle in up to 1 cup of lamb stock. Reduce the heat to low and simmer, covered, for 15 to 20 minutes, stirring occasionally.

7   With a fork, beat the egg yolks in a small mixing bowl. Add a very generous pinch of salt, lots of pepper and the cheese. Add 1 heaping tablespoon of the parsley. Halve and juice the lemon into the egg mixture, beating with the fork.

8   Remove the frying pan from the heat and let it cool for 1 to 2 minutes. Remove and discard the bay leaves. Pour the egg mixture into the juices around the lamb and stir vigorously to form a runny egg sauce. If the sauce seems too thin or uncooked, return the skillet to low heat and stir for 30 to 60 seconds. If it seems too dry, stir in a tablespoon or more of the hot lamb broth.

9   Sprinkle in the remaining 1 tablespoon parsley and serve immediately.

Easter Monday:
Roman Spring Picnicking Rites

*E*aster Monday—what the Romans call *Pasquetta*—is a lighthearted day for *una scampagnata fuori porta* (a picnic excursion beyond the old city gates). You pack up the leftovers—*corallina salame,* leavened Easter *pizza pasquale* or *torta salata,* boiled eggs, cold roast lamb and a bottle of chilled Frascati white wine—or head to an *osteria,* trattoria or *ristorante* to continue the Easter feast in a sylvan setting, perhaps with *abbacchio brodettato* (see page 158), a *Pasquetta* specialty. I have always been amazed by the skill Romans deploy in preparing *Pasquetta* picnics. The family Fiat (nowadays probably a BMW or Volvo) is packed with folding table and chairs. While junior is bringing it around down pedestrian-only streets, grandma is boiling the fettuccine, cooking it extra al dente, dressing it with classic *alla romana*–style sauce (see page 122) and returning the pasta to the still-hot pot mummified in dish towels for insulation. Then it's a dash to the car before the traffic cops arrive!

Some inhabitants of the Eternal City, predicting a bumper-to-bumper snarl on the Via Appia and other arteries, stray no farther than the lawns and bay-shaded lanes of Rome's central parklands, the Villa Borghese. Back in the 1960s, my family sometimes went to Ostia Antica to picnic among the ruins, where spearmint grows wild and, crushed underfoot, mixes with the scent of the nearby Mediterranean. Friends went to Tivoli, northeast of Rome, site of the famous waterworks at Villa d'Este, while my wife's family went north to the shores of Lake Bracciano—all excellent and venerable picnicking spots.

The Romans' favorite spring excursion destination, though, has always been the Alban Hills—a series of volcanic, grapevine-stitched knolls southeast of the capital. They're dotted with ancient towns, such as Frascati and Marino, where the same-name wines originate, Nemi, Grottaferrata and Castel Gandolfo, site of the Pope's summer residence overlooking Lake Albano. When I say "always" I mean always. Frascati was the holiday hangout of Rome's upper classes about two thousand years ago, before Easter Monday had been invented. Castel Gandolfo, known in its ancient incarnation as Alba Longa, was founded several hundred years before Rome. It's been the backdrop to countless rites of spring that were surprisingly similar to contemporary Easter Monday picnics, whose historical significance as a celebration of the rebirth of the Earth after the death of winter is largely overlooked by most modern merrymakers.

Down the centuries, picnicking Easter Monday pilgrims—most of them more interested in feasting than in worshipping pagan deities or blessing the paschal lamb—have spawned dozens of cheerful, country-style trattorias in the Alban Hills. Many of them started out as *osterie* (taverns) where day-trippers would stop to drink local wines and snack on simple dishes but have evolved into full-blown restaurants.

As you drive around the Alban Hills looking for a picnic spot or place to nap, keep your eyes open for bonfires. Locals might be roasting *carciofi alla matticella,* whole artichokes jabbed into embers made from dried grapevine cuttings from the previous fall (see page 256).

Grottaferrata, famous for its thousand-year-old fortress abbey, is only about 3 miles from Castel Gandolfo as the crow flies, but many times that by tortuous road. Local spring specialties there include fettuccine with fresh fava beans or tender leeks, spicy lamb stew (see *Agnello alla Cacciatora in Bianco Disossato,* page 154) and fresh strawberry tiramisù (see *Tiramisù con le Fragole,* page 286).

Easter egg at Confetteria Moriondo e Gariglio

Abbacchio al Forno con le Patate

ROAST SUCKLING LAMB WITH POTATOES

8-pound bone-in leg of lamb, preferably milk-fed (see Sources, page 297)

4 tablespoons extra-virgin olive oil

1 head garlic

2 heaping tablespoons fresh rosemary leaves

Kosher salt or coarse sea salt and freshly ground black pepper

2 cups Italian dry white wine, preferably Frascati or Marino

1½ pounds small new potatoes, halved

SERVES 6 TO 8

In spring, Romans roast whole lambs—including the head—for the paschal feast. While lamb brains are considered a delicacy, and the lungs, offal and intestines go into gutsy dishes such as *coratella* or *pajata* (see On the Lamb, page 155), you can make a much less daunting version of this dish by simply roasting a leg of baby lamb Roman-style, with lots of garlic and rosemary. To specify "baby lamb" isn't redundant—a whole Roman *abbacchio* usually weighs less than 15 pounds and is exclusively milk-fed. Unless the lamb you've purchased is particularly fatty, there is no need to roast it on a rack. Lamb juices—what Romans call *il sughetto*—keep the meat moist by direct contact in the pan. Also, the potatoes are even more scrumptious when they soak up a portion of garlicky, herbed *sughetto*. Romans roast their *abbacchio* until well done and crispy on the outside.

1   Preheat the oven to 400°F.

2   Trim any fat or gristle off the lamb and rub the leg with 2 tablespoons of the oil. Place the lamb in a large oven pan. With a paring knife, make incisions ½ to 1 inch deep up and down on both sides.

3   With a paring knife, peel and halve about two-thirds of the garlic cloves, discarding the green shoots. Reserve the remaining one-third whole cloves to scatter over the lamb.

4   Rinse, pat dry and mince the rosemary leaves with the halved garlic cloves and a generous pinch each of salt and pepper. With the side of a knife blade, mash them into a thick paste. Poke the paste into the incisions with your fingers.

5   Season both sides of the lamb leg with salt and pepper. Scatter the remaining garlic cloves on top and around the leg and drizzle with the remaining 2 tablespoons oil.

6   Roast the lamb for about 30 minutes, until the top of the lamb is brown. Reduce the heat to 350°F and add the wine. Toss the potatoes into the pan. Roast for about 75 minutes (or 60 minutes if you prefer the lamb medium-rare). Turn the potatoes occasionally as the lamb cooks, crisping them on all sides.

7   Pour the pan juices into a sauceboat. Transfer the lamb to a cutting board and slice it. Arrange the slices on a large serving dish, surround them with the potatoes and garlic cloves and serve immediately, with the sauceboat on the side.

Crostini d'Abbacchio

LAMB KEBABS WITH PANCETTA, SAGE AND TOASTS

2 pounds boneless lamb (shoulder or leg)

40 to 50 fresh sage leaves

1½ cups Italian dry white wine

14 to 16 slices country-style bread

8 ounces pancetta or bacon strips

2 tablespoons extra-virgin olive oil

Kosher salt or coarse sea salt and freshly ground black pepper

SERVES 4

*C*rispy outside and moist inside, this peasant dish seasoned with sage or bay leaves and Parma ham or pancetta is popular throughout Latium and much of south-central Italy. When made with mutton, locals call it *rostini.* My friend Antonio Paolini, an Italian wine expert and food-loving economics reporter at Rome's biggest daily, *Il Messaggero,* likes to marinate his kebab lamb in white wine, an improvement on the traditional recipe of which I fully approve. If you have a barbecue, use it to make this recipe, or broil the lamb skewers in your oven. The recipe yields sixteen 6-inch skewers, four per person.

1   Rinse the lamb and sage under cold running water and pat dry on paper towels. Cut the lamb into 1½-inch cubes. Combine the lamb and 4 sage leaves in a medium-sized mixing bowl. Pour the wine over and mix well. Cover and refrigerate for several hours.

2   Toast the bread medium-dark and cut off the crusts. Divide each slice into 4 to 6 mini toasts, about the same size as the lamb cubes, making 1 mini toast per lamb cube.

3   Cut the pancetta into small squares or rectangles about the same size as the lamb cubes, making 1 square per lamb cube.

4   Remove the lamb from the refrigerator, pour off the wine, discard the sage and spread the cubes on paper towels to dry.

5   Make one skewer at a time. Slide 1 mini toast to the base of a skewer. Slide 1 square of pancetta next to it. Slide 1 sage leaf on and follow with 1 lamb cube. Repeat the sequence—toast, pancetta, sage, lamb—until the skewer is full. Finish with a mini toast. Prepare skewers until the toasts, pancetta, sage and lamb are used up.

6   Preheat a broiler or gas grill, or build a medium-hot fire in a barbecue.

7   Distribute the skewers over one or more baking trays, or directly on the barbecue grill. With a pastry brush, brush them with the oil. Sprinkle them, turning, with a generous pinch each of salt and pepper.

8   Broil or grill the skewers, turning often until the meat is well done, 20 to 25 minutes.

9   Allow the skewers to cool until easy to handle before serving.

"Eat the suckling lamb, the flock's tenderest, with more milk than blood in it, that has not lost its virginity by eating grass . . ."

Juvenal (A.D. 60–130)

Maiale in Tegame al Latte

PORK BRAISED IN MILK WITH GARLIC AND ROSEMARY

My friend Claudio Volpetti, co-owner with his brother Emilio of the celebrated Volpetti delicatessen in the Testaccio neighborhood, did a little jig when I asked him to show me how he makes this classic recipe, which is claimed by Lazio and several other Italian regions (including Emilia-Romagna and Campania). "*Che buono!*" he enthused, a nostalgic twinkle in his eye. "We used to eat it as children. . . ."

I've heard this refrain from many Italian friends. Why pork braised in milk should be associated with happy childhood memories is a mystery. I suspect it's the milk; in Italy, milk is a food reserved almost entirely for babies and small children.

Claudio Volpetti has lived in Rome for more than thirty years, but he's originally from the neighboring region of Umbria. To ensure we executed the recipe in the state-of-the-art Roman manner, he called upon Anselmo Blasilli to season and bind the meat. Anselmo is from Rieti, a town on the northern edge of Rome's region, and before joining the Volpettis, he worked for eighteen years as a specialized pork butcher—a *norcino.* Anselmo confirmed what I'd read in several scholarly texts: This favorite children's recipe goes back to antiquity. The Romans of old didn't have refrigeration

and used salt to preserve meat, especially pork. To remove the salt, they braised the meat in milk. Marcus Gavius Apicius, the food-loving general credited with compiling the recipes that went into the world's first known cookbook, *De re coquinaria,* explains the process. Some Romans think the technique was actually developed even earlier by the Etruscans, though this is pure speculation. The Roman or Lazio

3-pound pork roast, preferably neck, shoulder or loin

6 whole sprigs fresh rosemary

6 cloves garlic

Fine salt and freshly ground black pepper

2 tablespoons extra-virgin olive oil

8 cups milk

SERVES 6

version calls for browning the pork first, then adding boiling milk, whereas most other versions say the pork and milk should be cooked together from the start. I like the Roman version best, because the browning process sears the meat and makes it more flavorful. It's absolutely normal for the milk sauce to come out lumpy—the great nineteenth-century cookbook writer Pellegrino Artusi in his recipe #551 suggests spreading the lumps on toast. As with many Roman recipes, it's the flavor not the aesthetics that counts.

Later, as we feasted on the exquisitely moist and creamy pork we'd cooked together, Claudio, Emilio and Anselmo confirmed between bites another interesting tidbit I'd heard about milk-braised pork and related stews, including the celebrated *baekeoffe* of the Alsace region in France. Until the post–World War II period, it seems, many rural bakers would charge a nominal fee to bake food for fieldworkers. On the way home, the peasants would pick up their slow-cooked lunch or dinner. In central Italy and especially around Rome, pork braised in milk was one of these dishes. You'd be hard-pressed nowadays to find bakers willing to rent space in their ovens, but the modern stovetop cooking method given below seems to work pretty well, judging by the tears of pleasure it elicits among milk-braised-pork aficionados.

1   Rinse the pork and pat it dry with paper towels. With a sharp knife, make eight incisions up to 2 inches deep at regular intervals along its length, between the strings binding it. Flip the roast over and make eight comparable incisions.

2   Rinse the rosemary sprigs, pat them dry with paper towels and break four of them into four sections, each 1 to 2 inches long.

3   Peel the garlic cloves and quarter them with a paring knife, discarding the green shoots. With your fingers, push 1 broken section of rosemary and 1 quarter garlic clove into the bottom of each incision. Flip the roast and repeat the operation. Carefully lift the strings binding the roast and slide under the remaining 2 whole sprigs of rosemary, 1 sprig on top and 1 on the bottom.

4   Sprinkle the roast with several generous pinches each of salt and pepper. Rub the seasonings over the meat and into the incisions with your fingertips.

5   Heat the oil in a large, heavy-bottomed stainless steel or earthenware pot big enough to hold the roast snugly over medium heat. Brown the roast on all sides and on both ends, flipping and turning with a large cooking fork and steel spatula, about 10 minutes. Pour off the fat.

6   Pour 4 to 6 cups of the milk into a medium-sized saucepan and bring it to a boil without letting it froth, spill out and burn. Slowly pour enough of the boiling milk over the pork to almost cover it. Bring the milk back to a slow boil without letting it froth over. Lower the heat and simmer the pork, covered, at a slow boil for 20 minutes, turning several times to keep the pork moist.

7   Uncover the pot, adjust the heat to maintain a slow boil and cook, uncovered, for about 2 hours, turning every 20 minutes. Add the remaining 2 to 4 cups milk, $\frac{1}{2}$ cup at a time, to keep the meat covered and moist. To test for doneness, poke the pork with the tines of a large cooking fork or the blade of a carving knife; the juices, if any, should run clear.

8   With a large fork and a steel spatula, transfer the pork to a cutting board, slice it thinly and transfer the slices to a platter. Let them cool.

9   With a skimmer, remove any remaining fat from the milk sauce. Increase the heat under the sauce and reduce it, stirring frequently, until thick and creamy, with lots of lumps, 10 to 15 minutes. If you object to the lumps, spoon-crush the hot sauce through a sieve, or simply pour it over the room-temperature sliced pork and serve.

NOTE: If you can, make this dish a day ahead and refrigerate it. It comes out even tastier. Do steps 1 through 7 above. Let the pork sit unsliced in the pot with the milk sauce in the refrigerator for up to 24 hours. Remove the congealed fat. Slice the meat and arrange it on a platter. Let it warm to room temperature. Reheat and reduce the milk sauce, straining it if you wish, and pour it over the sliced pork. Serve immediately.

Norcini: Rome's
Umbrian Pork Butchers

In the hierarchy of Rome's food specialty shops, *norcinerie* hold pride of place alongside *salsamenterie*, *salumerie*, *pizzicherie* and *gastronomie*—all four covering what we'd call the deli business. That's because *norcinerie* sell every imaginable delicacy derived from pork, cured or fresh. Romans are crazy for pork. The repertoire boasts dozens of recipes for it roasted, grilled, pan-fried, stuffed and spitted. Carbonara and amatriciana would be impossible without guanciale (salt-cured pork jowl) or pancetta (unsmoked Italian bacon). The city's *norcinerie* are run by *norcini,* a term meaning both "pork butchers" and "people from Norcia," as if everyone from this small town in Umbria just north of the Lazio border were in the pig-processing trade.

As a matter of fact, Norcia has been celebrated for its swineherds, boar and pork butchers for so long that the term *norcino* has come to mean exactly that in standard Italian. Every year, from November through March, itinerant *norcini* range over the peninsula, preparing pork products as far north as Parma, land of prosciutto crudo and *culatello* hams.

Why Norcia? The Etruscans. They domesticated wild boar in the area long before Rome was founded. Horace in his *Satires* describes Umbrian range-raised boar, fattened on acorns from the boundless dark forests that gave the region its name (Umbria means shady, leafy land). Until the advent of refrigeration, pigs destined for making cured pork products were always slaughtered in cool weather from fall to spring, which meant *norcini* were seasonal workers and thus had to round out their income doing other jobs. When they weren't butchering pork, they herded swine and farmed, and became famous for a sideline in Umbrian brined broad beans (*fusaglie*) and straw hats, both sold by the wayside and ever since associated with *norcini* in the minds of many Italians. In the 1600s, the *norcini* formed a guild in Rome and persuaded a powerful saint to protect them: Santa Maria dell'Orto. She's the patron, among others, of barrel-makers, greengrocers, chicken farmers and wine merchants. Her same-name church is in the Trastevere neighborhood. By 1900, Rome's *norcini* had created a capillary network of hole-in-the-wall shops selling either pork products or straw hats,

L'Antica Norcineria. From left, Alberto Simoni, Danilo Sordi and Giuseppe Simoni

run by extended families that eventually settled permanently in the capital. The Volpetti family is probably the best known of them, in part because at least seven brothers of one branch of the tribe from the village of Nortosce near Norcia hit the streets of Rome between 1900 and 1920, prospered and proliferated. Today there are two famous, unaffiliated Volpetti shops in central Rome, owned by distant cousins. Third-generation Emilio and Claudio Volpetti run the shop in Testaccio. A gaggle of multigenerational, eager Volpetti youngsters runs the place in Via della Scrofa (Sow Street). Both Volpetti shops are now more delicatessen than *norcineria,* selling everything from fine wine and rare cheese to take-out foods, bread and pastry.

Three other celebrated, centuries-old *norcini* clans operate nearby. Giuseppe Simoni and his son Alberto flanked by cousins fresh from the Umbrian hills run l'Antica Norcineria, which just happens to face the Volpetti shop in Via della Scrofa. Guarded over by a mounted boar's head, the Simonis still cure pork jowl, pancetta and other pork products right in their shop. Five minutes away on foot down twisting alleys is Carilli in Via di Torre Argentina, near the Pantheon. Here Salvatore Carilli and his many brothers and cousins produce all the traditional delicacies. Salvatore travels several times a week to his hometown in Umbria, where he makes not only ham and cured pork products but also honey and wine, rising at 4 A.M. to fit it all in. He's so passionate about the quality of his pork that he accompanies each of his range-raised pigs to the slaughterhouse and makes sure the pork he receives at the end of the process comes from the pigs he raised—not a given in these days of huge slaughterhouses, where hundreds or thousands of animals are processed at a time. Salvatore transforms the pork meat himself into products like mountain ham, air-dried for 2 years. The Antica Norcineria Viola, run by the Viola clan, is an Aladdin's cavern of hams, jowls and pancetta, a Campo de' Fiori institution since 1890 that anchors the market square in these turbulent times of round-the-clock nightclubs and organized pub crawls.

Maiale Porchettato

BACON-WRAPPED PORK ROAST SEASONED WITH PEPPER, GARLIC, FENNEL AND DILL

Spitted whole pig (*porchetta*) stuffed with wild fennel, garlic and lots of black pepper is a regional specialty that goes back to Homeric times. The first sacrifice Aeneas made after landing near the mouth of the Tiber was a friendly but luckless sow who showed him where to found his settlement. *Porchetta* still features at every Rome-area *festa,* from block parties to political rallies, arts and crafts shows to bacchanalian romps honoring patron saints or the heroics of local soldiers or sailors. The city of Viterbo at the northern end of Rome's region claims to make the best *porchetta,* though several Alban Hills communities such as Grottaferrata, Marino and Ariccia contest this. Wild fennel is the herb of choice though some prefer *porchetta* with rosemary.

Given the logistical difficulties of roasting whole pigs in a big city like Rome, the task is left nowadays to pork butchers equipped with giant rotisseries. Called *norcini,* most of these butchers are originally from Norcia in Umbria (see *Norcini*: Rome's Umbrian Pork Butchers, page 169). Their shops are called *norcinerie.* Several dozen *norcini* keep Romans in constant supply of ready-to-eat *porchetta.* It usually winds up as sandwich meat.

If you don't happen to have a giant rotisserie in your kitchen, or a backyard barbecue big enough to roast a whole pig in, try this method of making pork roast, *porchetta*-style. The recipe comes from an old *norcineria* in Trastevere called Iacozilli, where there's always a whole roasted pig displayed in the window. The technique emulates the effect of cooking the pig in its juices trapped in its skin, which is what makes *porchetta* so mouthwateringly moist. To achieve this, ask your butcher to bone a rib roast for you so that there is a cavity in the pork. You season the roast inside and out, wrap it in strips of bacon and seal it tightly in aluminum foil. Since wild fennel isn't readily available in America, I use a domestic fennel bulb and fresh dill instead, with a generous pinch of fennel seeds or aniseeds. The result is authentic-tasting, delicious Viterbo-style *porchetta.* You'll need a large roasting pan and extra-wide heavy-duty aluminum foil for wrapping.

8 ounces bacon strips

4 cloves garlic

1 heaping tablespoon aniseeds or fennel seeds

1 small bulb fennel

10 whole sprigs fresh dill

Freshly ground black pepper

Kosher salt or coarse sea salt

4-pound boneless pork rib roast

SERVES 8

1 Stretch enough aluminum foil across the bottom of a roasting pan and beyond it on both sides to completely and comfortably envelope the roast. Lay half of the bacon strips side by side across the aluminum foil in the center of the pan, corresponding to the length of the roast.

2 Peel the garlic, eliminate the green shoots and mince. Sprinkle a quarter of it over the bacon. Sprinkle a quarter of the aniseeds over the garlic.

3 Thinly slice the fennel bulb; scatter a quarter of the slices over the aniseeds. Lay 3 to 4 sprigs of the dill on top of the fennel. Sprinkle on a generous pinch of pepper and a small pinch of salt.

4 Pat the pork roast dry with paper towels. If there is no cavity in it, use a carving knife to create one by making a 4-inch-deep slash lengthwise down its length. Use your fingers to flatten it open. Fill the cavity with three-quarters each of the remaining fennel slices, garlic, aniseeds and dill. Sprinkle in a small pinch of salt and a generous pinch of pepper.

5 Tie up the roast tightly with kitchen string. Place it on top of the bacon strips and seasonings in the pan.

6 Preheat the oven to 375°F.

7 With your fingers wrap the bacon strips as far up as they will go around the roast. Sprinkle it with the remaining fennel slices, garlic, aniseeds and dill. Place the remaining bacon strips side-by-side atop the roast so that the roast is fully wrapped in bacon. Gather and lift the aluminum foil and crimp it together to form a tight, sealed envelope.

8 Roast for 1½ hours. Carefully open the foil. To test for doneness poke the roast with a knife. The juices should run clear. Transfer the pork to a cutting board.

9 Slice the pork thick, arrange on a platter, swirl the pan juices over the pork slices and serve immediately.

Cinghiale in Agrodolce

SWEET-AND-SOUR WILD BOAR OR PORK

With the exception of grated dark chocolate, none of the ingredients in this luscious recipe comes from the New World. I've sampled sweet-and-sour boar, a fall-winter dish, at various trattorias and restaurants in and around Rome, among them La Carbonara. The recipe is especially popular in rural districts where wild boar roam—wreaking havoc. Environmental protection laws passed since the 1980s and a lack of natural predators have led to an explosion in boar numbers all over Italy. It's estimated they account for 80 percent of the damage to crops in the country. That's why various government entities now encourage licensed hunters to cull boars and feral porkers (wild pigs and crossbreeds of wild or domestic pigs and boars). It explains why this venerable delicacy, cited in the 1830s by the ever-famished Roman dialect poet Giuseppe Gioachino Belli, has made a big comeback of late.

I've used both wild boar and domestic pork to make *cinghiale in agrodolce.* The results are very different but equally delicious, and I wouldn't know which to recommend as first choice. The trick, if using pork, is to cut the 24-hour marinating time to a couple of hours, since pork is infinitely less tough and less gamy than boar.

5-pound wild boar or lean pork roast

2 carrots

1 large white onion

2 cloves garlic

1 celery stalk

3 cloves

1 bay leaf

2 heaping teaspoons fresh thyme

2 cups Italian dry white wine, preferably Frascati or Marino

1 cup white wine vinegar

Kosher salt or coarse sea salt and freshly ground black pepper

1/4 cup extra-virgin olive oil

4 ounces pancetta or bacon

Hot water

2 tablespoons raisins

2 dates

2 dried figs

2 tablespoons sugar

3 heaping tablespoons semisweet chocolate, powdered or crushed or cut into chips

2 tablespoons pine nuts

SERVES 8

1 Rinse the meat, pat it dry with paper towels and place it in a nonreactive pot big enough to easily hold the roast and all the other ingredients.

2 To make the marinade, peel the carrots, onion and garlic, discarding the garlic's green shoots, and mince. Remove the stringy parts of the celery and mince it. Combine half the minced vegetables in a medium-sized saucepan. Add the cloves, bay leaf and thyme. Pour in 1 1/2 cups of the wine and 3/4 cup of the vinegar. Sprinkle in a generous pinch each of salt and pepper. Bring the liquids to a slow boil, stirring occasionally, and simmer for 5 minutes. Remove the saucepan from the heat and let the marinade cool.

3 Pour the cooled marinade over the meat. Cover the pot and marinate the boar in the refrigerator for 24 hours, turning several times. Marinate the pork, if using, for 2 to 3 hours in the refrigerator, turning every half hour.

4 Transfer the meat from the pot to a cutting board. Pat it dry with paper towels. Pour the marinade into a bowl and reserve it.

5 Heat the oil over medium-high in the pot in which the meat was marinated. Add the meat and brown it thoroughly, stirring, flipping and scraping with a wooden spoon or spatula, 8 to 10 minutes. Mince the pancetta and brown it with the meat, 1 to 2 minutes. Pour in the remaining 1/2 cup wine and boil to evaporate it, 1 to 2 minutes.

6 Stir in the remaining minced vegetables and sauté for 1 to 2 minutes. Pour in the marinade and add enough hot water to cover the meat about halfway. Bring the liquid to a boil, lower the heat to minimum and simmer, covered, for 1 1/2 hours.

7   Meanwhile, soak the raisins in 1 cup of warm water for 15 minutes. Drain them in a sieve.

8   Pit the dates. Mince the dates and the figs.

9   When the meat is done, transfer it to a cutting board and cover it with aluminum foil. Remove and discard the bay leaf. Pour the contents of the pot into a food processor and process until smooth, or pass through a food mill. Return the mixture to the pot and add the remaining 1/4 cup vinegar, the sugar, chocolate, raisins, dates, figs and pine nuts. Turn the heat to high and reduce the sauce, stirring until it is thick enough to coat the back of a wooden spoon evenly. Pour half of the sauce into a sauceboat.

10   Slice the meat, arrange it on a platter and pour the remaining sauce from the pot over it. Serve immediately with the sauceboat on the side.

Latte e vvino, veleno fino.
(Milk drunk with wine makes fine poison.)

—Old Roman saying

Pollo in Padella

Chicken Sautéed in a Frying Pan with Bay Leaves, Rosemary, Onions and Garlic

One of the easiest and tastiest in the Roman poultry repertoire, this recipe differs from a standard chicken *alla cacciatora* in that it has no tomatoes or mushrooms, relying instead on the earthy pungency of bay leaves and the aromatic power of fresh rosemary, with a pleasant sweetness from the sautéed onions. Countless homemakers and chefs have come up with variations on the theme of *pollo in padella*—which simply means "chicken (sautéed) in a frying pan," *padella* being the pan. Anna Mangioli, a great home cook who volunteers by day as a museum guard at Trajan's Market (Emperor Trajan's Imperial marketplace, now an art exhibition space), adds chopped Gaeta olives to her *pollo in padella*. Others might change the mix of herbs or toss in a few strips of minced pancetta, but I like this straightforward, old-fashioned recipe best.

Probably the tastiest *pollo in padella* my wife and I have ever made was the result of a serendipitous morning walk across the wooded knolls of Rome's Villa Borghese park. The park bristles with bay trees. It had rained that morning, and we could smell the trees as we picked our way among the splashing fountains and mossy statuary. I gathered a handful of tender bay leaves and slipped them into my pocket. A few hours later, at our local butcher shop, I put my hand in my pocket, remembered the bay leaves and showed them to the butcher. What was his favorite recipe for using them, my wife wondered. *Pollo in padella,* he answered without hesitation. We bought his best range-raised fryer, asked him to chop it into pieces for us, then crossed the street to the outdoor market and bought onions, garlic and fresh rosemary. We trotted home laden with the fixings for our lunch. It was so good we barely had any chicken left over for dinner that night.

5-pound range-raised whole chicken or parts (mix of thighs, breasts and wings)

5 tablespoons extra-virgin olive oil

1 large onion

2 cloves garlic

4 whole fresh bay leaves

3 heaping tablespoons fresh rosemary leaves

Kosher salt or coarse sea salt and freshly ground black pepper

¾ cup Italian dry white wine, preferably Frascati or Marino

SERVES 6

1 If necessary, cut the chicken into individual parts. Rinse the pieces and pat them dry with paper towels. Remove and discard any fat.

2 Heat 3 tablespoons of the oil in a large, heavy frying pan over medium-high heat. Add the chicken parts and sauté, turning, flipping and scraping with a steel spatula until thoroughly browned, 8 to 10 minutes. Transfer the chicken parts to a bowl, and pour off the fat and oil from the frying pan.

3 Peel the onion and garlic, discarding the garlic's green shoots, and mince.

4 Return the frying pan to medium heat. Pour in the remaining 2 tablespoons oil, add the minced onion and garlic and sauté, stirring often, until the onion becomes translucent, 3 to 4 minutes. Stir in the bay leaves and 2 heaping tablespoons of the minced rosemary.

5 Add the chicken, 1 piece at a time, flipping and turning to coat it with the oil and minced seasonings. Add a generous pinch each of salt and pepper and sauté for 1 minute. Pour in the wine and boil to evaporate it, 1 to 2 minutes. Add the remaining 1 heaping tablespoon rosemary, lower the heat to minimum and simmer, covered, for 45 minutes.

6 With a slotted spatula, remove the bay leaves. Serve immediately.

Villa Borghese gardens

Rome's Far Side: Trastevere

The Trastevere neighborhood across the Tiber River from central Rome has long been one of the keepers of the flame of Roman cooking. Three main factors influenced Trastevere's cooking style. First, for centuries the area wasn't administratively or geographically considered part of central Rome and wasn't taxed or regulated in the same way, so it attracted Italians from far-flung regions. Also, from Imperial times right up to the creation of the Ghetto across the river from Trastevere in 1556, it attracted a large Jewish population. This led to culinary diversity. Second, most of the fishermen who worked the Tiber for eels, sturgeon, perch and other freshwater species lived in Trastevere, and so did many sailors based in Rome's seaport, Ostia. This added a lot of fish-based recipes to the repertoire. Third, the countryside ran right up into Trastevere until recently. There were market gardens, vineyards and orchards all around, so vegetable specialties abounded. When I first lived in Rome from 1965 to 1966, the arm-span-wide alleys and hidden courtyards of Trastevere doubled as poultry runs, with market gardens creeping up the sides of the Gianicolo hill, planted with spiky artichokes that vied with giant, flowering zucchini plants.

To this day, many Roman recipes are identified with an "*alla trasteverina*" suffix to show they originated in Trastevere, among them stuffed eggplant (see *Melanzane Ripiene alla Trasteverina,* page 246). *Trasteverini,* as locals are known, call their prized artichokes *mamme,* while across the river, Romans call them *cimaroli* (tip-toppers) or *mammole* (big mothers). Reflecting the Jewish influence in the neighborhood from centuries past, *Trasteverini* still make home-

D'Augusto Trattoria, Trastevere

made beef jerky. Peer into a half-shuttered, breezy old Trastevere apartment, and you might see bits of meat hanging from a laundry line and covered with gauze to keep the flies off.

Crowded and noisy, Trastevere may never have been the land of milk and honey, but several thousand years ago, it became celebrated for its free-flowing wine and a miraculous fountain that spurted olive oil. The site of the olive oil gusher is now occupied by one of Rome's homelier birdbath fountains, facing the church of Santa Maria in Trastevere. The neighborhood's vinous heritage is reflected in the curious 1927 drinking fountain one hundred yards away, down the aptly named Via della Cisterna (Cistern Street). Water gushes from the fountain's stone wine barrel, amid sculpted wine measures and a crushing vat. When first hooked up, the Fontana della Cisterna flowed red and white with local wines; back then Trastevere warehoused Rome's potables.

Despite centuries of crosspollination, immigration, plague, pestilence and war, *Trasteverini* still consider themselves "the original Romans" or "Romans from Rome," with family roots sunk into a largely mythical classical past. To this day, they call themselves *noiantri*—us guys—and refer to other Romans as *voiantri*—you all. They have long spoken a subdialect of Romanaccio with even more exaggerated pronunciation than in the rest of Rome. The city's two great dialect poets, Giuseppe Gioachino Belli (1791 to 1863) and Trilussa (Carlo Alberto Salustri, 1871 to 1950), are immortalized in Trastevere by monuments, streets, bars, pizzerias and restaurants named after them (see In the Belly of the Poet: G. G. Belli, Rome's Famished Bard, page 59).

Partying and gourmandizing have always been the neighborhood specialty. In *Fasti,* Ovid (43 B.C. to A.D. 17) describes the ancient, wild and woolly Trastevere festival, originally held annually on June 24. Nowadays the Festa de' Noiantri (Our Festival), held for eight days during the last half of July, fills Trastevere's tangle of laundry-strung alleys and cluttered piazzas with religious processions honoring the Madonna del Carmine, and even more craft stands and street musicians than usual. The air is scented with toasting bruschetta (see page 15), bubbling pots of chicken and sweet peppers (see page 182), fried salt cod and spitted stuffed pig—*porchetta* (see page 172).

Pollo coi Peperoni alla Romana

CHICKEN SAUTÉED WITH SWEET PEPPERS, ROMAN STYLE

5-pound whole range-raised chicken or parts (mix of thighs, wings, breasts)

1 large white onion

2 ounces pancetta or bacon (2 to 3 strips)

2 tablespoons extra-virgin olive oil

1 *peperoncino* (hot chili pepper), shredded, or ¼ teaspoon crushed red pepper flakes

½ cup Italian dry white wine, preferably Frascati or Marino

1 (16-ounce) can Italian plum tomatoes, preferably San Marzano

Kosher salt or coarse sea salt

4 to 5 large sweet peppers (mix of yellow and red), roasted, skinned and seeded (see How to Roast, Skin and Seed a Sweet Pepper, page 65)

1 heaping tablespoon minced fresh marjoram or oregano

SERVES 6 TO 8

This recipe for sweet, spicy, succulent chicken sometimes goes by the name *pollo alla trasteverina* (chicken cooked in the style of Trastevere). Everyone in Rome agrees that whatever the name, chicken with stewed peppers is *the* archetypal Roman chicken dish, traditionally made for the Festa de' Noiantri and Ferragosto, respectively the mid-July and mid-August holidays that go back to antiquity. The recipe is still made by countless home cooks and often appears on the menus of trattorias in Trastevere, where it was probably invented centuries ago. Making it in the traditional way involves blackening and peeling the sweet peppers before stewing them, a messy process that's richly rewarding because scorched peppers are tastier and sweeter than un-scorched ones. A perennial argument among this dish's devotees revolves around the roasting, scorching and peeling methods and whether onion or garlic or both should count among the ingredients. You'll need a large, high-sided frying pan with a lid to make this recipe.

1   If necessary, cut the chicken into individual parts. Rinse the pieces and pat them dry with paper towels. Remove and discard any fat.

2   Peel and roughly chop the onion with the pancetta.

3   Heat the oil in a large, high-sided frying pan over medium. Add the onion and pancetta. Sauté, stirring with a wooden spoon or spatula, until the onion becomes translucent and the pancetta barely starts to crisp, about 3 to 4 minutes. With a slotted spoon, remove them from the pan to a bowl and cover with a lid.

4   Add the *peperoncino* to the pan and stir. Increase the heat to high, add the chicken parts and brown them thoroughly, stirring, flipping and scraping, 8 to 10 minutes. If the chicken is very fatty, pour off some of the fat. Return the sautéed onions and pancetta to the pan and stir thoroughly.

5   Pour in the wine and boil to evaporate it, 1 to 2 minutes. Add the tomatoes with their packing juices and a pinch of salt. Sauté for 5 minutes, stirring and crushing the tomatoes with a wooden spoon or spatula. Lower the heat to minimum and simmer, covered, while preparing the sweet peppers.

6   Slice the skinned, seeded peppers into strips $\frac{1}{2}$ to 1 inch wide and $1\frac{1}{2}$ to 2 inches long. Stir them into the frying pan with the chicken. Sprinkle in the marjoram and adjust the salt. Simmer, partially covered, until the chicken is tender enough to flake apart with the tines of a fork, 15 to 25 minutes.

7   Serve immediately.

Poultry shop

Pollo Ripieno alla Papalina

THE POPE'S ROAST CHICKEN STUFFED WITH CHESTNUTS, PORCINI, TRUFFLE AND SAUSAGE MEAT

The Umbrian hill town of Norcia a few miles north of the Latium border was a gastronomical stronghold of the Papal States, the Vatican's former earthly domain extending over much of central Italy. For centuries, Norcia supplied the papal court with skilled butchers and delicatessen men called *norcini* (see Rome's Umbrian Pork Butchers, page 169). Norcia also supplied—and still does—most of Italy's black truffles, the celebrated *tartufi neri di Norcia*. Botanically similar truffles grow near another former papal stronghold, Avignon, in France. It might have been during the "Babylonian captivity" (1309 to 1378) of the popes in the walled city of Avignon that this festive truffled chicken recipe was invented. It bears the hallmarks of a venerable dish of the upper classes: the use of (formerly precious) nutmeg, truffles and wild mushrooms. It's also reminiscent of that classic Old France recipe, *poulet en demi-deuil* (chicken shrouded in a mantle of black truffles). Remarkable, too, is the absence of plebian onions or garlic—unnecessary and unworthy seasonings, perhaps, for the miter-wearing class.

This is not a trattoria or even a restaurant dish. The private cooks of the papal court have given way nowadays to eager home cooks. In truth, many Romans buy their *pollo ripieno* from specialized butcher shops, like Angelo Feroci, a century-old institution near the Pantheon. The recipe is also made with turkey or capon. This is my adaptation of a Feroci stuffed chicken, integrating elements from a *pollo alla papalina* recipe in Vittorio Metz's cookbook, *La cucina del Belli* (see In the Belly of the Poet: G. G. Belli, Rome's Famished Bard, page 59).

4-pound chicken,
preferably a range-raised
roaster, with liver

8 ounces sweet Italian
sausage or lean ground
pork

3 tablespoons extra-virgin
olive oil

I cup chicken broth
(see page 62)

8 ounces stale bread
(about 3 large slices)

8 to 10 fresh chestnuts,
or 1 (28-ounce) can
chestnuts packed in water,
drained

2 ounces dried porcini
(about 2 cups)

I cup warm water

I large egg

Pinch of nutmeg

Kosher salt or coarse
sea salt and freshly
ground black pepper

I large black truffle or
3 tablespoons truffled
olive oil

SERVES 6

1. Rinse the chicken and pat it dry with paper towels. Clean the liver, removing any hard or discolored sections with a paring knife. Rinse and dice it.

2. Remove the sausage meat from its casing and break it or the ground pork into roughly ½-inch pieces. You should have about 1½ cups.

3. Combine the sausage with 1 tablespoon of the oil in a large frying pan and sauté over medium heat until browned, 2 to 3 minutes, stirring frequently with a wooden spoon or spatula. Stir in the liver and 2 tablespoons of the chicken broth and sauté for 15 minutes, stirring, flipping and scraping.

4. Remove the frying pan from the heat. Lift out the liver and pork with a slotted spoon and set aside.

5. Mix the remaining broth into the meat juices in the skillet. Dice the bread. You should have about 6 cups. Stir it in and let it absorb the broth and juices, 2 to 3 minutes.

6. Preheat the oven to 450°F.

7. If you are using fresh chestnuts, score them, put them on a baking tray and roast, flipping several times, for about 15 minutes. Or grill them until tender, 10 to 12 minutes. Let them cool. With a paring knife, peel and halve them, discarding the hairy inner skin. If you are using canned chestnuts, rinse them under cold water, pat dry and halve them.

8. Soak the dry mushrooms in a small bowl in the water for 15 to 20 minutes. When the mushrooms are tender, use a slotted spoon to remove them from the bowl.

Wipe them carefully with paper towels to absorb excess liquid. With your fingers, clean off any remaining soil. Cut away and discard any tough parts or imperfections. Filter the soaking water through a fine-mesh sieve or strainer lined with a paper towel or a paper coffee filter. Cut the mushrooms into rough ¼- to ½-inch pieces.

9   Combine the bread, egg, chestnuts, mushrooms, 2 tablespoons of the strained mushroom water, a generous pinch of nutmeg and the liver-and-sausage mixture in a food processor. Process until homogenous, about 1 minute. Transfer the paste to a large mixing bowl and season it generously with salt and pepper.

10   If you are using a fresh truffle, brush it with a scrub brush, eliminating dust or dirt. Rinse it under cold water and pat it dry with a paper towel. Remove any imperfections and slice the truffle into slivers. Add three-quarters of them to the stuffing mixture. If you are using truffle oil, pour in about 2 tablespoons. Mix gently with a spatula or wooden spoon.

11   Put the chicken in a large roasting pan. With your fingertips, carefully lift the skin up and away from the meaty parts of the chicken breasts and slide the remaining truffle slivers between the skin and flesh. If you are using truffled oil, drip the remaining 1 tablespoon oil under the skin and over the chicken.

12   With a spoon and your fingers, fill the chicken cavities front and back with the stuffing. Pin the cavities closed with toothpicks.

13   Lower the oven temperature to 350°F.

14   Drizzle the chicken with the remaining 2 tablespoons oil and sprinkle in a small pinch each of salt and pepper. Roast for 75 to 90 minutes, basting occasionally with chicken juices and the remaining strained mushroom water. To check for doneness, prick the thigh; the chicken is cooked when the juices run clear with a hint of pink.

15   To serve, pour the pan juices into a sauceboat and scoop the stuffing into a bowl. Carve the chicken and serve it hot with the stuffing and sauceboat on the side.

TIP: You can carefully sew this stuffed chicken closed, but I use toothpicks for the job. Sewing ensures a sturdier seal. Toothpicks are faster and, in this case, if they give way, the stuffing just inside the opening of the cavity will get extra crispy and be even more delicious. There's little chance it will fall out—there's no need to flip the chicken over. Even if some stuffing does fall into the cooking juices, this too will be scrumptious. Make sure to remove the toothpicks before serving!

If you've made more stuffing than you can force into the chicken's cavities, form it into golf-ball-size dumplings and scatter them around the oven pan like potatoes. Crispy outside and moist inside, they're fabulous. If you have leftover chestnuts, wait until about 15 minutes before the chicken is cooked and toss them into the pan.

Galletto alla Diavola

SPICY GRILLED CHICKEN WITH LEMON, GARLIC, ROSEMARY, BACON AND HOT CHILI PEPPER

Cocky is a good way to describe this palate-bucking dish that crops up on the menu of many a trattoria. In Rome the recipe is traditionally made, not with regular chicken but with *galletto* (bantam cock). Lavishly mustachioed restaurateur Giovanni Coletti looks more like a walrus than a rooster, but he's nonetheless nicknamed *Galletto*. His much-loved Osteria Ar Galletto on the corner of Vicolo del Gallo and Piazza Farnese in the heart of old Rome has worn its name since at least 1815, and may well have been serving *galletto alla diavola* since the fifteenth century, when the Vicolo del Gallo was rammed through, linking the Campo de' Fiori to Palazzo Farnese. With two elaborate marble bathtub fountains splashing in the square and the immense Renaissance palazzo as backdrop, it seems incongruous to feast on such rustic fare. But that's one of Rome's paradoxes: Storied splendor and rusticity have always thrived side-by-side in everything from urbanism to cuisine.

The best way to cook *galletto alla diavola*—literally, the devil's bantam, so named for its spiciness—is to grill it. Romans flatten the poultry and use clamp grills, like big old-fashioned hot dog grills, sometimes called "fish baskets," to keep it splayed. But you can also broil *galletto alla diavola* in your oven. The essential thing is to let the poultry marinate in the spice mix for at least an hour, and preferably overnight, before cooking it. Some cooks use only coarsely ground black pepper, but most prefer using black pepper in tandem with *peperoncino*.

4-pound chicken or two
2-pound game hens

2 cloves garlic

6 whole sprigs fresh
rosemary

2 lemons

1 tablespoon extra-virgin
olive oil

2 *peperoncini* (hot chili
peppers), shredded,
or ¹/₂ teaspoon crushed
red pepper flakes

2 strips bacon

Fine salt and coarsely
ground black pepper

SERVES 4 TO 6

1   Rinse the poultry and pat it dry. With a carving knife and a cleaver, split the carcasses in half. Cut along each side of the backbone. Remove the backbone. Spread the poultry open and flatten it with a mallet or rolling pin. Put the split poultry in 1 or more high-sided oven pans.

2   Peel the garlic, eliminating the green shoots, and mince. Transfer the garlic into a small mixing bowl.

3   Rinse the rosemary, pat it dry and remove the leaves from 2 of the sprigs. Mince the leaves and add them to the garlic. Set aside the other 4 sprigs.

4   Rinse the lemons, halve and juice them into the mixing bowl. Flatten the squeezed halves and set aside. Pour the oil into the mixing bowl along with the *peperoncini*. Stir thoroughly. Use a pastry brush to apply the mixture evenly to both sides of the split poultry.

5   Put 1 strip of bacon on the inside of each chicken or game hen and pin it down with a toothpick. Put 2 whole sprigs of the remaining rosemary on top of each strip of bacon. Top them with the flattened lemon halves. Sprinkle the chickens with a generous pinch each of salt and of coarsely ground pepper. Cover with aluminum foil or plastic wrap and refrigerate for at least 1 hour, preferably overnight.

6   Build a medium-hot fire in a barbecue or preheat the grill or broiler in your oven.

7   Lift one chicken or game hen at a time with its dressing and lay it on a clamp-type grill (the kind used for hot dogs). Clamp the grill shut and grill or broil the poultry until cooked through, turning often, about 30 to 35 minutes. To test for doneness, insert the tines of a fork; the juices should run clear with just a hint of pink. If you don't have a clamp-type grill, place the poultry directly on the barbecue grill or in a pan under the broiler and flip it often with a steel spatula, being careful not to let the loose rosemary sprigs or flattened lemon halves fall off.

8   Serve immediately.

Gallinaccio in Tegame

TURKEY THIGH BRAISED IN WHITE WINE AND BROTH,
WITH FRESH HERBS AND PANCETTA

𝒯urkey has been so popular in Rome for so long that most Romans don't realize the
bird is native to Central and North America, brought to Europe in the 1500s, probably by
marauding Spaniards. I've seen wonderful nineteenth-century photographs of turkey
ranchers driving their flocks through Rome's ruined monuments, just as shepherds,
goatherds and cowherds once did (the Forum was long called the Cow Pasture). For
centuries, turkey has been on Roman dinner tables, often stuffed and roasted, or braised
on the stovetop with an abundance of wild herbs as in this recipe, which is said to have
originated in the *osterie* (wine bars) of old. It was probably a bunch of soused *osteria* patrons
who dubbed turkey *gallinaccio*. *Gallina* means "hen," and by adding the pejorative masculine
suffix *-accio,* the term makes the bird sound like a brutish cross-dresser. The original
Osteria del Gallinaccio recalled by Roman writers like Adolfo Giaquinto, Vittorio Metz
and Livio Jannattoni disappeared long ago. A handful of *trattorie* and restaurants still serve

gallinaccio in tegame, also known as *arrosto
morto di gallinaccio,* but the recipe is
mostly made at home these days.
Some of our friends use chicken or
rabbit instead of turkey, with
excellent results. The longer and
slower it cooks, the better it is. You
can even make it ahead and reheat it
the next day.

Dining out at Osteria Ar Galletto

1 cup chicken broth
(see page 62) or water

3-pound turkey thigh

2 cloves garlic

2 heaping tablespoons
fresh rosemary leaves

Kosher salt or coarse
sea salt and freshly
ground black pepper

4 ounces guanciale
(see Sources, page 297),
pancetta or bacon

2 tablespoons extra-virgin
olive oil

2 heaping teaspoons
fresh thyme

1 cup Italian dry white
wine, preferably Frascati
or Marino

SERVES 4

1   Heat the broth over medium-low.

2   Rinse the turkey thigh and pat it dry with paper towels. With a paring knife, make incisions ½ to 1 inch deep up and down it on both sides.

3   Peel the garlic cloves, cut them open and discard the green shoots. Mince the rosemary and garlic with a pinch each of salt and pepper. With the side of the knife blade, mash them into a thick paste. With your fingertips, poke the paste into the incisions. Season both sides of the thigh with salt and pepper, rubbing with your fingers.

4   Roughly chop the pork; you should have about ¾ cup. Scatter it around a large nonreactive pot. Pour in the oil and heat it over medium. Melt the pork fat without browning or crisping the meat, stirring often with a wooden spoon or spatula, 2 to 3 minutes. With a slotted spoon or spatula, transfer the pork to a plate covered with paper towels.

5   Add the turkey thigh, raise the heat to medium-high and brown it on both sides, 12 to 15 minutes. If the turkey is fatty, drain off some of the fat.

6   Return the pork to the pot and sprinkle in the thyme. Pour in the wine and boil to evaporate it, 1 to 2 minutes. Pour in ½ cup of the broth. Lower the heat to minimum and braise, covered, for 90 minutes or more, turning every 15 minutes. Add 2 tablespoons of hot broth at a time to keep the thigh from drying out. When done, it should flake off at the flick of a fork.

7   Transfer the turkey to a cutting board, slice it and put the slices on a serving platter. Pour half the herbed juices over the slices and the rest into a sauceboat. Serve immediately with the sauceboat on the side.

Martino al Forno

MONKFISH BAKED ON A BED OF LEMONY POTATOES

2 pounds fresh monkfish, cleaned and filleted

2 pounds potatoes, preferably Yukon gold or yellow Finn

4 tablespoons extra-virgin olive oil

Kosher salt or coarse sea salt and freshly ground black pepper

4 heaping tablespoons fine bread crumbs

4 cloves garlic

4 heaping tablespoons minced fresh flat-leaf parsley

Juice of 1 lemon

SERVES 4

Monkfish, also known as anglerfish because of the unusual "fishing pole" projecting from its grisly mouth, has half a dozen different names in Italian, demonstrating the popularity of this Adriatic native. *Rospo* (toad) and *rana pescatrice* (fishing frog) are the most common appellations; but, in Rome, monkfish goes by the genteel moniker *martino*. The dangling "bait" at the end of the monkfish's natural fishing pole is called the *loffia*. This peculiar organ emits a liquid that stuns small fish that nibble at it. The tricky monkfish then gobbles them up. In Rome and elsewhere in Italy, to say someone is *loffio* means they're tricky, sleazy or untrustworthy. This simple yet succulent recipe lets the flavor and texture of the monkfish shine through. The seasonings are crushed garlic, salt and pepper, parsley and freshly squeezed lemon juice in tandem with extra-virgin olive oil. They and the juices of the baking fish slowly permeate the bed of thinly sliced potatoes. I learned how to make it from third-generation fishmongers Anna Elisa Scipioni, her husband Ugo Pantano and his aunt Fernanda Pantano, whose stand has appeared on Tuesdays and Fridays at the Piazza di San Cosimato open market for the better part of the last hundred years. Buy firm potatoes, such as Yukon gold or yellow Finn; they absorb juices and hold up better than most other varieties.

1   Preheat the oven to 375°F.

2   Rinse the fillets, put them on a platter covered with paper towels and pat them dry.

3   Peel and slice the potatoes about ⅛ inch thick. Place them in the bottom of a large baking pan or ovenproof casserole and drizzle with 2 tablespoons of the oil. Sprinkle in a generous pinch each of salt and pepper. Toss the potatoes until evenly coated. Sprinkle in half of the bread crumbs and toss. Arrange the potatoes into an even layer in the bottom of the pan.

4   With the heel of your hand or the flat part of a wide-bladed knife, crush the unpeeled garlic. Arrange the garlic evenly spaced over the potatoes.

5   Sprinkle a generous pinch of the parsley over the potatoes and garlic.

6   Remove the paper towels from under the monkfish. Drizzle 1 tablespoon of the oil over the fish. Rub the oil into the fillets. Sprinkle in the remaining bread crumbs, rolling and flipping the fillets until coated. Transfer the fillets to the bed of potatoes and garlic. Sprinkle in the bread crumbs left behind on the platter.

7   Sprinkle 1 tablespoon of the lemon juice over the fillets and potatoes. Sprinkle in a small pinch each of salt, pepper and parsley. Bake until the potatoes are tender inside and crisp around the edges, 30 to 35 minutes.

8   Remove the pan from the oven, sprinkle the remaining parsley over the fish. Drizzle the remaining 1 tablespoon oil and the rest of the lemon juice on top. Serve immediately.

Graté di Alici o Sogliole

GRATIN OF FRESH ANCHOVIES, SARDINES, MACKEREL OR SOLE

3 pounds fresh anchovies, sardines, mackerel or sole, cleaned, boned and flattened or filleted

6 cloves garlic

4 to 5 teaspoons extra-virgin olive oil

About 1½ cups fine bread crumbs

4 heaping tablespoons minced fresh flat-leaf parsley

3 to 4 tablespoons Italian dry white wine, preferably Frascati or Marino

2 *peperoncini* (hot chili peppers), shredded, or ½ teaspoon crushed red pepper flakes (optional)

1 lemon

Kosher salt or coarse sea salt and freshly ground black pepper

SERVES 6

Right up there with salt cod, Rome's other cult fish is the anchovy, usually called *alice* or *aliciotto* when fresh and *acciuga* when preserved. Of the dozens of ways to elevate it from bait to delicacy this is among my favorites: baked in layers with a garlicky bread crumb crust. The term *graté* is a corruption of gratin. It was probably the French during the two Napoleonic occupations of Rome (1798 to 1814 and 1849 to 1870) who repopularized the age-old gratin technique. This recipe crops up on most homemakers' tables, especially in the former Jewish Ghetto, and in many a traditional Roman eatery, like Da Gino. The place's affable owner, Luigi del Grosso, showed me how to make his succulent, peppery version of *graté*. You can make it very successfully with fresh sardines or mackerel, since fresh anchovies are tough to get in the United States. I've also eaten a similar fish casserole elsewhere in Rome made with sole. To Romans, sole is a noble fish prized for its mild flavor. So if you prefer sole, use fillets of sole and, so as not to overwhelm them, forgo the hot chili pepper.

1 Preheat the oven to 375°F.

2 Rinse the fish under cold, running water and put them on a platter covered with paper towels. If you are using anchovies, sardines or mackerel, put them on a cutting board, one by one, and spread them open flat like a book, pressing down firmly with your fingers. Pat them dry with more paper towels and return them to the platter.

3 Peel the garlic, discarding the green shoots, and mince. In a small bowl, reserve 1 heaping teaspoon of the minced garlic.

4 With 1 teaspoon of the oil, oil a 7-by-12-inch oven pan. Spread out one-third of the flattened fish or fish fillets side-by-side in the bottom of the pan and drizzle them with about one-third of the remaining 3 to 4 teaspoons of oil.

5 Sprinkle in about ⅓ cup of the bread crumbs, one-third of the minced garlic and one-third of the parsley. Over this, sprinkle 1 tablespoon of the wine, a tiny pinch of *peperoncino,* a squeeze of lemon juice and a small pinch each of salt and pepper. Build another layer over the first and sprinkle it with the same ingredients in the same order and proportions. Build a third layer.

6 With a fork, stir the remaining bread crumbs (about 4 heaping tablespoons) into the bowl with the reserved minced garlic. Top the last layer of fish with an even sprinkling of the garlicky bread crumbs, a drizzle of oil and a drizzle of lemon juice.

7 Bake for 20 minutes.

8 Serve immediately.

Filetti di Sogliola con Patate, Cipolla, Funghi e Carciofi

FILLETS OF SOLE WITH POTATOES, ONION, MUSHROOMS AND ARTICHOKES

2 pounds fresh sole fillets

1 lemon

4 medium-sized artichokes

4 medium-sized potatoes, preferably Yukon gold, yellow Finn or russet

Kosher salt or coarse sea salt

8 ounces fresh mushrooms (*champignons de Paris,* cremini or portobello or a mixture)

2 cloves garlic

1 small white onion

4 tablespoons minced fresh flat-leaf parsley

4 tablespoons extra-virgin olive oil

Freshly ground black pepper

SERVES 6

Not photogenic but lip-smacking good, this rustic stewed-vegetable-and-sole recipe comes from the coast south of Rome near Anzio, a farming district celebrated in particular for its artichokes. The vegetables balance each other nicely, the potatoes providing a natural thickening agent, and the fish comes almost as a surprise—a very pleasant one. This is the kind of old-fashioned dish you'll only find served at home in Rome. It comes to us via our friend Verdella Caracciolo, a talented home cook with three discerning young children who love sole. Make sure to use tender artichokes, whittled to the heart, firm-fleshed potatoes, such as Yukon gold or yellow Finn, and mild fresh button or portobello mushrooms. Porcini fresh or dry would overwhelm the delicate flavor of the sole. If you use whole sole as opposed to fillets you're guaranteed to face the challenge of picking out fins and tiny bones.

1   Rinse the fillets under cold running water, put them on a platter covered with paper towels and pat them dry.

2   Juice half the lemon into a bowl of cold water big enough to hold the artichokes. Reserve the other half.

3   Clean and trim the artichokes to remove all inedible parts (see How to Clean Artichokes, page 40).

4   Peel and halve the potatoes. Combine them in a medium-sized saucepan with a pinch of salt and about 8 cups of water. Bring the water to a boil. Boil for 3 minutes. Add the artichokes and boil for another 10 to 12 minutes, until both vegetables are very al dente. Lower the heat to minimum and keep the water simmering. With tongs, remove the vegetables to a colander, run cold water over them for 1 minute, transfer them to a cutting board and let them cool.

5   Clean the mushrooms carefully with moistened paper towels. With a paring knife, cut off the bases of the stems and thinly slice the mushrooms and attached stems. You should have 2$^1/_4$ cups.

6   Peel the garlic and onion and remove and discard the garlic's green shoot. Mince together the garlic and onion. Combine with the parsley.

7   Quarter the cooled artichokes, slicing off and discarding the hairy choke and any remaining sharp inner leaves. Thinly slice each quarter. Dice the potatoes into 1-inch cubes.

8   Heat the oil in a very large frying pan over medium. Add the garlic, onion, parsley and a pinch each of salt and pepper. Sauté, stirring with a wooden spoon or spatula, for 2 to 3 minutes. Toss in the potatoes, artichokes and mushrooms and sauté for 8 to 10 minutes, until tender when poked with a fork. Flip, scrape and stir frequently, and add boiling water, 1 tablespoon at a time, if the vegetables seem too dry.

9   Slice the fillets into strips about 1 inch wide. Lay them on top of the vegetables, sprinkle in 2 tablespoons of boiling water, cover the pan and steam the fillets on each side for 3 to 4 minutes, flipping carefully once with a spatula.

10 Adjust the salt and pepper, squeeze the remaining lemon half over the fillets and serve immediately.

Baccalà in Agrodolce alla Romana

SWEET-AND-SOUR SALT COD, ROMAN STYLE

The daily spectacle of seagulls circling Rome's terra-cotta rooftops is a constant reminder of the sea. The mouth of the Tiber River opens a mere 10 miles from the Forum, yet this recipe featuring salt cod, a North Atlantic fish, has long been a favorite among Romans. Salt-preserved fish was a specialty of the Gauls before the Roman conquest of what's now France in A.D. 52 and has been known in Italy since antiquity.

A wide variety of fish, from sardines and anchovies to herring, haddock and cod were preserved in this way in the days before refrigeration. The technique survives despite depleted fish stocks, primarily in Iceland and the Scandinavian countries, Newfoundland, Greenland and Canada (New Brunswick). It has almost disappeared from the northeastern United States, where salting cod was a major industry right into the twentieth century. Despite its popularity in Gaul and other parts of the Empire, Romans in Rome probably began eating salt cod, which they and most other Italians call *baccalà,* around the eighth century. A cult food in the Eternal City, *baccalà* is featured in about a dozen recipes in the Roman repertoire, ranging from simple pan-fried fillets (one venerable Rome fry shop, Filetti di Baccalà, serves them exclusively) to more complex concoctions. It's not that locals don't eat fresh fish—they do—but salt cod has a flavor and texture all its own, lending itself to many-layered recipes such as this one, which is less interesting when made with fresh cod. For one thing, *baccalà* stands up beautifully to long, slow simmering and is ideal for flouring and frying.

Some people are put off by the fishy smell of *baccalà* before it's cooked. The amazing thing is how un-fishy prepared salt cod smells and tastes. Once upon a time it was a cheap convenience food, available year-round. All you had to do was soak it in water and cook it

2 pounds salt cod

1 cup all-purpose flour

6 tablespoons extra-virgin olive oil

1 heaping tablespoon raisins

1 white onion

2 cloves garlic

2 tablespoons minced fresh flat-leaf parsley

1/2 cup Italian dry white wine, preferably Frascati or Marino

2 tablespoons white wine vinegar

1 tablespoon sugar

2 cups peeled, seeded and chopped medium-sized fresh Italian plum tomatoes (about 1 pound) (see How to Peel and Seed a Tomato, page 93)

1 small red or yellow delicious apple

6 to 8 prunes

1 lemon

1 tablespoon pine nuts

Kosher salt or coarse sea salt and freshly ground black pepper

1 *peperoncino* (hot chili pepper), shredded, or 1/4 teaspoon crushed red pepper flakes

Hot water (optional)

SERVES 6

in any of a dozen ways that every Italian cook knew by heart. Now *baccalà* is an expensive delicacy, but it's still offered in trattorias and features on most Roman family tables, especially on Fridays, traditionally the lean day of the week. *Baccalà in agrodolce* is equally at home in the former Jewish Ghetto, where many think the recipe originated hundreds of years ago.

In Rome when you want to convey the idea that someone is tense, you say, "*Rigido come un baccalà*" (stiff as salt cod). That's because once upon a time, *baccalà* was sold flat, dry and hard, and strung up that way in the kitchen. These days all Roman fishmongers desalt *baccalà* for their clients.

In the United States, Italian, French, Spanish and Portuguese specialty food stores and a surprising number of supermarkets sell salt cod. Those that do not stock it can usually order it. Most salt cod available in America comes from Canada, is folded neatly in little wooden boxes, and is semisoft. You need only soak it overnight in the refrigerator in several changes of cold water to eliminate both the salt and the fishy smell. If you do find whole, stiff salt cod you should soak it for 24 to 36 hours in many changes of cold water or under a slow-running tap.

1   Buy presoaked cod or soak the cod for 12 to 36 hours in several changes of cold water. Rinse the cod thoroughly. Cut it into roughly 2-inch by 3/4-inch strips.

2   In a medium-sized mixing bowl, dredge the cod strips in the flour. Place them on a platter. Spread several layers of paper towels on another platter.

3   Heat the oil in a large frying pan over medium until bubbling but not smoking. With a slotted spatula, carefully lower the floured cod strips into the oil and fry until golden, turning twice, 3 to 4 minutes. Transfer the fried cod to the paper towels to drain. Cover them with a sheet of aluminum foil to keep them warm. Remove the frying pan from the heat but do not discard the oil.

4   Soak the raisins for 15 minutes in 1 cup of warm water. Drain them through a sieve or strainer. Set aside.

5   Peel the onion and garlic, removing and discarding any green shoots from the garlic, then mince. Return the pan to medium heat. Add the onion, garlic and parsley and sauté, stirring and scraping frequently, until the onion becomes translucent, 2 to 3 minutes.

6   Pour in the wine, vinegar and sugar, stirring and boiling to evaporate the liquids, 1 to 2 minutes. Lower the heat to medium-low and simmer.

7   Stir the tomatoes into the frying pan. Increase the heat to medium-high, stirring frequently while preparing the other ingredients.

8   Peel and slice the apple about ¼ inch thick. Pit and halve the prunes. Rinse the lemon. Mince or grate the zest. Add the apple, prunes, raisins, pine nuts, lemon zest, a generous pinch each of salt and pepper and the *peperoncino* to the frying pan. Stir thoroughly, lower the heat to minimum and simmer, uncovered, for 15 minutes.

9   Return the cod strips to the frying pan, mix them carefully with the sauce and simmer, covered, for 15 minutes, stirring occasionally and adding hot water 1 tablespoon at a time if the sauce seems excessively thick.

10 Serve immediately.

Recipe for a Roman Street-Corner Symphony

Scientists may someday confirm that the Roman passion for noise is genetic. Rome rates among the world's most acoustically endowed cities. Sounds are prolific chilled but are most luscious when served piping hot, from March through October and sometimes even in November and December.

SERVES 3.5 MILLION

1 Take 1 vintage Vespa and rev it for 2 to 3 minutes to 4,000 rpm, preferably between 2 A.M. and 6 A.M., though any time is acceptable. Speed along cobbled alleys, scattering pedestrians like enemy gladiators while sounding your horn, until the noise echoes through every window within a mile, 30 to 40 minutes.

2 Park within inches of a trattoria table and, when the customers shout loud enough to be heard over the engine, you may turn it off. Immediately pull out your cell phone, call your grandmother and tell her to toss the pasta into the boiling water—you're almost home. You might have to repeat the instructions several times to make yourself heard over the other Vespas, shouting patrons, municipal buses, tourist buses, streetcars, trains on the overhead tracks heading to Termini Station, roadworkers

with hammers and chisels reshaping old stone, fishmongers about to close up for the evening, artichoke and watermelon sellers crooning the merits of their wares, dishwashers banging heavy pots outside restaurant kitchen doors, bakers beating giant pans in stony courtyards and several thousand merrymakers tuning radios, zapping TVs and singing soccer chants in the ancient dwellings stacked around.

3   Bound up the steps of your building, throw open the windows, turn on the stereo, and sing along in *Romanaccio* dialect, even if the tune is Neapolitan. Lean out and call down to your many friends on the terraces below, who are busy spinning *spaghetti alla carbonara* onto their forks while chatting, guffawing and bantering. Wave at your neighbor across the laundry-strung alley and show her your new cell phone. Go through each of the fifty possible rings from Bach to Samba and Italian rap. Repeat the exercise several times.

4   Lean farther out. Yell down the block at Sandro the deli man who's closing his rolling metal shutters. Ask him to pull the shutters up and bring you the 100 grams of sliced, translucently thin prosciutto you promised to buy but somehow forgot. Over the roar of the metal shutters agree to meet in the café below. Tell grandma to hold dinner. Rush out before she or your parents can protest.

5   Clatter down the stone steps and decide on an espresso though it's not the appropriate hour. Stir in the sugar, making sure to tinkle the spoon against the cup like everyone else, 3 to 4 minutes. Make conversation with the barman over the grinding fury of the coffee grinder, the whining of the milk steamer and the slamming of the coffee basket over the waste can. When Sandro arrives, offer him a drink, switch to Frascati to keep him company and argue loudly about which is better, Roma or Lazio. Simultaneously answer your cell phone and reassure your grandmother that you'll be up within two minutes with the promised prosciutto.

6   Dash upstairs. Converse with your great aunt as she fries popping artichokes in the kitchen, and with your father as he uncorks a bottle in the dining room, and with your siblings and cousins at table, busy serving and laughing and gobbling while a radio blares, 90 to 120 minutes. Make sure to bounce your nephew on your knee while

singing Roman-dialect *stornelli* drinking songs and playing all fifty rings on your *telefonino* cellular unit.

7   Walk around the corner to your favorite ice-cream parlor. Order a cone, drag metal chairs to several locations and decide finally to perch with seventeen other vociferous friends on the edge of a night-lit, splashing fountain's bowl. Shout over the gushing water and the bleating accordion music, the tour guides simultaneously speaking six languages and the barking of traffic cops through bullhorns.

8   Sidestep the legions of pilgrims dragging suitcases amid swirling clouds of cooing pigeons. Turn off the squealing alarm on your Vespa, rev up, load a friend on the back and ride into the night with seagulls crying overhead, horses clip-clopping around the Coliseum, church bells ringing and voices, voices, voices.

Orata al Forno con Finocchio Selvatico e Succo d'Arancia

BAKED GILTHEAD, BREAM OR SEA BASS WITH AN ANISE
AND ORANGE JUICE REDUCTION SAUCE

2 pounds gilthead, bream or sea bass (1 or more fish), cleaned

10 to 12 sprigs fresh anise or dill

1 large orange

1 clove garlic

4 tablespoons plus 1 teaspoon extra-virgin olive oil

Kosher salt or coarse sea salt and freshly ground black pepper

6 tablespoons Italian dry white wine, preferably Frascati or Marino

SERVES 4

When hard-core Roman foodies tell you the only authentic Roman fish recipes are for anchovies, shark, eel, mollusks and salt cod, you can always remind them that, according to Columella (first century A.D.), the world's earliest fish farms were developed by two Roman military men, Sergius Orata and Licinius Murena. While Murena adopted the Latin name of the eels he raised (*myraina* in Greek, whence our word moray eel), General Orata took the Latin name for gilthead (*orata*). This Mediterranean fish isn't related to, but tastes like, bream and sea bass, which are readily available in America, and suggested here as substitutes.

Romans have always loved many types of freshwater and saltwater fish and eat them in great quantities. This recipe comes from the Viterbo area, an inland region north of Rome that, oddly enough, boasts one of Italy's biggest fish processing and trucking industries. The authentic main seasoning is wild fennel, a plant that grows like a weed there and throughout Rome's region, but is unfindable in America outside the San Francisco Bay area, where Italian immigrants planted it in the mid-1800s. Fresh anise or dill work just as well, possibly even better.

1   Preheat the oven to 375°F.

2   Rinse the fish, put it on a platter covered with paper towels and pat it dry inside and out.

3   Rinse the anise and pat it dry. Rinse the orange, pat it dry and with a paring knife or vegetable peeler, remove the colored zest. Reserve the peeled orange.

4   Peel the garlic, eliminating the green shoot. Mince the anise, orange zest and garlic. Combine them in a small mixing bowl. Moisten them with 1 teaspoon of the oil, stirring with a fork.

5   Put the fish in a large ovenproof casserole and sprinkle it inside and out with a generous pinch each of salt and pepper. Stuff it with the minced seasonings and drizzle it with the remaining 4 tablespoons oil and 4 tablespoons of the wine. Bake for 20 to 25 minutes, until the flesh is no longer translucent but still firm at the flick of a fork.

6   Juice the orange into a small saucepan, add the remaining 2 tablespoons wine and reduce the liquids over medium heat until thickened and bubbling, stirring frequently, 8 to 10 minutes.

7   With two steel spatulas, transfer the fish from the casserole to a warmed serving platter and cover it with aluminum foil.

8   Stir the juices from the casserole into the saucepan with the orange juice and wine. Remove the aluminum foil from the fish and nap with the sauce. Serve immediately.

Filetti di Spigola alle Olive di Gaeta

SEA BASS WITH BLACK GAETA OLIVES, CHERRY TOMATOES AND FENNEL SEEDS

4 skinless sea bass fillets (about 2 pounds)

1 medium-sized white onion

2 anchovy fillets

4 tablespoons extra-virgin olive oil

Kosher salt or coarse sea salt

½ cup Italian dry white wine, preferably Falerno

6 to 8 large or 12 to 16 small cherry tomatoes (about 1½ cups)

¾ cup pitted, chopped Gaeta or other Italian or Greek black olives

1 tablespoon fennel seeds

SERVES 4

*S*ea bass has joined the ranks of "Roman" fish only in the last fifty years or so. But it's now as popular, perhaps even more popular, than some of the old standards—salt cod, anchovies, eel and shark. I've seen many fish recipes calling for Gaeta olives—the best table olives from the Rome region. This recipe, as perfected by celebrated Roman seafood chef Alberto Ciarla, is one of my favorites. The cherry tomatoes provide sweetness and acidity to balance the olives' earthy flavor, while the fennel seeds give a surprising licorice taste and crunchy texture, transforming this easy-to-make recipe into a subtle delight.

1   Rinse the sea bass fillets, put them on a platter covered with paper towels and pat them dry. Warm a baking sheet in the oven at 250° F.

2   Peel and mince the onion.

3   If you are using salted anchovies, desalt them (see Desalting Anchovies, page 24). If you are using anchovy fillets packed in oil, remove them with a fork and drain them on paper towels.

4   Heat 2 tablespoons of the oil in a large frying pan over medium-low. Add the onion and the anchovy fillets. Sauté, stirring with a wooden spoon or spatula to crush the anchovies, until the onion becomes translucent, 5 to 6 minutes.

5 Raise the heat to medium-high, add a pinch of salt, pour in the wine and boil to evaporate it, 1 to 2 minutes.

6 Add the cherry tomatoes. Add half the olives. Sauté, stirring frequently, until the tomatoes wilt and begin to collapse, 1 to 2 minutes.

7 Lower the heat to medium and carefully add the sea bass. Cook the fillets for 2 to 3 minutes on each side, turning once with a slotted steel spatula. Use the spatula to transfer the fillets to the warmed baking sheet.

8 Quickly spoon the olive-tomato-and-onion sauce from the frying pan onto four dinner plates. Top each plate with one fillet. Scatter the remaining olives and the fennel seeds on top and drizzle the fillets with the remaining 2 tablespoons oil. Serve immediately.

Il Moro Fountain, Piazza Navona

Fritto Antico

FRIED BABY SQUID, CALAMARI AND SHRIMP

As extroverted and opinionated as he is talented, Roman chef-restaurateur Alberto Ciarla serves some of the capital's best fish dishes, including this mixed seafood fry. I first ate it with my wife at Ciarla's extravagantly luxurious same-name restaurant on Piazza di San Cosimato in the Trastevere neighborhood, where customers sit like pearls in comfy chairs in the red, black and crystal interior, which is lined by half a dozen huge aquariums. Ciarla is a former Italian league rugby star and his muscles bulge from his fine suits, but his passion for sports is equaled by his devotion to fine cooking. He comes from a family of restaurateurs and knows a lot about Rome's culinary traditions. While many of his menu offerings are of his own invention, he insists that this seafood fry is as old as the Coliseum. Though I've never encountered the recipe or anything like it in Apicius or other ancient sources, there's reason to believe Ciarla may be right; the Romans adored fresh fish and seafood, and frying was a common cooking technique. But most of Ciarla's clients don't care when it was invented. This crisp, light seafood fry is among the best I've ever tasted anywhere. Ciarla's trick is to use only fresh—never frozen—seafood and to coat it with a mix of semolina and dried herbs. He flash-fries it in a light-bodied extra-virgin olive oil. The herbs perfume the oil, and the semolina prevents the seafood from absorbing too much of it. "The herbs and semolina won't stick properly to frozen seafood, believe me," he insists, flexing. "It's worth it to use fresh!" He's right.

I rarely attempt frying more than four servings of *fritto antico* at a time because it's important to get the seafood to the table while it is still piping hot. Remember: Always heat olive oil slowly and never let it smoke. Be careful when frying food to protect yourself from the hot oil, which can splatter; wear kitchen gloves and an apron.

1 Gently rinse the seafood in a colander and let it drip dry.

2 Spread about 2 cups of the semolina in the middle of a baking sheet to a depth of at least 1 inch. Line a platter with waxed paper.

8 ounces fresh small calamari rings

8 ounces fresh cleaned baby squid (see How to Clean Squid, page 133)

1 pound fresh shelled shrimp

4 cups semolina (about 1 pound)

3 heaping tablespoons mixed dried herbs (shredded bay leaf, parsley, thyme, basil)

3 to 4 cups light extra-virgin olive oil for frying

Fine salt

4 tablespoons minced fresh flat-leaf parsley

1 lemon, cut into wedges

SERVES 4

3 Place about one-third of the still-damp mixed seafood items side-by-side on top of the semolina. Sprinkle the seafood with one-third of the dried herbs (1 heaping tablespoon) and gently flip and roll it in the semolina until thoroughly coated. Transfer the coated seafood to the platter covered with waxed paper and top it with another layer of waxed paper. Repeat the operation, adding fresh semolina to the baking sheet, until all the seafood has been seasoned and coated.

4 Pour the oil into a large frying pan or medium saucepan to a depth of 1 to 2 inches and heat it over medium-low to 350°F, until bubbling hot but not smoking. To check for hotness without a thermometer, step back and carefully flick a drop of water onto the surface, making sure you don't get splattered. The oil should sizzle, dance and evaporate within seconds.

5 Line a platter with several layers of paper towels. With tongs, transfer the seafood in small batches to the frying pan and fry for 2 to 3 minutes, turning frequently. Transfer the seafood to the towel-lined platter and sprinkle it with salt.

6 Once all the seafood has been fried, serve it immediately on individual plates, topped with the parsley, with the lemon wedges on the side.

VARIATION: A variant to this recipe is *fritto di molluschi guarnito con carciofi a spicchi* (seafood with slivered artichokes). Back in the 1920s, Italian cookbook writer Ada Boni noted in *La cucina romana* that Romans liked their fried seafood with *carciofi fritti dorati* (slivered fried artichokes). While you'll rarely find this variation today, I've made it at home and think it is delicious. Halve the quantities given above for seafood. Halve the quantity of artichokes in *Carciofi Fritti Dorati alla Romana* (page 252), doing steps 1 through 3 of the recipe. Moisten the slivered artichokes with lemon juice, roll them in the semolina and fry them with the seafood as explained above.

Mazzancolle al Coccio

PAN-FRIED JUMBO SHRIMP WITH WHITE WINE AND LEMON JUICE

3 pounds fresh shelled
jumbo shrimp or prawns,
or spiny lobster or crayfish
tails

2 lemons

4 to 6 heaping tablespoons
all-purpose flour

Kosher salt or coarse
sea salt and freshly
ground black pepper

¼ cup extra-virgin
olive oil

1 cup Italian dry white
wine, preferably Frascati
or Marino

SERVES 6

A classic of the Roman fish repertoire, this is a wonderfully simple, fast and low-calorie way to enjoy shrimp, prawns, spiny lobster or crayfish. The variety of crustacean most often available in Rome is known as *mazzancolle* (*gamberoni* elsewhere in Italy) and has a delicate flavor enhanced by the recipe's wine and lemon juice. Romans swear that you have to cook *mazzancolle* in an earthenware pot (*coccio*), but I find a heavy iron frying pan works well, too.

1   Rinse the shrimp, pat them dry with paper towels and lay them out on a platter. Warm another platter.

2   Juice 1 lemon into a cup and slice the other into thin rounds.

3   In a medium-sized mixing bowl, combine the flour with a very generous pinch each of salt and pepper. Dredge the shrimp in the seasoned flour and return them to the platter.

4   Heat the oil in an earthenware casserole or heavy iron frying pan over medium-high. Carefully add the shrimp to the pan in a single layer and sauté for 3 minutes per side, flipping with a spatula. Pour in ½ cup of the wine and boil to evaporate it, 30 to 60 seconds.

5   Transfer the shrimp to the clean, warmed platter. Pour the lemon juice, remaining ½ cup wine and a pinch each of salt and pepper into the pan, stirring and scraping for 1 minute.

6   To serve, pour the pan juices over the shrimp and top with the lemon slices. Serve immediately.

Seppie Ripiene coi Piselli o Salsicce di Mare

CARLA'S STUFFED CUTTLEFISH WITH PEAS

This is how our friend Carla Bertini makes stuffed cuttlefish (and squid) with peas, a Roman seafood classic. She calls the recipe "seafood sausages" because that's what the stuffed cuttlefish come out looking like. A photography researcher, Carla is passionate about food. She learned to cook from her mother and grandmother and upholds Roman tradition by inviting friends and family to regular dinner parties where she excels at the entire regional repertoire.

Stuffed cuttlefish, squid or calamari with peas is a favorite springtime dish. It's also made with artichoke hearts. With frozen peas, you can make this recipe any time of year.

2 cups water

2 pounds small fresh or frozen cleaned cuttlefish or squid (see How to Clean Squid, page 133), (about 10, each 2½ inches wide by 6 inches long)

4 tablespoons minced fresh flat-leaf parsley, plus several whole sprigs parsley

3 cloves garlic

1 large egg

2 thick slices white bread

3 pounds fresh, tender young peas in their pods or 1 (1-pound) package frozen peas

3 tablespoons extra-virgin olive oil

½ cup Italian dry white wine, preferably Frascati or Marino

Kosher salt or coarse sea salt and freshly ground black pepper

SERVES 4

1   Make the squid stock. Bring the water to a boil in a small saucepan. Toss in 1 cleaned squid with several whole sprigs of parsley and boil for 4 to 5 minutes. Lower the heat and simmer.

2   To prepare the squid tentacles, remove and discard the bulb-like beaks at the base after pushing them out. Rinse under cold running water to remove any remaining sand. Mince and reserve the tentacles.

3   Peel 2 of the garlic cloves, discarding the green shoots, and mince. Combine the garlic, minced parsley and tentacles in a bowl. Crack in the egg and beat it.

4   Pour 1½ cups of the squid stock into a shallow bowl. Tear the bread into tatters; you should have about 2½ cups. Drop the bread into the bowl. Once the bread has softened, remove it with a slotted spoon and, holding it over the sink, with your fingers press out the stock, squeezing and forming the bread into a small ball. Crush and blend it into the mixture with the tentacles until pasty and homogenous.

5   With a small spoon such as a teaspoon, stuff each squid about two-thirds full with the paste. Close the ends with a toothpick. Save any leftover stuffing.

6   Shell the peas by running your index finger along inside the pods; you should have about 2⅔ cups.

7   Heat the oil in a large earthenware casserole or heavy skillet over medium-low.

8   With the heel of your hand or the flat part of a wide-bladed knife, crush the remaining clove of garlic on a cutting board. Spread the clove open with your fingers. Discard the skins and green shoots. Add it to the oil, sauté for 2 to 3 minutes and discard it.

9   Increase the heat to medium. Add the squid in a single layer and sprinkle in any leftover stuffing. Sauté for 2 minutes, flipping the squid once, until the squid are slightly swollen and pink.

10 Pour in the wine and boil to evaporate it, lifting and flipping, 1 to 2 minutes.

11 Add the fresh or frozen peas to the squid with a generous pinch of salt and pepper, cover the pan, and simmer over low heat for 15 to 20 minutes, adding stock, 1 tablespoon at a time, to keep the squid moist.

12 To serve, transfer the squid to a serving platter and remove the toothpicks. Moisten the squid with pan juices and serve hot.

Quer che nu'strozza 'ngrasse.
(If it doesn't kill you, it'll make you hardier.)

—Old Roman saying

Polipi in Padella alla Luciana

OCTOPUS WITH SPICY TOMATO SAUCE

3 pounds octopus, cuttlefish, squid or calamari, fresh or frozen, cleaned and thawed (see How to Clean Squid, page 133)

2 cloves garlic

5 tablespoons extra-virgin olive oil

1½ *peperoncini* (hot chili peppers), shredded, or ½ teaspoon crushed red pepper flakes

1 tablespoon anchovy paste

Kosher salt or coarse sea salt and freshly ground black pepper

½ cup Italian dry white wine, preferably Frascati or Marino

1 tablespoon white wine vinegar

1 (28-ounce) can Italian plum tomatoes, preferably San Marzano

6 slices country-style bread

4 heaping tablespoons minced fresh flat-leaf parsley

SERVES 6

No one in Rome remembers Luciana, but whoever she was, she gave this recipe to the local repertoire at some point in the last two hundred years or so, when tomatoes and red hot chili peppers became popular. The recipe is perpetuated among countless Romans who don't like it when food historians suggest the real name is *polipi in padella alla lucana;* i.e., from the Lucania region south of Rome. The recipe was transmitted to me in various versions by home cooks and fishmongers, among them the friendly and ever-helpful Anna Elisa Scipioni, a native of Tarquinia north of Rome near the border with Tuscany. As Anna Elisa says, *polipi in padella* is easy to make and wonderfully spicy, and who cares if Luciana really existed or not? If you can't find baby octopus, use large octopus, squid, cuttlefish or calamari instead and chop them into bite-sized bits. Like squid, calamari and cuttlefish, octopus is great either fresh or frozen, since the freezing process actually helps to tenderize the flesh.

1   Rinse the octopus or other squid, calamari or cuttlefish under cold running water, pat dry on paper towels and cut into bite-sized pieces.

2   With the heel of your hand or the flat part of a wide-bladed knife, crush the garlic on a cutting board. Spread the cloves open with your fingers. Discard the skins and green shoots.

3   Heat 3 tablespoons of the oil in a large, high-sided frying pan over medium-low heat. Add the garlic and *peperoncini.* Stir with a wooden spoon or spatula for 1 minute. Stir in the anchovy paste, dissolving it in the oil.

4   Increase the heat to medium-high, add the octopus and sauté for 5 to 6 minutes, adding a small pinch of salt and several turns of the peppermill. Pour in the wine and vinegar and boil to evaporate them, 2 to 3 minutes.

5   Add the tomatoes and their packing juices, stirring and crushing. Bring the mixture to a boil, lower the heat to minimum and simmer, uncovered, for 45 minutes until thick.

6   Toast the bread medium-dark and cut each slice into 4 crostini. Put 4 into each of six deep soup bowls.

7   Divide the stew among the soup bowls, garnish with the parsley, drizzle with the remaining 2 tablespoons oil and serve immediately.

The Fountains of Rome

*W*hen the Goths sacked Rome for the first time in A.D. 410, 11 aqueducts fed 1,212 public fountains, 11 Imperial thermal establishments and 926 public baths. In 537, Vitiges the Goth cut the last functioning aqueducts, ushering in the "waterless" Middle Ages, a period that lasted about nine hundred years.

Frittata con le Zucchine

ZUCCHINI FRITTATA WITH FRESH MINT AND PECORINO ROMANO

8 large eggs

4 heaping tablespoons freshly grated Pecorino Romano

Fine salt and freshly ground black pepper

1 pound small zucchini

3 to 4 tablespoons extra-virgin olive oil

4 heaping tablespoons minced fresh spearmint

SERVES 4

La frittata is Italy's answer to the omelet, but it is easier and quicker to make since you don't have to flip or fill it—the filling is blended into the beaten eggs, or vice versa. In Rome, favorite frittata ingredients range from leftover pasta to onions, pancetta and fresh vegetables, especially zucchini, sweet peppers and artichokes, though the first recorded frittata, from Apicius twenty centuries ago, calls for fresh peas.

This is an iconic food: Just think of the unforgettable scene in Ettore Scola's masterpiece *Una giornata particolare* (*A Special Day*) in which Sophia Loren, as a housewife, cooks up a frittata for Marcello Mastroianni, her mysterious, ambiguous anti-Fascist neighbor, as Mussolini parades in the streets below. Frittatas are the ultimate comfort-seduction food, symbolic of domesticity, abundance and fertility. They are served in simple trattorias, but above all at home, usually for a table of two. In Rome, the expression *fare la frittata* means more than just "making a frittata"—it has all kinds of hidden meanings, some political, most sexual. It's tough to make a perfect frittata for four: I prefer making two perfect ones for two, or I use two frying pans side by side. Zucchini and mint make a delicious combination but if you prefer you can also mix the eggs with about half the yield of the following recipes: spicy zucchini and basil (see *Concia di Zucchine,* page 251), stewed sweet peppers (see *Peperonata,* page 249), amatriciana sauce (see *Bucatini all'Amatriciana,* page 90).

1. Beat the eggs in a medium-size mixing bowl and blend in the Pecorino Romano with a pinch of salt and plenty of pepper.

2. Rinse the zucchini, pat them dry and slice them into thin rounds.

3. Heat the oil in one very large or two medium-sized nonreactive frying pan(s) over medium. Add the zucchini and sauté, stirring, flipping and tossing for 5 to 6 minutes. Lower the heat to minimum, cover the frying pan(s) and simmer until tender, 3 to 4 minutes.

4. Add the mint, a tiny pinch of salt and pepper, and pour in the beaten eggs. Lift and tilt the pan to distribute the contents. Cook, covered, until the frittata is firm but moist.

5. Slice and serve immediately.

Bridges over the Tiber River, with Saint Peter's Dome in the background

Uova in Trippa

FRITTATA STRIPS WITH SPICY TOMATO SAUCE, MINT AND PECORINO ROMANO

1 recipe *Sugo Finto* (page 89) tomato sauce

1 *peperoncino* (hot chili pepper), shredded, or ¼ teaspoon crushed red pepper flakes

2 heaping tablespoons minced fresh spearmint

6 large eggs

3 tablespoons milk

4 tablespoons freshly grated Parmigiano-Reggiano

Fine salt and freshly ground black pepper

2 tablespoons extra-virgin olive oil

2 heaping tablespoons freshly grated Pecorino Romano

SERVES 4

This simple, traditional recipe combines a classic frittata and *trippa alla romana* (see page 149)—without the tripe. The designation *in trippa* refers to the fact that the frittata omelet strips look like tripe, and the tomato sauce used here is nearly identical to standard tripe topping, but there's no meat of any kind in this gutsy delicacy. Our friend Carla Bertini, an enthusiastic home cook who delights in her family's umpteen-generation culinary repertoire, learned to make *uova in trippa* from her mother and grandmother and shared the recipe with me.

1   Prepare the *Sugo Finto,* heat it over medium-low, and add the *peperoncino.*

2   Stir in a pinch of the mint and keep the sauce simmering.

3   Beat the eggs in a mixing bowl with the milk, 2 tablespoons of the Parmigiano-Reggiano and a pinch each of salt and pepper.

4   Heat the oil in a very large, nonreactive frying pan over low heat. Slowly pour in the egg mixture, tilt, shake, and cover the pan. Cook the frittata on one side only until firm, 4 to 5 minutes. With a spatula, transfer the frittata to a cutting board and slice it into strips about 1 inch wide.

5   Return the frying pan to medium-low. Add the frittata strips and spoon the tomato sauce over and around them. Sprinkle in the remaining mint and 2 tablespoons Parmigiano-Reggiano. Add the Pecorino Romano, cover the pan, turn off the heat and wait 1 minute before serving.

Uova in Tegame con Asparagi e Pancetta

Eggs Sunny-Side Up in a Frying Pan with Asparagus, Pancetta and Pecorino Romano

2 pounds green asparagus

1 clove garlic

2 ounces pancetta or bacon (2 to 3 strips)

1 tablespoon extra-virgin olive oil

4 large eggs

About 1½ cups freshly grated Pecorino Romano

Freshly ground black pepper

Serves 4

Asparagus have been on Roman tables since the first local shepherd plucked one, found it tasty and survived to tell his story about three thousand years ago, but who's counting? The ancient Roman foodie Apicius gives a recipe (#133) for what we'd probably call an asparagus frittata, and it's known that everyone from the caesars and the popes to the lowest slave or monk fed on asparagus spears before, during and after the Roman Empire. Nowadays, you can usually find several types of asparagus at the same time in Roman markets throughout the spring months: pencil-thin wild asparagus, slightly plumper cultivated "wild asparagus" and various thicknesses of local green and northern Italian or French white asparagus. Our friend Claudio Zampa, greengrocer extraordinaire at the Campo de' Fiori market, told us about this way to "accommodate" the pungent vegetable. I love it for its simplicity and rustic flavors.

Wild asparagus

1   Rinse the asparagus and cut off the woody lower sections.

2   Bring about 1 cup of water to a boil in a wide saucepan or a deep frying pan. Add the asparagus and cook until barely al dente, 3 to 5 minutes. Transfer the asparagus to paper towels to dry the spears. Chop them into roughly ½-inch sections, leaving the tips whole.

3   Peel and halve the garlic with a paring knife, discarding the green shoots. Roughly chop the pancetta. You should have about ½ cup.

4   Heat the oil in a large frying pan over medium heat. Add the pancetta and garlic and sauté until the garlic colors and the pork barely begins to crisp, 2 to 3 minutes. Transfer the pancetta to a plate with paper towels to absorb excess fat. Discard the garlic. Drain off about half of the fat in the frying pan.

5   Add the asparagus to the frying pan and sauté for about 1 minute over medium heat, stirring and scraping with a wooden spoon or spatula. Lower the heat to minimum and stir the pancetta back in.

6   Crack the eggs carefully atop the asparagus, making sure not to break the yolks. Sprinkle 4 heaping tablespoons of Pecorino Romano and a generous pinch of pepper on top. Cover the frying pan and steam the eggs until the whites are firm and the cheese has melted, 3 to 4 minutes.

7   Serve immediately with the eggs sunny-side up and a bowl of the remaining Pecorino Romano on the side.

"Let it be done in less time than it takes to cook an asparagus!"
—common expression during the reign of Augustus Caesar (63 B.C. to A.D. 14)

Carciofini in Fricassea

FRICASSEED BABY ARTICHOKES IN A HERBED EGG CREAM

These tulip-sized artichokes are eaten whole after fricasseeing in a buttery, creamy egg sauce redolent of fresh mint. An old recipe, it has a papal feel because of the luscious dairy products it uses instead of poor folks' olive oil.

Caravaggio, who arrived in Rome poor and unknown but became rich and famous, preferred oil to butter with his artichokes, and this preference gave rise to one of the more celebrated episodes in the irascible baroque painter's life. A regular patron of La Locanda del Moro alla Maddalena, a popular Rome tavern back in the 1590s, Caravaggio ordered his usual artichokes sautéed in olive oil and got them dripping in butter instead. Furious, he flung the food into the tavern-keeper's face and stormed out. The tavern-keeper got off lightly, since soon afterward Caravaggio proved himself capable of much greater violence—he was convicted of murdering a friend and had to flee Rome.

Needless to say, the pope, Caravaggio's main employer, made sure not to serve his protégé this particular artichoke recipe, which uses butter and cream and was even richer back in the artist's heyday and remained overwhelmingly rich right into the twentieth century. As Ada Boni instructs in her seminal 1920s cookbook *Il Talismano della Felicità,* to make *carciofini in fricassea,* first you slice the artichokes, flour them, dip them in egg, fry them in butter, then sauté them a second time with more butter, eggs and chicken broth.

For many years the most flavorful, tender artichokes in town were grown on the hill above the giant oval Piazza del Popolo, crowned for the last two hundred years by the Pincio belvedere and the Villa Borghese. Back in Imperial times, the site had orchards and kitchen gardens belonging to the Roman general and notorious gourmand Lucius Licinius Lucullus Ponticus, a.k.a. Lucullus (ca. 117 to 56 B.C.), credited with bringing certain species of cherry trees to Rome from the Near East (see A Lucullan Repast, page 223). Lucullus's land abutted the game park of Quintus Hortensius and both remained a vast vegetable patch known in Latin as the *Collis Hortulorum* until about three hundred years ago. From the fall of the Empire until about 1800, the best speci-

1 lemon

16 tiny, tender artichokes
or 8 medium-sized
artichokes

3 heaping tablespoons
minced fresh spearmint

3 heaping tablespoons
minced fresh flat-leaf
parsley

5 eggs, at room
temperature

6 tablespoons heavy cream

Kosher salt or coarse
sea salt and freshly
ground black pepper

4 tablespoons butter

SERVES 4

mens it produced usually wound up on the pope's table. That's another reason to suppose this recipe may have originated in the Vatican's kitchens, once a crucible of culinary creativity. Fricasseed artichokes have never been a restaurant dish and are almost always made at home and eaten as a main course, like a frittata. The recipe works best with tiny artichokes that you can pop whole into your mouth.

1 Halve the lemon. Juice one half into a bowl of cold water big enough to hold the artichokes and their stems. Juice the other half into a small mixing bowl. Use the squeezed lemon halves to rub the artichokes as you work.

2 Clean and trim the artichokes to remove all inedible parts (see How to Clean a Globe Artichoke, page 40). If the trimmed whole artichokes are bigger than about 1½ inches in diameter, cut them into bite-sized halves or quarters. Trim and peel the stems. Chop the pith into sections about 1 inch long.

3 Combine the mint and parsley in the small mixing bowl with the lemon juice. Add the eggs, cream and a generous pinch each of salt and pepper. Whisk until fully blended.

4 Bring 2 cups water to a boil in a medium-sized saucepan. Toss in the artichokes and stems and boil them, covered, until tender, 12 to 15 minutes. Drain them in a colander and let them drip dry.

5 Melt the butter in a large frying pan over medium-low heat. Add the artichokes and stems and sauté for about 5 minutes, stirring, flipping and scraping with a wooden spoon or spatula. Lower the heat to minimum and pour in the herbed cream mixture, stirring and coating the artichokes, 2 to 3 minutes. Turn off the heat and stir until the eggs are set, 30 to 45 seconds.

6 Serve immediately.

A Lucullan Repast

$\mathcal{W}$ho was Lucullus, the gourmandizing Roman general whose legendary feasts gave rise to the expressions "a Lucullan repast" or "a feast fit for Lucullus"? Lucius Licinius Lucullus Ponticus was born circa 117 B.C. and died in 56 B.C., having garnered more fame for feasting in his retirement than for his brilliant military career in Asia Minor under Sulla. Among his varied achievements, he's credited with bringing to Rome in 72 B.C. grafts or seeds of at least one variety of cherry tree from Cerasus (the origin of the word "cherry"), near his military posting on the Black Sea. Wild, inedible cherries were already known in Italy and France, but Lucullus's cherries, probably stolen from the gardens of defeated Mithridates VI, King of Pontus, eventually caught on among Roman food lovers. This alone is enough for Lucullus to deserve eternal thanks. Some modern Italian cherry varieties may be descended from the general's trees, and what would Roman cooking be without sour cherry *crostata* (see page 292)? Lucullus was also known among fellow patricians for his peculiar habit of force-feeding thrushes and for his countless banquets, including a certain dinner party costing a hideously huge sum and designed for three guests only: himself, Cicero and Pompey the Great. Though he had a luxurious villa on the coast near Naples, for which he ordered slaves to dig a tunnel to bring seawater into a lake stocked with the fish he delighted in eating, Lucullus also owned prime land in Rome. His house, game park and gardens spread over parts of what's now the Pincio, Villa Borghese and Trinità dei Monti above the Spanish Steps. It was during the erection of the obelisk atop the staircase that Goethe, in 1787, discovered precious fragments from the general's gardens. Until the late 1800s, before air pollution and architecture got in the way, you could see from Lucullus's property across the "wide-spreading *campagna* till a silver line marks the sea melting into the horizon beyond Ostia," as Augustus Hare put it in *Walks in Rome* (1871). While standing in his celebrated vegetable patch shaded by cherry trees, as his servants hunted game or fetched fattened thrushes from the surrounding parklands, Lucullus could observe his fresh fish arriving at Ostia's seaport, then making their way alive in tanks in a flat-bottomed boat up the Tiber, up the hill and onto his table, where they were killed before enchanted guests and served alongside exotic fare—flamingo tongues, perhaps? Luckily, "a Lucullan repast" today in Rome really just means "Wow, what a great meal!"

CONTORNI

VEGETABLES AND SIDE DISHES

THE WORD *contorno* (*contorni* is the plural) means frame, as in the edge around something central. In terms of an Italian meal, vegetable-based *contorni* frame the main course and correspond roughly to what we'd call a vegetable side dish. To Romans, the role of the *contorno* is a question not only of aesthetics—a plate for each course and each course in its plate— but also of eating foods in what the Romans believe, based on ancestral tradition, is a healthful and pleasant progression. Some *contorni* may seem more like first or even main courses—stuffed sweet peppers and eggplants, or fricasseed artichokes, for example. Artichokes are a special case, falling into appetizer, starter, main course and vegetable side categories, thereby causing confusion to outsiders. But locals have no trouble with the concept, and my advice is to compose your meal as you wish and eat these *contorni* at whatever point in your meal you feel most comfortable with.

Only-in-Rome *contorni* revolve around the perennial stars of local produce, some of which come from market gardens right on the edge of town: puntarella chicory (with anchovy dressing), salads made with a myriad of mixed baby lettuces, Romanesco artichokes and Romanesco broccoli. Other favorites include broccoli rabe, peas, spinach, sweet peppers and zucchini prepared in any number of ways. Baking, deep-frying or pan-frying with olive oil and garlic are popular techniques. Like chicory, zucchini are unsung heroes of many central- and southern-

Italian regional cuisines, and they're worshipped in Rome. In the Imperial era, Roman patricians employed what may have been the first hothouse technology to grow them year-round, and they're available year-round to this day. The local variety (called *zucchine romanesche*) is pea-green, fluted like a marble column and harvested when only 4 to 5 inches long. You can find them in farmers' markets and specialty greengrocers' shops in the United States. Romans prefer small, tender vegetables as a general rule; when it comes to zucchini, they believe the younger and paler they are the better. Avoiding overlarge, seed-filled vegetables is a sound principle to follow when making any of these recipes.

The sign reads "Real Roman [Zucchini], Not Bitter."

Broccoletti Strascinati

PAN-FRIED BROCCOLI RABE WITH GARLIC AND CHILI PEPPER

1½ pounds fresh
broccoli rabe

Kosher salt or coarse
sea salt

2 cloves garlic

3 tablespoons extra-virgin
olive oil

1 *peperoncino* (hot chili
pepper), shredded,
or ¼ teaspoon crushed
red pepper flakes

SERVES 6

The Italian verb *strascinare* means literally "dragging," but when applied to cooking technique in Rome, it means "sautéing in a frying pan" with olive oil, garlic and *peperoncino*. The technique is applied to many leaf vegetables. Broccoli rabe features high on the best-loved *strascinare* list, alongside chicory.

1   Soak the broccoli rabe in cold water, rinse and spin it dry. Get rid of woody or damaged leaves or stalks.

2   Bring 3 to 4 quarts of water to a boil in a big pot. Toss in the broccoli rabe with a pinch of salt and boil for 5 minutes. Drain, squeeze to remove excess liquid and coarsely chop it. You should have about 4 cups.

3   With the heel of your hand or the flat part of a wide-bladed knife, crush the garlic on a cutting board. Spread the cloves open with your fingers. Discard the skins and green shoots.

4   Heat the oil in a large, heavy frying pan over medium. Add the garlic and *peperoncino*. Sauté, stirring with a wooden spoon or spatula, until the garlic begins to color, 1 to 2 minutes. Remove and discard the garlic. Add the broccoli rabe and sauté until tender, 3 to 4 minutes.

5   Serve immediately.

NOTE: You can also serve broccoli rabe *all'agro;* i.e., without sautéing, using olive oil and lemon juice or vinegar instead. Follow steps 1 and 2 above, adding the garlic to the cooking water. Once the broccoli is cooked, discard the garlic. Dress with 2 tablespoons of extra-virgin olive oil, 1 tablespoon fresh lemon juice or vinegar and a pinch each of salt and freshly ground black pepper. Toss. Serve warm or at room temperature.

About Puntarella

$\mathcal{E}$ach head of puntarella, a kind of chicory, produces up to 20 shoots in its center. They look surprisingly like white asparagus spears—albeit stubby baroque asparagus spears twisted like the Bernini columns in Saint Peter's. The shoots appear in spring and, if allowed to mature, turn into tall, hollow seed-bearing stalks. The trick is to harvest puntarella when the stalks are young, tender and tasty, and anywhere from 2 to 4 inches long. Once they thicken and start hollowing out, they're already past their prime.

Romans carefully slice the shoots and float them in basins of cold water so that they curl and look like fiddleheads. Few bother to do this at home, preferring to buy puntarella presliced from experts, such as Mirella Angelini (*left*), a lifer at the Campo de' Fiori outdoor market. One day Mirella showed me exactly how to *capare* (clean and trim) this peculiar plant. It's a lot easier than you'd expect.

First, working with a paring knife, Mirella removes the green dandelionlike outer leaves from the head and cuts the asparaguslike stalks—*le punte*—off the plant's tough, flame-shaped body. She trims off the base of each *punta* so that it's flat. Then she peels the *punta* all around, as if she were peeling the base of an asparagus spear, to remove the slightly bitter exterior. Having revealed the tender, pale-green pith, she slices it in half down the center, lengthwise, and then works on one half of it at a time. She cuts the half into two, three or four matchstick-size sections, depending on the pith's thickness. She then repeats the operation with the other half of the pith and drops the sliced puntarella sections into a basin of cold water. They curl up effortlessly in 30 to 40 minutes.

"You can keep them in cold water for hours," Mirella says. "They stay fresh, crisp and curly, especially if you put the water container covered in the fridge."

Most Romans make a peppery, garlicky pounded-anchovy dressing for their puntarella. Like me, Mirella likes the taste of garlic but finds it hard to digest raw. So she hand-crushes 2 cloves and lets them steep for 10 to 20 minutes with the anchovies, vinegar and olive oil. After that she tosses in the puntarella and lets the salad sit for 5 minutes, then removes the crushed garlic and serves.

Puntarelle in Salsa d'Acciughe

PUNTARELLA CHICORY SALAD WITH ANCHOVY DRESSING

1 large head puntarella
with tender shoots
(or 1 head curly endive
or 4 Belgian endives)
(about 2 pounds)

2 eggs (optional)

3 anchovy fillets

2 cloves garlic

2 tablespoons white wine
vinegar

4 tablespoons extra-virgin
olive oil

Kosher salt or coarse
sea salt and freshly
ground black pepper

SERVES 4

*T*he endive and chicory families remind me of my own extended family, which includes every imaginable mix of southern, central and northern European, North and South American and African genes. In other words, it's a family with many cousins. As regards chicory and endive, confusion reigns when it comes to distinguishing between two cousins, *Cichorium intybus* (chicory) and *Cichorium endivia* (endive). This age-old Roman salad recipe calls for puntarella, a very specific kind of chicory—or endive, depending upon whom you ask. Puntarella is a very close relative of Catalonia (also spelled Catalogna). The name "Puntarella" derives from *punta,* meaning point, sprout or tip. Puntarella is increasingly available at American produce markets and farmers' markets and is well worth seeking out for its refreshing flavor and incomparable crispness. I've seen it sold as puntarella chicory, puntarella endive and puntarella radicchio.

While most puntarella salad recipes you encounter in Rome these days don't call for boiled eggs, those in many old cookbooks do, including Ada Boni's seminal *La cucina romana* (1929). I make puntarella salad both ways and find them equally delicious, so I've listed the eggs as an option. Try the salad without eggs the first time around, and with eggs the second, then decide which you prefer. By the way, don't throw away the outer leaves of the puntarella; they're delicious, too. Save them for other uses. For example, mince and toss them with mild lettuce or other salad greens dressed with the anchovy sauce recipe below, or with olive oil and lemon juice. Alternatively you can boil them for 10 minutes, squeeze them dry, mince and sauté them with olive oil, garlic and hot chili pepper. If you can't find puntarella, use chopped Belgian endive, curly endive or radicchio instead and skip step 3.

1   Rinse the puntarella, shake it dry and cut away the spindly outer green leaves. (Wrap them in damp paper towels and keep them in the crisper drawer of your fridge for other uses—see recipe introduction.)

2   Put the eggs, if using, into a small saucepan filled with cold water. Bring the water to a boil and simmer uncovered for 12 minutes, exactly. Immediately pour off the boiling water and run cold water over the eggs until they're easy to handle. Peel, roughly chop and set aside.

3   Fill a large pot or basin with very cold water. Cut the asparaguslike stalks away from the puntarella head and trim their bases flat. Working with one stalk at a time, peel off the skin, leaving only the pale-green pith. Slice it in half lengthwise. From each half, slice two, three or four matchstick-size sections and drop them into the cold water. Repeat the operation with the other half. Trim and slice the remaining stalks, tossing the sliced sections into the cold water. Let them float for 30 to 40 minutes until they curl like fiddleheads.

4   If you are using salted anchovies, desalt them (see Desalting Anchovies, page 24). If you are using anchovy fillets packed in oil, remove them with a fork and drain them on paper towels. Put the anchovy fillets into a medium-sized salad bowl and, with a fork, crush them into a paste.

5   With the heel of your hand or the flat part of a wide-bladed knife, crush the garlic on a cutting board. Spread the cloves open with your fingers. Discard the skins and green shoots. Add the garlic to the salad bowl and stir. Pour in the vinegar, oil, a small pinch of salt and a generous pinch of pepper. Stir thoroughly. Add the eggs, if using, and toss. Let the sauce sit until the puntarella have curled.

6   Remove the puntarella curls from the water, shake them dry and add them to the salad bowl. Toss thoroughly and let the salad sit for 5 minutes. If desired, remove and discard the raw garlic.

7   Serve immediately.

Grow Your Own:
A Roman Kitchen Garden

Most Roman vegetables, greens and herbs are now available at American farmers' markets, Italian produce markets and specialty shops, and some supermarkets. But you can easily order seeds or seedlings and grow your own. This is especially desirable if you like authentic Roman mixed salad, *la misticanza,* a wildly flavorful blend of mild and peppery arugula varieties, up to five different varieties each of chicory and endive, baby borage, watercress, baby lettuces and field greens.

Here's my short list of essential Roman produce and herbs. See Sources (page 297) for seed suppliers.

SPADONA CHICORY: Mule-ear cutting chicory that's drought- and heat-resistant. Sowing-to-harvest: 60 days. Plant it February to September. Once the leaves are about 6 inches long, cut them off at the base. They regenerate seven to eight times. Eat spadona chicory raw or cooked.

CATALONIA OR DENTARELLA CHICORY: A serrated-edge chicory that looks like a big dandelion. Planting and harvest is the same as for spadona. Use the tender leaves and sprouts raw in salads, or boil and pan-fry the whole plant.

PUNTARELLA CHICORY: This is a variant form of Catalonia, with twisted spears used in salad. It's grown like the other two chicories above and is especially cold-resistant.

ARUGULA: Wild or garden varieties of this peppery green grow anywhere—in beds or pots, even indoors or on a windowsill, just about any time of year. Arugula shoots up and is ready to harvest in 30 days. Snip it off at the base and it regenerates several times. It's the main component of *la misticanza* but goes into many other recipes.

ROMANESCO BROCCOLI: The spiral-topped broccoli Romans favor will grow anywhere in the continental United States. It takes about 5 months to grow (it is usually planted in May and harvested in September or October).

CHERRY AND PLUM TOMATOES: Sow seeds in early spring, plant out in April, harvest in full summer. Tomatoes need heat, so if you live in a cool area, grow them in a hothouse, forcing tunnel or indoors.

ROMANESCO ZUCCHINI: These pale green fluted columns should be harvested when about 5 inches long. They'll grow anywhere from Maine to New Mexico, producing flowers you can harvest for stuffing. To bear fruit, they need heat and lots of room. Plant after the last frost, harvest throughout the summer into fall.

FAVA BEANS: Plant them in late fall in temperate zones, and by Easter, they'll be ready to harvest. Elsewhere, favas should be sown in early spring for summer harvesting. It's practically impossible to keep a fava from thriving. Eat them raw with Pecorino Romano or use them in a dozen Roman recipes.

HERBS: The big four are flat-leaf parsley, spearmint (and nepitella or pennyroyal), basil and marjoram. Buy seeds or small potted plants and grow them in spring, summer and fall, in beds or pots. Parsley and spearmint regenerate endlessly for several years if you pinch off a few leaves or sprigs at a time, or cut them off at the base with care. Marjoram and basil should always be pinch-harvested and will regenerate for several months (basil) or years (marjoram).

Lattughe Farcite

STUFFED LETTUCE HEADS

6 small heads mild lettuce, preferably butter lettuce, or escarole

2 cloves garlic

12 to 15 anchovy fillets

1 tablespoon capers (see page 88)

1½ cups pitted, chopped Gaeta or other Italian or Greek black olives

½ cup extra-virgin olive oil

Freshly ground black pepper

Kosher salt or coarse sea salt

SERVES 6

*D*ifficult though it may be to believe given the sheer number of artichoke recipes in the Roman repertoire, a few locals actually object to the robust flavor of artichokes. To satisfy such palates, some clever Roman cook devised this dish, which uses mild lettuce heads instead of artichokes. The lettuce heads are braised in the style of *carciofi alla romana* (see page 34). Here, though, the garlic, capers and anchovies give this surprising dish a delicious piquancy. Some snide pundits might claim that thrifty homemakers invented this recipe as a means to use up tired produce—when you cook lettuce, no one can see that it was wilted. Naturally, the recipe works best when made with fresh, crisp lettuce, the milder the better. You won't find this on Roman restaurant or trattoria menus nowadays, though apparently it was once popular in the former Jewish Ghetto, where it was probably born several centuries ago. These days it's strictly a home-style dish with a distinctly homely look; the lettuce literally wilts into a green mound. But it's so delicious, you can't help forgiving its aesthetic shortcomings.

1   Clean the lettuce by soaking the heads in a large basin in several changes of cold water. Rinse them under cold running water. Remove and discard the outer leaves, keeping the heads intact. Set the heads base-upward to drip dry in a dish rack.

2   Peel and halve the garlic, discarding the green shoots. Mince it.

3   If you are using salted anchovies, desalt them (see Desalting Anchovies, page 24). If you are using anchovy fillets packed in oil, remove them with a fork and drain them on paper towels. Mince the anchovies. You should have $\frac{1}{4}$ cup.

4   Combine the garlic, anchovies, capers, olives, $\frac{1}{4}$ cup of the oil and a generous pinch of pepper in a bowl. Mix thoroughly.

5   In a Dutch oven or deep saucepan with a lid, place the lettuce heads base-down, side-by-side, as tightly as possible. With your fingers carefully open the leaves and fill them with the anchovy mixture. Drizzle the remaining $\frac{1}{4}$ cup oil over the lettuce and sprinkle in a small pinch of salt.

6   Carefully pour about $\frac{1}{2}$ inch of cold water around the bases of the lettuce heads. Cover the pan and simmer for 25 minutes. Remove the lid and cook, uncovered, for 5 minutes.

7   With a slotted steel spatula or slotted spoon, lift the heads one by one, let them drain back into the pan and transfer them to a platter. Serve hot or at room temperature.

Markets New and Old

*L*ong before the sun rises over Rome, workers at its eternal marketplaces are busy setting up, unloading and sweeping, or wolfing quick breakfasts of *cornetti* (croissants) and olive oil–anointed *pizza bianca* (flatbread) sent down with thimbles of black espresso or tiger-striped foamy cappuccinos. Things start getting interesting around 3 A.M. at the wholesale fruit, vegetable and fish market south of the Ostiense train station, near the gasworks' giant skeleton. Here, hundreds of hard-driven trucks swarmed by greengrocers and fishmongers disgorge tons of dewy zucchini flowers and flipping-fresh anchovies. The dickering begins before the crates hit the floor. Within minutes, some products are speeding down the capital's sclerotic arteries into arm-span-wide capillaries to the dozens of squares large, small and microscopic, where shoppers will begin their daily marketing ritual by 7 A.M., a vigorous workout lasting until the markets close in the early afternoon, usually by 1:30 P.M.

Campo de' Fiori, strategically placed between Piazza Navona and Piazza Farnese, is abuzz at dawn, still seething with the vinous merrymakers who've turned the square into a round-the-clock open-air club. Around them spring flower stalls, fruit and vegetable stands and an increasing number of hawkers of household items, clothing and souvenirs. To out-of-towners, this is Rome's greatest outdoor market. But there are many others.

South of the Aventine, about 20 minutes on foot from the Campo, business is under way at the Testaccio neighborhood's covered market. The particularly well stocked butchers' shops and *salumerie* delis here are a reminder that the municipal slaughterhouse operated nearby for centuries.

Across the Tiber in Trastevere, at the triangular Piazza di San Cosimato, a similar scene is unfolding. Locals with string bags are gathering at Sacchetti, a pastry shop–café on the square, breakfasting while watching the sun umbrellas pop open over bundles of chicory, mountains of mushrooms and pyramids of globe artichokes.

Central Rome's biggest, liveliest open market, though, animates the unsung Trionfale neighborhood between the Vatican and Monte Mario. This is an authentically Roman haggling ground and fills an entire city block off Via Andrea Doria, a major artery. It's possibly the only place downtown where you can still find ten types of tomatoes from Lazio and elsewhere on offer daily, year-round, not to mention salt cod presoaked in a converted aquarium, locally cured pork products and homegrown chicory or arugula. Not far from the Termini train station, Rome's most ethnically mixed inner-city market, recently relocated, splays ragtag stalls down streets fanning from Piazza Vittorio, a large, bedraggled square dedicated to United Italy's first king, Vittorio Emanuele II, with the requisite crumbling ancient ruins in its center. African and Asian herbs and spices vie with necklaces of local *peperoncini* (chili peppers).

Every district in town still has its covered *mercato rionale* (neighborhood market), and sprinkled between are other, usually minuscule, open markets. One of my favorites is wedged at the foot of the Quirinale presidential palace behind the Trevi Fountain. Another fills the pocket-size Piazza delle Coppelle north of the Pantheon, while others add color to Via della Pace, west of Piazza Navona and Via G. B. Ferrari near the octopuslike traffic circle of Piazza Mazzini. Beyond the peddlers of auto parts and fake Persian carpets at the Porta Portese flea market is the Via Ettore Rolli market, hidden along an abandoned train viaduct. Here you'll rarely see a face from outside this blue-collar bastion.

Rome's *mercati* are as old as the city itself. Three of the earliest documented markets go back to the second century B.C.: the fruit and vegetable Olitorium sited near the Portico d'Ottavia in what's now the Ghetto, the Forum Boarium livestock market near the Aventine and Testaccio, and the Macellum, the city's first covered market, built near the Forum in 179 B.C. Emperor Trajan's celebrated market, built between 109 A.D. and 113 once rose to a height of six floors, with 150 shops. The fishmongers occupied the top level so that the salt water piped in from Ostia and the freshwater from an aqueduct could circulate in tanks full of live fish.

Trionfale market scene

While to the casual observer all seems well at Rome's magical markets, things are changing behind the scenes. Supermarkets undercut prices, stay open longer and offer climate-controlled environments modern Roman shoppers love. Supermarket buyers also sidestep traditional middlemen and market gardeners. This is one of the factors that have led to the decline of the wholesale market, which is being evicted from central Rome, ostensibly to make way for urban development. Its new site is 20 miles farther out, making it practically unreachable by mom & pop retailers who already rise at 3:30 A.M. to start their days. If poverty preserves, prosperity brings rapid change; city authorities are gentrifying some neighborhood markets out of existence, like the ones at Piazza di San Cosimato and Piazza Vittorio, whose stallholders are retiring in droves because they can't afford to remodel. The face and demographics of Rome are changing, too. The Campo de' Fiori district's rents have skyrocketed as foreigners snap up prized real estate, driving out the last longtime market folk. Increasing noise and massive crowding at night, with British- or German-organized club and pub crawls, amplified street music and squads of drunken rowdies, make the Campo—historically a lively

place—increasingly difficult for early risers. The numbers tell all: There were several hundred food vendors in the 1950s. Only a fraction hangs on: two fishmongers, perhaps twenty fruit and vegetable sellers, and not a single butcher. The survival of Rome's colorful inner-city marketing tradition is threatened as never before—exception made for the Goths' and other unwanted visitors' historic sackings of the city.

ABOVE AND OPPOSITE: *Campo de' Fiori*

Involtini di peperoni

SWEET PEPPER ROLLS STUFFED WITH CHEESE AND ANCHOVY

6 ripe mixed yellow and red sweet (bell) peppers, roasted, skinned and seeded (see How to Roast, Skin and Seed a Sweet Pepper, page 65)

8 ounces fresh Italian mozzarella, preferably cow's milk *fior di latte*

8 ounces provolone

3 tablespoons ricotta, preferably Italian ewe's-milk ricotta

8 to 12 anchovy fillets

SERVES 6
(16 TO 20 SMALL ROLLS)

I first tasted these succulent, roasted stuffed sweet peppers at the home of our friend Verdella Caracciolo, on a rooftop terrace overlooking countless cupolas and the famous Fountain of the Turtles in the Piazza Mattei. We ate many delicious dishes that night, but this is the recipe that stuck in my mind. Verdella is a talented home cook with three rambunctious, food-loving children to feed. It was a fellow shopper at one of Rome's outdoor markets who gave Verdella the recipe. Good recipes travel fast. I later tasted similar sweet pepper rolls at several Rome restaurants. It turns out *involtini di peperoni* are a cinch to make, the natural outgrowth of age-old recipes like *saltimbocca alla romana* (see page 138) and *fiori di zucca fritti* (squash flowers stuffed with mozzarella and anchovy, see page 46). I use three cheeses: mozzarella, provolone and ricotta, filling a third of the rolls with each because they all go well with anchovy and sweet pepper. You can serve these rolls as a vegetable side dish or appetizer.

1   Preheat the oven to 350°F.

2   Slice each pepper into three sections following the natural ribbing, each about 2½ inches wide. Arrange the pepper sections flat on one or more baking sheets.

3   Slice the mozzarella and provolone into sticks roughly the same width as the pepper sections. Distribute the cheese sticks equally over the sections, one-third each.

4   With a small spoon, scoop up the ricotta
    1 teaspoon at a time and fill the
    remaining pepper sections.

5   If you are using salted anchovies desalt
    them (see Desalting Anchovies, page 24).
    If you are using anchovy fillets packed in
    oil, remove them with a fork and drain
    them on paper towels. Slice the anchovies
    into 1-inch strips. Lay the strips on top of
    the cheese sticks or ricotta, using one
    strip per pepper section.

6   Roll the pepper sections like jellyrolls and
    pin them with toothpicks. Bake until the
    mozzarella and provolone melt and ooze
    out, 15 to 20 minutes.

7   Transfer the rolls to a serving dish,
    remove the toothpicks and serve hot or
    at room temperature.

Pomodori Ripieni di Riso

TOMATOES STUFFED WITH RICE

12 large round firm tomatoes, not too ripe

12 heaping tablespoons risotto rice, preferably carnaroli, arborio or vialone nano

6 tablespoons extra-virgin olive oil

2 cloves garlic

2 heaping tablespoons minced fresh mint leaves

3 heaping tablespoons minced fresh flat-leaf parsley

Kosher salt or coarse sea salt and freshly ground black pepper

2 medium-sized potatoes, preferably Yukon gold, yellow Finn or russet

SERVES 6

Greengrocer Claudio Zampa has one of the best-stocked stands at the famous Campo de' Fiori outdoor market in Rome's historic heart. When they're not cleaning, chopping and bagging fresh vegetables for folks too busy to do such tedious tasks themselves, Claudio and his sister-in-law Lina De Clemente spend their time giving their clients recipes. Lina is a great tomato lover. She showed us how to make this popular Roman perennial that transforms firm round tomatoes into convenient containers for mint-perfumed risotto rice.

1   Working on one tomato at a time, with a paring knife, cut a ring about 2 inches in diameter around the top and carve out a cap as on a jack-o'-lantern. Remove the cap, cut off and discard any woody material, and reserve. With a serrated spoon, such as a grapefruit spoon, scoop out the insides of the tomatoes and transfer them to a cutting board. Eliminate the seeds and cut away and discard the core. Roughly chop the edible pulp and transfer it into a small mixing bowl. Repeat the operation until all the tomatoes have been emptied. Place the tomatoes in a large ovenproof baking dish.

2 Stir the rice and 4 tablespoons of the oil into the tomato pulp.

3 Peel the garlic, discarding any imperfections and green shoots. Mince the garlic. Stir the garlic, mint and parsley into the mixing bowl with a generous pinch each of salt and pepper. Let the mixture sit for 30 minutes.

4 Peel the potatoes. Slice them about ¼ inch thick. Slip the potato slices between and around the tomatoes.

5 Preheat the oven to 375°F.

6 Fill each tomato almost to the top with the stuffing mixture and replace the caps. Drizzle the tomatoes and potatoes with the remaining 2 tablespoons oil. Bake for 45 to 60 minutes.

7 Serve hot or at room temperature.

Mysterious Misticanza: Rome's Favorite Salad

"To dress a salad right, you need four people:
a wise man to put in the salt, a miser to add the vinegar,
a wastrel to pour in the oil and a madman to mix and toss it."

Old Roman saying

Romans have been eating *la misticanza,* a salad of raw mixed wild lettuces, herbs and field greens, forever. The ancients called it *acetarium* because it was dressed with *aceto* (vinegar). The modern name *misticanza* comes from "mixture." And the perfect Roman *misticanza* mixes and matches twenty different green ingredients. The first written mention of it goes back to the fifteenth century.

La misticanza provides a genial pretext for citydwellers to commune with Nature. I've seen many Romans in spring gathering the makings of their salads right in town, especially around the Via Appia Antica and nearby Caffarella parklands, or the Circus Maximus. Where tourists see weeds, locals see free food. Usually, however, commercial growers sow a variety of seeds together and harvest in one go, thereby determining the future salad's composition. Often greengrocers and market stallholders—called *cicoriare,* meaning chicory specialists—mix myriad tiny plants, washing, trimming and bagging them for you. Among Rome's best-known *misticanza* mixers was *Maria la cicoriara,* "Chicory-Mary." She cleaned chicory and made her mysterious leafy blend for about 70 years at a stall on the Campo de' Fiori. Maria is retired now but I recall her as recently as the late 1990s reciting an untranslatable Catalogue Aria of the greens she favored. In Italian and *Romanaccio* dialect it came out sounding something like this: *acetosa, erba brusca, barba di frate, erba stella, burragine, bucalossi, caccialepri, cariota, cicorietta, erba noce, piedigallo, grespino, indiviola, lattughella, ojosa, piede-di-papavero, pimpinella, porcacchia, radicette, raponzoli, riccetta, rughetta . . .* It turns out this particular aria has been canonized over the decades not just by humble *cicoriare* but also by

Chicory, a component of misticanza

published poetasters and celebrated food writers.

To approximate Maria's classical-age Roman *misticanza,* combine about five types each of tender young chicories and endives with baby escarole and other suckling lettuces, tiny borage leaves, newborn turnip tops, juicy purslane and lots of spicy arugula (wild and sativa). The dressing: extra-virgin olive oil, lemon juice or red wine vinegar, fine sea salt and freshly ground black pepper. If you like, add a crushed anchovy to the dressing, a little raw garlic, and toss like mad.

Melanzane Ripiene alla Trasteverina

EGGPLANTS STUFFED WITH DRIED PORCINI

1 ounce dried porcini
(about 1 cup)

1 cup warm water

3 large purple eggplants

2 cloves garlic

6 tablespoons extra-virgin
olive oil

4 ounces stale bread, cut or
broken into crouton-sized
chunks (about 1½ cups)

1 stalk celery

3 heaping tablespoons
minced fresh flat-leaf
parsley

2 heaping tablespoons
freshly grated Pecorino
Romano

Kosher salt or coarse
sea salt and freshly
ground black pepper

SERVES 6

This is the Trastevere neighborhood's version of stuffed eggplants, as made by recently retired greengrocer Armanda Graziani. I love it for the hearty mix of mushroom and tomato flavors and the garlicky croutonlike bread crumbs sautéed in olive oil. There's no need to salt the eggplants to remove the bitter juice; the parboiling takes care of that. The recipe works equally well with tomatoes, sweet peppers and zucchini.

1   Combine the dry mushrooms in a small bowl with the water and soak for 15 to 20 minutes. When the mushrooms are tender, remove them from the bowl with a slotted spoon. Wipe them carefully with paper towels to absorb excess liquid. With your fingers, clean off any remaining soil. Cut away and discard any tough parts or imperfections. Filter the soaking water through a fine-mesh sieve or strainer lined with a paper towel or a paper coffee filter. Cut the mushrooms into rough ¼- to ½-inch pieces.

2   Bring 3 to 4 cups of water to a boil in a large saucepan. Toss in the eggplants and parboil for 4 to 5 minutes. Drain and cool the eggplants in a colander.

3   Cut off and discard the stems and halve the eggplants lengthwise. With a spoon, scoop out the seedy insides. Drop the insides into a food processor and process for 30 to 60 seconds, until pasty. Transfer the paste to a medium-sized mixing bowl.

4   With the heel of your hand or the flat part of a wide-bladed knife, crush the garlic. Spread the cloves open with your fingers. Discard the skins and green shoots.

5   Heat 4 tablespoons of the oil in a small frying pan over medium heat. Sauté the garlic and bread, stirring with a wooden spoon or spatula for 2 to 3 minutes, until the garlic starts to color. Stir the bread into the eggplant pulp.

6   Preheat the oven to 375°F.

7   Remove the stringy parts of the celery and mince it. Add the celery and parsley to the eggplant mixture. Stir in the mushrooms, 2 to 3 tablespoons of the mushroom water, the cheese, a small pinch of salt and several turns of the peppermill.

8   Place the empty eggplant shells in a large ovenproof baking dish. Fill each half to the top with the stuffing mixture. Drizzle the remaining 2 tablespoons oil over them. Bake for 45 to 60 minutes, until the eggplant shell is tender and the filling is crisp on top.

9   Serve hot or at room temperature.

Peperoni Ripieni col Tonno

SWEET PEPPERS STUFFED WITH TUNA AND BLACK OLIVES

6 large yellow, green and red sweet (bell) peppers

2 (6-ounce) cans Italian *ventresca* (underbelly) tuna packed in extra-virgin olive oil, or 2 (6-ounce) cans tuna packed in water, plus 6 tablespoons extra-virgin olive oil

¾ cup pitted, chopped Gaeta or other Italian or Greek black olives

3 heaping tablespoons minced fresh flat-leaf parsley

2 anchovy fillets

1 teaspoon fresh or dried oregano or marjoram

1 large egg

2 cups plus 2 tablespoons fine bread crumbs

Freshly ground black pepper

1 tablespoon extra-virgin olive oil for drizzling

SERVES 6

In Rome, the two most popular recipes for stuffed sweet (bell) peppers call for either ground beef and rice or tuna and bread crumbs. I like both, but I find that the tuna mixture is more flexible; it's delicious either hot or at room temperature. Since I'm partial to stuffed vegetables as a picnic food or snack, I usually go for the tuna. The olives and anchovy are salty enough to season the stuffing mixture. Be generous with the pepper.

1   Preheat the oven to 400°F.

2   With a paring knife, cut around the caps of each pepper, pull out and discard them. Slice the peppers in half lengthwise. Remove and discard the seeds and filaments. Put the halved peppers open-side up on a large baking sheet.

3   With a fork, flake the tuna directly into a food processor and add the packing oil. If you are using tuna packed in water, drain it before transferring it to the food processor with 6 tablespoons oil. Add the olives and parsley.

4   If you are using salted anchovies, desalt them (see Desalting Anchovies, page 24). If you are using anchovy fillets packed in oil, remove them with a fork and drain them on paper towels. Add the anchovies to the food processor.

5   Add the oregano, egg, 2 cups of the bread crumbs and a generous pinch of pepper. Process until homogenous, 45 to 60 seconds.

6   Spoon the mixture into the pepper boats and tamp it down with the back of the spoon. Sprinkle with the remaining 2 tablespoons bread crumbs and drizzle with the oil. Bake until the peppers begin to blister, split and ooze, 30 to 40 minutes.

7   Serve hot or at room temperature.

Peperonata

ROASTED SWEET PEPPERS SAUTÉED WITH ONION, GARLIC, BAY LEAF AND TOMATOES

One of my childhood jobs as domestic kitchen assistant to my mother was to get fresh bay leaves off the tree in the backyard of the Bay Area house where we lived. When in Rome, instead, my mother would send me to the pocket-sized gardens, near our apartment, flanking the Piazza del Popolo, which were shaded by old bay trees—

and full of young lovers. "Pick only the leaves growing as high up as you can reach," she'd say, with a vague reference to dogs and adolescents.

The bay went into all sorts of recipes, including this one for sweet pepper stew, a summertime favorite. I still enjoy going out to pick fresh bay leaves before making *peperonata,* and when I'm in Rome, I get them from the centuries-old trees in the Forum or the rambling hedges of the Villa Borghese—always from upper branches.

2 large white onions

2 cloves garlic

5 to 6 large sweet (bell)
peppers (mix of yellow
and red), roasted, skinned
and seeded (see How to
Roast, Skin and Seed a
Sweet Pepper, page 65)

3 tablespoons extra-virgin
olive oil

2 cups peeled, seeded and
chopped medium-sized
fresh Italian plum
tomatoes (about 1 pound)
(see How to Peel and Seed
a Tomato, page 93)

2 fresh bay leaves

Kosher salt or coarse sea
salt and freshly ground
black pepper

SERVES 6

1   Preheat the oven to 450°F.

2   Peel and roughly chop the onion. Peel and halve the
     garlic, eliminating the green shoots. Slice the peppers
     into strips about 1 inch wide.

3   Heat the oil in a large frying pan over medium heat.
     Add the onion and garlic and sauté, stirring frequently
     with a wooden spoon or spatula, until the onion
     becomes translucent, 2 to 3 minutes. Remove and
     discard the garlic. Stir in the tomatoes with the bay
     leaves and a pinch each of salt and pepper. Sauté for 5
     to 6 minutes.

4   Stir in the peppers and lower the heat to minimum.
     Simmer for 8 to 10 minutes, until the vegetables are
     extremely tender.

5   Remove and discard the bay leaves before serving the
     peperonata hot or at room temperature.

TIP: *Peperonata* makes a great filling for frittata (see page
216). Use half the yield of this recipe to fill an 8-egg frittata.

Concia di Zucchine
PAN-FRIED ZUCCHINI WITH VINEGAR AND HERBS

2½ pounds small zucchini

4 cloves garlic

¼ cup extra-virgin olive oil

1 *peperoncino* (hot chili pepper), shredded, or ¼ teaspoon crushed red pepper flakes

2 tablespoons white wine vinegar

4 heaping tablespoons minced fresh flat-leaf parsley

6 heaping tablespoons minced fresh basil leaves

Kosher salt or coarse sea salt

SERVES 6

Also called *zucchine marinate,* this Roman-Jewish recipe is great for jazzing up zucchini. It's a standard at many Ghetto-area trattorias and a favorite among home cooks. Some prefer to make their zucchini without garlic or chili pepper. Both are traditional ingredients, however, and I find them essential. These zucchini are good hot or cold and can be served as an appetizer or vegetable side.

1   Slice the zucchini into thin rounds.

2   With the heel of your hand or the flat part of a wide-bladed knife, crush the garlic on a cutting board. Spread the cloves open with your fingers. Discard the skins and green shoots.

3   Heat the oil in a large frying pan over medium heat until bubbling-hot but not smoking. Add the garlic, sauté for 2 to 3 minutes, then remove and discard it.

4   Add the *peperoncino* and the sliced zucchini and sauté, stirring, flipping and tossing, for 2 to 3 minutes. Drizzle in the vinegar and boil to evaporate it, 1 to 2 minutes. Lower the heat, cover the pan and simmer until the zucchini are tender, 4 to 5 minutes. Stir in the parsley and basil and a pinch of salt.

5   Serve hot or at room temperature.

TIP: You can also use half the yield of this zucchini recipe to fill an 8-egg frittata (see page 216).

Carciofi Fritti Dorati alla Romana

GOLDEN FRIED ARTICHOKE SLICES, ROMAN STYLE

2 lemons

6 young, tender large (or 12 small) globe artichokes

6 eggs, at room temperature

Fine salt and freshly ground black pepper

1 cup all-purpose flour

2 to 3 cups light extra-virgin olive oil

SERVES 6

There's an old Roman expression that goes, "Anything you fry will be delicious, even a stick!" Of course, you're better off avoiding sticks and frying naturally delicious and wholesome foods instead, especially fresh vegetables. The Romans' cult vegetable is the artichoke, so it comes as no surprise that this recipe for fried artichokes bears the *alla romana* mark of distinction. You can use any variety of artichoke to make *carciofi fritti dorati,* but I find the recipe works best with large globe types. They have a big heart that's easy to slice into wedges. Romans eat these fried artichoke slices as an appetizer, main dish or vegetable side. The usual dose for a main or side dish is one large or two small artichokes per person, with a ratio of one egg per large artichoke (or two small artichokes). The amount of olive oil you'll need depends on the size of your frying pan. For a high-sided pan 10 to 12 inches in diameter, I calculate approximately 2 to 3 cups of oil to fry 6 large artichokes. You should have more oil on hand just in case you need it to top up—some artichokes are more absorbent than others.

1   Juice 1 of the lemons into a bowl of cold water big enough to hold the artichokes and stems. Use the squeezed lemon to rub the artichokes as you work.

2   Clean and trim the artichokes to remove all inedible parts (see How to Clean a Globe Artichoke, page 40). Cut the trimmed artichokes and stems into slices and rounds ¼ inch thick and pat them dry on paper towels.

3   Beat the eggs thoroughly in a large mixing bowl while adding several generous pinches each of salt and pepper. Beat in the flour until the mixture has the consistency of very thick pancake batter. Let the batter sit for 15 minutes.

4   Spread several layers of paper towels on a large platter.

5   Pour the oil into the frying pan to a depth of about 1 inch. Heat it over medium to 350°F, until bubbling-hot but not smoking. To check for hotness without a thermometer, step back and carefully flick a drop of water onto the surface, making sure you don't get splattered. The water should sizzle, dance and evaporate within seconds.

6   With a slotted spoon or slotted steel spatula, drop 1 spoonful at a time of sliced artichokes into the batter and stir until coated. Lift one slice at a time, shaking the spoon to eliminate excess batter, and with your fingers carefully drop it into the hot oil. Fry the slices in small batches for 1 to 2 minutes on each side, flipping once, until crisp. Transfer the slices as you work to the paper towels to absorb excess oil. Continue to batter and fry the slices until all are used, adding oil to the pan as needed to maintain the same level.

7   Remove the paper towels, arrange the artichoke slices on the platter and sprinkle them with salt and pepper. Halve the remaining lemon and juice it over the artichokes. Serve immediately.

Cabbage Head, Roman Style

Two of Rome's favorite vegetables, artichokes and broccoli, are local shorthand for "dunce" or "cabbage head." Shout "*Carciofo!*" or "*Broccolo!*" and human heads will turn.

Broccoli Galati con Vino e Bucce d'Arancia

BROCCOLI BRAISED IN RED WINE WITH ORANGE ZEST

2 pounds Romanesco broccoli or 1 medium-sized cauliflower (about 1 pound) and 1 pound broccoli

2 cloves garlic

¼ cup extra-virgin olive oil

Kosher salt or coarse sea salt

1 *peperoncino* (hot chili pepper), shredded, or ¼ teaspoon crushed red pepper flakes

Zest of 1 orange, minced

1½ cups Italian dry red wine

SERVES 6

Our friend Marina Magri, a history teacher in Rome, learned how to cook from her mother Giuseppina in Alatri, a small town in the Ciociaria farming district south of Rome. Marina's family makes this recipe with white cauliflower and red wine. In the Alban Hills near there, the locals eat the same dish but with green *broccolo romano* (called Romanesco broccoli or minaret broccoli in America) and white wine instead, and they add orange zest. They call the recipe *broccoli affogati* (drowned broccoli) or *broccoli strascinati* (broccoli "dragged" through olive oil in a frying pan; i.e., sautéed).

Since *broccolo romano*—a lovely, spiral-shaped chartreuse-colored head that tastes like a cross between regular broccoli and cauliflower—isn't always available in America, I find this recipe works fine with regular broccoli or broccoli mixed with cauliflower. I prefer using red wine, Ciociaria-style, but I also like the Alban Hills' addition of orange zest. The zest and wine actually give the broccoli a pleasant scent. The result is a spicy, winey, unusual dish that goes great hot as a side with robust pasta or hearty meat dishes, or at room temperature as a summer salad.

1   Cut away and discard any woody sections or imperfections on the broccoli. Divide the vegetables into florets and dice the stems.

2   With the heel of your hand or the flat part of a wide-bladed knife, crush the garlic on a cutting board. Spread the cloves open with your fingers. Discard the skins and green shoots.

3   Heat the oil in a large frying pan over medium. Add the garlic, a pinch of salt and the *peperoncino*. Sauté until the garlic is browned, 2 to 3 minutes. Add the broccoli and sauté for 3 to 4 minutes, stirring, flipping and scraping.

4   Stir the zest into the frying pan.

5   Pour in the wine, stir thoroughly and boil it off, 2 to 3 minutes. Lower the heat to medium-low. Simmer, covered, for 15 minutes, stirring and flipping occasionally. With a slotted spoon or slotted spatula, transfer the vegetables to a warmed serving platter. Increase the heat and reduce the wine and juices for 3 to 4 minutes.

6   Nap the vegetables with the sauce and serve hot or at room temperature.

TIP: Buy seeds and grow your own *broccolo romano*. Several American suppliers, including The Cook's Garden, carry *broccolo romano* and other Italian vegetable seeds (see Sources, page 297).

Carciofi alla Matticella
EMBER-ROASTED ARTICHOKES

I first heard about *carciofi alla matticella* in the town of Castel Gandolfo, site of the Pope's summer residence, in the breezy Alban Hills south of Rome. This is Roman wine country, where Frascati, Velletri, Marino and other so-called Castelli Romani bottlings originate, so grapevines stipple the slopes. Traditionally, grape growers plant artichokes around the edges of their vineyards. The months of March and April, when the artichokes are at the height of their season, coincide with the second pruning of the vines (the first is in November). So vineyard workers gather the dead, dry grapevine cuttings and make raging bonfires with them. They harvest the nearby artichokes and jab them stem-down into the embers. Once the artichokes are roasted, they're stripped of their leaves. Their scorching hearts are dipped into olive oil with salt and gobbled with abandon, a wonderfully messy, sensual artichoke orgy. One famous Roman restaurateur I know, Alberto Ciarla, originally from the Alban Hills, throws a yearly bacchanalian *matticella* party for his birthday, with about five hundred guests, an excuse to sample not only artichokes but also the local wine Ciarla makes. The addition of hot chili or black pepper, garlic and wild mint or parsley to this recipe is a refinement that makes most authentic vineyard workers snicker. But I think it gives this rustically irresistible dish even more punch. Naturally, there's no agreement on the origin of the name, which is sometimes spelled *manticella* and might be a reference to the pruning shears of vineyard workers, the bellows used to get the bonfires burning, or might, as the *matticella*-loving Alberto Ciarla explains, be a reference to the local dialect word for bundles of grapevine cuttings. You'll need a pair of leather gardening gloves to handle the hot, roasted artichokes while removing their leaves. You will also need several bundles of grapevine cuttings or one 10-pound bag of natural charcoal, firewood and kindling.

12 medium-sized globe artichokes

¹/₂ cup extra-virgin olive oil

4 cloves garlic

2 *peperoncini* (hot chili peppers), shredded, or ¹/₂ teaspoon crushed red pepper flakes

4 heaping tablespoons minced fresh flat-leaf parsley

4 heaping tablespoons minced fresh spearmint

Kosher salt or coarse sea salt

SERVES 6

1 Build a wood-fueled fire in a barbecue using grapevine cuttings, wood or untreated charcoal only. Do not use chemically impregnated charcoal or chemical starters or lighter fluid.

2 Soak the artichokes in a basin of cold water, rinse thoroughly and shake dry. If the leaf-tips have sharp points, snip them off with a pair of kitchen scissors or put them on a cutting board and lop them off with a knife. With your fingers and a serrated-edge spoon like a grapefruit spoon or melon-baller, spread open the artichoke, insert the tool and scrape out the hairy choke in the center. Tug with your fingers to dislodge recalcitrant tufts.

3 Pour ¹/₄ cup of the oil into a small mixing bowl. Peel and halve the garlic, discarding the green shoots, and mince. Stir the garlic, *peperoncini,* parsley and mint into the oil with a generous pinch of salt.

4 Stand the artichokes upright, stems down, in a large mixing bowl. With a small spoon and your fingers, force about 1 teaspoon of the herbed-oil mixture into the heart and behind the leaves of each. Save any remaining mixture to add to the dipping oil.

5 Once the fire has burned down to red-hot embers, use metal tongs to place the artichokes directly among the embers or above them on a grill. Continue to feed the fire with kindling. Roast the artichokes, turning often with the metal tongs, for about 45 minutes or until tender when poked with a knife. Remove them with the tongs. Wear leather gardening gloves to remove and discard the blackened outer leaves.

6 Pour the remaining ¹/₄ cup oil, and any leftover herbed-oil, into a serving bowl and stir in a pinch of salt. Serve the artichokes hot with the bowl of dipping oil on the side.

NOTE: Once you've gone to the trouble of building a fire to roast these artichokes, you might as well cook up a few other barbecue favorites, such as *Bruschetta Classica* (page 15), roasted sweet peppers, or *Crostini d'Abbacchio* (page 164) and spicy *Galletto alla Diavola* (page 188).

Vignarola

SPRING STEW OF PEAS, ARTICHOKES, FAVAS, SPRING ONIONS AND POTATOES

*T*he favorite edible snails of Rome's region are called *vignarole,* probably because vineyard workers would gather them among the grapevines, *le vigne.* Once upon a time, vines were grown amid olive trees and vegetable patches. Country folk would plant artichokes, fava beans and peas in such patches, right among the grapevines. Whether that's how this recipe got its name is unclear; the etymology of many Roman food terms is a mystery.

This luscious, slow-simmered spring vegetable stew is an only-in-Rome delicacy, rarely found on restaurant menus. The reason is simple: It's labor-intensive. However, I've eaten great *vignarola* at La Briciola, in Grottaferrata, fief of chef Adriana Montellanico, and at Papà Giovanni, a curious high-end restaurant in central Rome. *Vignarola* is still a regular feature at Rome's oldest trattoria, La Campana, in constant operation since at least the eighteenth century.

As with many venerable Roman recipes, there are many, sometimes contradictory, versions of *vignarola.* One school militates for pancetta or guanciale while another insists this should be a vegetarian dish. Some cooks use red chili pepper while others prefer black pepper. Some add lettuce hearts, others potatoes. But the really contentious issue surrounds the cooking method: Do you employ one or many pots, and should *vignarola* be eaten immediately or cooked down and reheated?

As usual, my favorite recipe combines elements from divergent schools. It strikes me as essential to prepare the artichokes separately, for instance, because they're the only vegetable in the mix that should be braised in white wine. The wine tempers the artichokes' slight bitterness and, because it's a natural antioxidant, helps keep them appealingly green. You'll need two large saucepans for this recipe, and probably a glass or two of chilled white wine to keep you company as it cooks.

I've listed *vignarola* as a vegetable side dish because that's where it traditionally appears on Roman menus. But you can serve it as a main course, especially if you want a vegetarian meal. For a similar recipe with pork and hot chili pepper, see the note for *la scafata,* a variation on *Spaghetti con Fave, Lattuga e Pancetta* (page 116).

1 lemon

3 medium-sized artichokes

1 clove garlic

10 tablespoons extra-virgin olive oil

3 heaping tablespoons minced fresh spearmint

Kosher salt or coarse sea salt and freshly ground black pepper

¹/₂ cup Italian dry white wine, preferably Frascati or Marino

Water

3¹/₂ pounds fresh young fava beans in their pods

8 ounces new potatoes

2 small white onions

3 pounds fresh, tender young peas in their pods or 1 (1-pound) package top-quality frozen peas

3 heaping tablespoons minced fresh flat-leaf parsley

SERVES 6

1 Juice the lemon into a bowl of cold water big enough to hold the artichokes and stems. Use the squeezed lemon to rub the artichokes as you work.

2 Clean and trim the artichokes to remove all inedible parts (see How to Clean a Globe Artichoke, page 40). Slice the trimmed artichokes and stems ¹/₄ inch thick, drain them in a colander and pat them dry on paper towels.

3 Peel and halve the garlic, eliminating the green shoot, and mince.

4 Heat 4 tablespoons of the oil in a large saucepan over medium heat. Add the garlic, mint and a pinch each of salt and pepper and sauté for 1 minute. Pour in the wine and about ¹/₂ cup of cold water. Add the artichokes and stems and cover the saucepan. Increase the heat to high and bring the liquid to a boil. Lower the heat and simmer, covered, until the artichokes are extremely tender, 30 to 40 minutes.

5 Shell the favas by running your index finger along inside the pods. You should have about 2¹/₂ cups. If the shelled favas are bigger than a thumbnail, blanch them in boiling water for 2 to 3 minutes. Drain them and eliminate the skins by rinsing under cold water and gently pinching with thumb and forefinger.

6 Peel the potatoes, removing and discarding any imperfections. Slice them into rounds the thickness of a quarter. You should have about 1¹/₂ cups. Peel and thinly slice the onions.

7   Heat 4 tablespoons of the oil in a second saucepan over medium. Add the onions and sauté until translucent, 1 to 2 minutes.

8   Add the favas and potatoes to the onions and cover with cold water. Put a lid on the saucepan and bring the water to a boil.

9   Run your index finger along inside the pea pods to shell the peas. You should have about 2$\frac{1}{2}$ cups. Add them to the favas and potatoes, topping up with hot water to keep the vegetables covered. Cover the saucepan and bring the stew to a boil. (If you are using frozen peas, add them.) Lower the heat and simmer, covered, until the vegetables are tender, 20 to 30 minutes.

10   Remove the saucepan from the heat. With a slotted spoon, transfer the vegetables to the saucepan with the artichokes. Stir in a pinch each of salt and pepper and simmer, uncovered, for 30 minutes.

11   Stir in the parsley and serve the *vignarola* hot in soup bowls drizzled with the remaining 2 tablespoons oil.

DOLCI

DESSERT

IN SPRING, SUMMER AND FALL, bowls heaped high with tree- or vine-ripened fruit—cherries, figs, peaches, apricots, pears, grapes—are found on every Italian table, and Rome is no exception. Fruit fresh or dried is the standard dessert on many days of the week, sometimes served with cheese, as in *cacio e pere* (cheese and sliced pears) or sweetened ricotta with berries. One local berry is in a class all its own: *fragole* (strawberries). For the last two thousand years, some of the best anywhere have come from the Alban Hills town of Nemi. Romans eat them by the ton, as-is or marinated with lemon juice and sugar.

But it's an abiding myth that Italians don't make or indulge in more elaborate *dolci* (sweets). Romans routinely flank the fruit bowl with a spread of cakes, tarts, cookies, meringues and sweet buns, especially on Sundays. To many, the supreme expression of the Nemi strawberry is in the exquisitely rich layered confection *tiramisù con le fragole* (see page 286).

Possibly the oldest Roman dessert of all is the *mostacciolo,* a tooth-breaking rectangle of hard-baked flour and honey. Originally used in fertility rites about three thousand years ago, you can still buy *mostaccioli* in Roman pastry shops today, though they're moister and fancier than anything the ancients knew. I'll never forget the *mostacciolo* a friend of mine found in the Alban Hills town of Frascati, showing a three-breasted woman striking a ballerina pose and bearing a banner reading "Miss Frascati." The first documented layer cake was described by Cato the Censor in the second century B.C., the precursor, perhaps, of tiramisù and *zuppa inglese* (trifle). Other ancient desserts popular today are *pangiallo* (walnuts, almonds, hazelnuts, pine nuts, candied fruit, raisins and almond paste packed into a loaf) and *panpepato* (basically *pangiallo* with lots of powdered black pepper and, nowadays, usually a coating of dark chocolate). Other perennials illustrating the continuum of Rome's food culture are vanilla-flavored *maritozzi* (buns), buttery *crostata* (jam tarts, see

page 292) and *castagnaccio* (chestnut-flour cakes, see page 274)—adored by Roman gourmands since at least the 1830s or 1840s, heyday of food-loving poet Giuseppe Gioachino Belli.

Borghese Gardens statue with vase of grapes and pomegranates

Brutte ma Buone

Hazelnut and Citrus-Zest Meringues

Butter for greasing

8 ounces hazelnuts, blanched

Zest of 1 lemon

Zest of 1 orange

$\frac{1}{2}$ cup superfine granulated sugar

3 egg whites

Makes about 24 cookies

"Ugly but delicious," that's the literal translation of the name of these exquisite flourless cookies. They come out looking like unsightly lumps studded with chopped nuts, but the taste is heavenly—a crispy meringue surface with a soft center. Valentina Sassara from the town of Marta on Lake Bolsena gave me this recipe, which has been popular in and around Rome forever. Valentina belongs to the old school of Italian homemakers. She effortlessly and cheerfully puts up preserves; makes fresh pasta; bakes all her own cookies, pies and pastries; and buys freshly butchered pork from a relative to cure it, churning out prosciutto, pancetta, guanciale, sausages and cracklings. Her jovial husband, Mario, is a winemaker whose fruity whites go into her *ciambelline* (see page 267). *Brutte ma buone* cookies are a specialty of Valentina's neck of the lake on the northern edge of Rome's region bordering Umbria and Tuscany. That's because the hills thereabouts are planted with row upon row of ancient, lichen-frosted trees that grow some of the world's sweetest, plumpest hazelnuts. Another reason *brutte ma buone* are so popular is they represent a delicious way to use egg whites left over from yolk-only recipes. Similar meringues are made elsewhere in Italy, usually with almonds, and called *brutti ma buoni.* In certain areas north of Rome, nouns and adjectives are systematically changed from the masculine to the feminine, which explains the slight difference in the name.

1   Preheat the oven to 375°F. Butter a 10½-by-15½-inch cookie sheet.

2   Roughly chop or pound the hazelnuts and put them in a large mixing bowl.

3   Mince or grate the lemon and orange zests. Add the zests to the hazelnuts and stir in the sugar.

4 Whip the whites in a standing mixer until stiff and peaky. With a rubber spatula, gently fold the whites into the hazelnut mixture until fully blended.

5 With a soupspoon, scoop up the batter 1 spoonful at a time and use another, smaller spoon to scrape it off and drop it onto the cookie sheet. Leave about 1/2 inch free around each cookie. Repeat the operation until the batter is used up. Bake until firm, 20 to 25 minutes.

6 Let the cookies cool and harden on the cookie sheet. You can store these meringues in a cookie jar or sealed tin can for several weeks.

Giambelline col Vino

LIFESAVER-SHAPED WINE-DUNKING COOKIES

Most Roman desserts fall into two general categories: soft spoon sweets and hard cookies or biscuits. These wine-dunking cookies are served in just about every trattoria and wine bar in town, and they're lifesavers in more than just shape. You'll be glad to have them to help you soak up the last drop of Frascati in your glass after a long, pleasant feast that has run from multiple appetizers through first and second courses with side dishes. Light, crunchy and hard to the tooth, *ciambelline* are made with little sugar and no butter (the original sweetner was concentrated grape must or *sapa* and raisins). The flavoring comes from cinnamon, olive oil and the white or red wine baked inside and dipped into from without. The easiest way to make these is by hand. Serve them accompanied by glasses of chilled Frascati or other Italian dry white wines.

2¹/₂ cups all-purpose flour, plus 1 heaping tablespoon for flouring

³/₄ cup sugar

Large pinch of ground cinnamon

6 tablespoons extra-virgin olive oil

6 tablespoons Italian dry white wine, preferably Frascati or Marino

MAKES ABOUT 24 COOKIES

1   Preheat the oven to 375°F. Grease and flour two 10¹/₂-inch by 15¹/₂-inch cookie sheets.

2   Combine the flour, sugar and cinnamon in a large mixing bowl. Stir with a large fork. Pour in the oil and wine. Knead for 6 to 7 minutes, pinching and squeezing the dough through your fingers. Alternatively, combine the flour, sugar and cinnamon in the bowl of a standing mixer or food processor. Mix or process at low speed for 15 seconds. Pour in the oil and wine and mix or process for 4 to 5 minutes, forming a granular dough. Turn or scoop the dough out onto a floured cutting board or marble slab and finish kneading by hand until the dough has the consistency of modeling clay, 1 to 2 minutes.

3   Make one *ciambellina* at a time. With your fingers, pinch off a pecan-sized piece of dough. Roll it on a clean work surface into a snake 4 to 6 inches long. Lift the snake and join the ends, pinching to form a lifesaver. Gently flatten it with a rolling pin or your palm to a thickness of about ¹/₄ inch. Transfer the *ciambellina* to the cookie sheet. Continue to roll out snakes and pinch them into lifesavers until the dough is used up.

4   Bake until the *ciambelline* begin to color, 15 to 20 minutes.

5   Turn them out onto a wooden board or rack while still hot and let them cool until rock hard, about 1 hour. You can store *ciambelline* in a cookie jar or sealed tin can for several weeks.

Castagnaccio Romano

FLAT CHESTNUT-FLOUR CAKE WITH PINE NUTS AND RAISINS

½ cup extra-virgin olive oil

4 heaping tablespoons raisins

2 cups chestnut flour (about 8 ounces)

¾ cup cold water

¾ cup sugar

4 heaping tablespoons pine nuts

SERVES 8 TO 10

Roman cookbook writer Giuliano Malizia collaborated on a massive tome entitled *La cucina romana e del Lazio.* In it he recalls how Roman schoolkids homeward bound in the days before fast food would rush for their slices of just-baked *castagnaccio* from the *bottega de zio*—the corner snack shop run by an avuncular old guy whose entire being was dedicated to the baking of this humble chestnut-flour sweet. Back in the 1960s I was one of those greedy kids. My brothers and I would gobble our naturally sweet, earthy *castagnaccio* wrapped in corn-yellow paper as we ambled home near Piazza del Popolo. The days of those corner *castagnaccio* sellers are over, but Roman bakers still turn out acres of this snack-cum-dessert, especially in the fall and winter, when the chestnut flour is fresh. *Castagnaccio* is a perennial of home cooks, too, because it's so easy to make, healthful and delicious. One of Rome's most talented, generous and refined pastry chefs, Gianni Cavaletti, is also wild about homemade *castagnaccio.* Some kids never grow up. This is his recipe.

1 Preheat the oven to 350°F. Grease a 10½- by 15½-inch baking sheet with 1 teaspoon of the oil.

2 Soak the raisins for 15 minutes in 1 cup of warm water. Drain them in a sieve or strainer.

3 In a medium-sized mixing bowl, whisk the chestnut flour while adding the water. Whisk in the remaining oil, sugar, raisins and pine nuts to make a runny batter.

4 Pour the batter into the baking sheet and shake the pan. Bake until the *castagnaccio* puckers and splits, about 30 minutes.

5 Turn the *castagnaccio* out while still hot onto a cutting board. Let it cool. Slice it into brownie-sized rectangles.

Fichi Ripieni

DRIED FIGS STUFFED WITH RICOTTA AND ALMONDS

18 large dry figs

6 tablespoons ricotta, preferably Italian ewe's-milk ricotta

18 almonds

SERVES 4 TO 6

Until recently, Christmas was a pretty lean, stripped-down holiday in Italy, observed by almost everyone as a religious and, therefore noncommercial, event. Gift-giving time was Epiphany, in early January, called *La Befana* in Italian, after the good witch who supposedly brings presents to well-behaved kiddies. All that has changed. Nonetheless Romans still eat traditional foods at Christmastime, along with more recently adopted treats, and the religious element, though tempered, is still felt by millions up and down the peninsula. This recipe is for a truly old-fashioned Christmastime dessert that is naturally sweet, sugarless and flourless yet astonishingly delicious. Stuffed figs have been around forever; the ingredients were staples of shepherds living in central Italy before Rome was founded, and therefore long before Christmas had been invented. Fresh or dried figs and goat's cheese is still a popular combination in rural regions of central Italy. Our friend Antonio Paolini, an economics and food writer at Rome's biggest daily, *Il Messaggero*, showed us how to make these sweet mouthfuls. In Rome, you can sometimes find them at Sacchetti, a celebrated café and pastry shop in Trastevere. Figure that you'll want at least three figs per person for a light dessert, good any time of year, but especially in the cold-weather months when dried fruit of any kind is the most appealing. Serve them accompanied by a glass of chilled dry or sweet Italian white wine such as Frascati, Frascati Cannellino, Marino or a late-harvest Grechetto.

1   With a paring knife, slit a pocket in the figs, cutting from the base toward the stem.

2   Spoon into each about 1 tablespoon of ricotta.

3   Slip an almond into the ricotta and gently pinch the figs closed. Arrange them on a serving dish. Pop them in your mouth.

Castagnole con la Ricotta

RICOTTA LEMON FRITTERS WITH SAMBUCA

1 lemon

2 large eggs, at room temperature

¼ cup sugar

½ cup ricotta, preferably Italian ewe's-milk ricotta (about 4 ounces)

1 tablespoon sambuca liqueur

1 cup all-purpose flour

1 package active dry yeast (¼ ounce or about 2¼ tablespoons)

Olive oil for frying (1 to 2 cups)

1 tablespoon confectioners' sugar

MAKES 16 TO 18 FRITTERS

Castagnole with or without ricotta and lemon are a carnival and Christmastide dessert made both at home and at street fairs, where boiling vats of olive oil perfume the air and kids dance around, clamoring for their rations of hot fritters. The Christmas fair at Piazza Navona in the heart of old Rome may be more commercial than it was decades ago, but it's still fun, especially for kids, and you can count on finding *castagnole* and other fried desserts there. Ditto at carnival (Mardi Gras), when Roman kids dress up in costumes and run amok. These *castagnole* are supposed to be the size and shape of chestnuts (*castagne*), but in fact look to me like Rorschach inkblot dumplings. They have the unique flavor duo of lemon and sambuca, the potent fennel-seed liqueur from Viterbo and Civitavecchia north of Rome. Similar fritters are made in other parts of Italy, but I know of no others with sambuca.

1   Grate the lemon zest directly into a medium-sized mixing bowl. Halve the lemon and squeeze 2 teaspoons of juice over the zest.

2   Add the eggs and beat with a handheld electric mixer or whisk while adding the sugar, ricotta, sambuca, flour and yeast. Beat until the batter is thick enough to hold a whisk upright, 2 to 3 minutes. Cover the bowl and let it sit in a warm, draft-free spot for 1 hour.

3 Pour the oil into a narrow, tall saucepan to a depth of about 3 inches. Heat it over medium-low to 350°F, or use a deep fryer set to 350°F. To check for hotness without a thermometer, step back and carefully flick a drop of water onto the surface, making sure you don't get splattered. The water should sizzle, dance and evaporate within seconds. Line a platter with paper towels.

4 Scoop up a tablespoon of batter and use a smaller spoon to drop it into the hot oil. Fry 4 to 6 fritters at a time until golden, about 2 minutes, turning several times. Transfer the fritters to the platter to absorb excess oil.

5 Dust the fritters with confectioners' sugar and serve immediately.

Castagnole *and other desserts in a handwritten recipe book*

Roman Carnival

"... [I]t attains, on the concluding day, to such a height
of glittering colour, swarming life, and frolicsome uproar,
that the bare recollection of it makes me giddy at this moment."

—Charles Dickens, *Pictures from Italy,* describing carnival in Rome in 1845

New Orleans, Rio de Janeiro and Venice are world-famous for their carnivals, also known as Mardi Gras. Rome once had a long tradition of supremely wild carnivals, starting hundreds of years before the birth of Christ with the so-called Saturnalia festival. During Saturnalia, slaves and the poor were allowed to feast and make merry with Roman aristocrats and even sit at the same table as the emperor. In the Christian era, carnival came to mean the period, usually 7 to 10 days, immediately prior to Lent. The word "carnival" comes from *carne vale,* literally "it's all right to eat meat," and for strict Catholics derives its significance from the fact that during Lent meat is not all right—lean eating is observed. The Roman carnival was famous, some would say notorious, especially in the Renaissance and Baroque periods, for its masks, parade floats, horse races on the Via del Corso, and crazy *Moccoletti* candle festival (everyone held a taperlike *moccoletto* candle and tried to keep it lit among flying confetti, dancing and wrestling). Roman carnival officially ended in the 1880s when Italy's Queen Margherita of Savoy pronounced it too dangerous.

Yet the old saying *È carnevale, ogni scherzo vale* (It's carnival, anything goes) is a yearly refrain. The custom of throwing carnival dinner parties at home and taking small children in costumes out to street-corner fairs lives on. During carnival, Romans still eat lots of meat. Most of all, people indulge in sweets, because Lent's other food stricture concerns sugar. The most popular sweets of all are fritters sprinkled with powdered sugar. Fritters go by various names in other parts of Italy, where similar traditions hold, but in Rome they're called *frappe* (the word's origin is mysterious) and *castagnole* (because they're vaguely the size and shape of chestnuts, *castagne*). *Frappe* are simple dough fritters, whereas *castagnole* are dough fritters leavened with yeast and often flavored with other ingredients.

Zuppa Inglese

ROMAN CREAM AND JAM TRIFLE

As the grand old man of Roman gastronomy Livio Jannattoni put it in his massive volume, *La cucina romana e del Lazio,* the only thing English about *zuppa inglese* is the adjective in the name—otherwise it's as Roman as can be. Oddly, Jannattoni then gives a recipe for what most Romans would call a *Monte Blanco,* a liqueur-soaked, domed pudding cake topped with meringue, similar to a baked Alaska. My mother makes *zuppa inglese* without meringue and so does every home cook I know in Rome, including Tèa Bo-Codignola, who walked me through her version of the recipe. Tèa's apartment overlooks one of the most colorful outdoor market squares in town, the Piazza di San Cosimato, which also happens to be surrounded by a dozen or more excellent food shops, pastry shops and bakeries, where she can buy the main components of the recipe—custard and *savoiardi* cookies—ready made. Tèa's clever trick is to grate one cookie and use it to coat the outside of the *zuppa inglese,* thereby imitating the meringue without any of the fuss.

What's in a name? You can't help remarking that *zuppa inglese* has a mysterious moniker meaning "English soup." It might be that the hoity-toity travelers of the eighteenth-century Grand Tour who came to Rome for their culture, sometimes accompanied by their chefs, introduced trifles to the Eternal City. I have also heard Romans claim that the name honors Admiral Nelson's defeat of Napoleon's fleet at Abukir in 1798 or possibly in 1805 at Cape Trafalgar. According to this version, Nelson, who spent a great deal of time in Naples with his mistress Lady Hamilton, adored trifles. Presumably the Neapolitan chef who supplied Nelson with his trifle fix brought the secret to Rome, where it was adapted to the indigenous palate.

Whatever its origin, *zuppa inglese* has been popular in Rome for the last two centuries. The dialect poet Giuseppe Gioachino Belli speaks of it in one of his satirical sonnets from the 1830s. It's just possible that *zuppa inglese* is also the precursor to that world-famous dessert tiramisù, which is made in much the same way. Both are built around *savoiardi* (ladyfinger cookies).

3 cups whole milk

Zest of 1 lemon, grated or minced

1½ cups superfine granulated sugar

¾ cup all-purpose flour

4 egg yolks

36 Italian ladyfinger cookies (1½ packages)

¾ cup marsala

¾ cup cold water

2 heaping tablespoons unsweetened powdered chocolate

4 heaping tablespoons top-quality fruit jam (sour cherry, blackberry, apricot, peach)

SERVES 8 TO 10

1 To make the custard, bring the milk to a gentle boil in a 3-quart or larger pot. Stir in the lemon zest and ¼ cup of the sugar.

2 In a large mixing bowl, whisk together the flour and remaining 1¼ cups sugar. Ladle in about ¾ cup of the boiling milk, whisking until lump-free.

3 Whisk in the egg yolks until fully blended. Pour the mixture into the pot of boiling milk, whisking energetically for 3 to 4 minutes to form a thick custard that almost holds the whisk upright.

4 Remove the pot from the heat and cool it to room temperature. Chill the custard for 45 minutes.

5 With a serrated knife, slice 20 of the ladyfingers in half lengthwise to make 40 thin halves, reserving the other 16 cookies whole.

6 Pour the marsala into a shallow bowl and dilute it with the water, stirring with a spoon. Quickly dip 20 of the ladyfinger halves, one at a time, into the marsala, turn once and use them immediately to line the bottom and sides of a shallow round bowl or glass dish about 3 inches deep and 9 inches in diameter.

7 Transfer about a quarter of the chilled custard (just over 1 cup) to a small mixing bowl and stir in the powdered chocolate.

8 To assemble the dish, build layers. With a rubber spatula, build an even layer of white custard about ½ inch thick over the ladyfingers in the bowl. With a small spoon, flick 2 tablespoons of the jam in small lumps randomly over the custard. Dip 10 of the ladyfinger halves into the marsala and arrange a layer over the jam. Spread all the chocolate custard over it. Dip the remaining 10 ladyfinger halves into the marsala and layer them over the chocolate cream. Cover it with a layer of white custard and fleck this with the remaining jam.

9   Dip 13 of the whole ladyfingers into the marsala and arrange them on top as the final layer. Cover with plastic wrap and chill the *zuppa inglese* for 2 hours. Refrigerate any leftover custard.

10 Remove the plastic wrap. Place a large round serving dish over the top of the bowl. Flip the bowl over onto the dish and rap with your knuckles to loosen the contents. If the *zuppa inglese* doesn't come free, float the bowl in a basin of hot water for 1 minute, flip it over and rap again.

11 With a rubber spatula, spread any remaining custard carefully over the outsides of the *zuppa inglese*. Working over a plate or cutting board, grate the remaining 3 whole ladyfingers into crumbs. With your fingers and a rubber spatula, dust and pat the *zuppa inglese* with the crumbs. Serve chilled.

NOTE: Packages of imported Italian *savoiardi* usually weigh 200 grams (7 ounces) and contain twenty-four cookies measuring roughly 1 inch wide by 5¼ inches long by ½ inch thick.

Il Tartufo dei Tre Scalini

THE TRE SCALINI'S CHOCOLATE TRUFFLE ICE CREAM

*P*iazza Navona is the elongated oval centerpiece square that graces the heart of one of Rome's oldest neighborhoods. It's famous for Gian Lorenzo Bernini's Four Rivers fountain, the church of Sant' Agnese in Agone by rival architect Francesco Borromini, and for a café-restaurant called Tre Scalini, birthplace of the renowned Tartufo—a ball of chocolate ice cream filled with a candied sour cherry and coated in chunky semisweet chocolate bits. Much imitated in Italy and abroad, the Tre Scalini's truffle has remained unchanged since 1931, largely because the establishment is still owned and operated by the same family, the Ciampini. It was Francesca Ciampini (her maiden name was Colasanti) who actually created the first Tartufo, working with her husband Giuseppe. He came from a village called Monteleone di Spoleto in Umbria—black truffle country. So when he saw his wife's ice-cream creation, he exclaimed, "It's a truffle!" Francesca and Giuseppe passed the secret to their son Nando, current scion of the Ciampini dynasty.

"This is our pride and joy," Nando told me, watching eagerly as I devoured a truffle in the sun, with Bernini's fountain splashing in the background. Presidents, prime ministers, popes and royalty have made their way to the Tre Scalini for its chocolate truffles. So eager was Nando for me to understand how to make the dessert properly that he took me by the elbow and showed me himself each step of the process. "Simple, no?" he asked. "We have nothing to hide!" Nando and his team of ice-cream makers turn out on average 500 truffles a day, that's about 180,000 truffles a year. They're sold not only at the Tre Scalini but also at the extended Ciampini family's other café-restaurants around town, notably in the Piazza San Lorenzo in Lucina and above the Piazza di Spagna in Via Trinità dei Monti.

4 cups whole milk,
preferably extra rich

1 cup whipping cream

1½ cups sugar

12 ounces semisweet
chocolate

6 candied sour cherries

SERVES 6

1 Combine the milk and cream in a medium-sized stainless steel pot over medium-high heat and bring to just under a boil. Lower the heat to minimum. Slowly pour in the sugar, stirring with a wooden spoon or spatula.

2 Chop the chocolate into rough, irregular raisin-sized chunks. Add the equivalent of 4 squares (4 ounces) of the chunks to the saucepan and stir until thoroughly melted. Scatter the remaining chocolate chunks across a platter or cookie sheet lined with parchment or waxed paper.

3 Remove the saucepan from the heat and let it cool for at least 30 minutes. Pour the cool chocolate mixture into an ice-cream maker and follow the manufacturer's instructions to make ice cream. Line a freezer tray with parchment or waxed paper or set out a large plastic container.

4 Make one truffle at a time. Scoop out a generous lump of ice cream the size and shape of a medium-sized potato. Put it on top of the chocolate chunks. With your index finger, poke 1 candied sour cherry into the center. Roll the truffle rapidly in the chunks until coated and studded with chocolate. Use a spatula to transfer it to the freezer tray. Put the tray in the freezer immediately. Continue to make truffles, one at a time, until the ingredients are used up.

5 Freeze the truffles for 12 hours, preferably overnight. Remove them from the freezer 5 minutes before serving to partially thaw. You can store truffles in a sealed container in the freezer for several weeks.

Il Cremolato di Pesca del Café du Parc

THE CAFÉ DU PARC'S FROZEN FRESH PEACH MASH

What could be easier and more delicious than fresh, ripe fruit crushed and frozen, then topped with unsweetened whipped cream? There's no additional sugar (unless the fruit isn't ripe), you don't need fancy equipment and, if you leave off the whipped cream, there's no fat.

Ever since they opened it in 1960, Valentino Seri and his family have been running the Café du Parc, a Rome institution right out of a film by Fellini. The tiny café faces

the Pyramid of Caius Cestius, spreading under a long canvas canopy into the Park of the Resistance edging the Aventine Hill. This Dolce Vita hangout is the only place left in town with fresh fruit ices of this kind.

Valentino explained to me how he makes his *cremolato*. "You buy fresh, ultra-ripe fruit like blackberries, apricots, bananas, peaches or pears. You clean and pat it dry and crush it by hand with a wooden spoon until it's reduced to a pulp—blenders and processors are no good for this because they ruin the texture! You freeze the pulp for half an hour or 45 minutes, take it out and crush it around with the spoon, refreeze it for 15 to 30 minutes and keep crushing and refreezing every 15 minutes until the *cremolato* is frozen and flaky—but not too stiff to spoon out. It should have the consistency of sherbet. You top it with fresh unsweetened whipped cream. That's it." When pressed, Valentino conceded that if the fruit isn't perfectly, totally ripe, it's all right to add a pinch of sugar—but no more than 2 percent of the total volume. Also, with bananas, melons and certain other kinds of fruit, I suspect even the Seri clan use knives, potato-mashers, food mills and, who knows, a food processor. I've made this *cremolato* recipe with everything from strawberries or pears to papaya and melon. It's hard to beat ultra-ripe peaches, though.

10 ultra-ripe peaches (about 2½ pounds)

1 tablespoon sugar (optional)

½ cup whipping cream (optional)

SERVES 6

1. Peel and pit the peaches and slice them into a large freezer-safe plastic or Pyrex bowl. Sprinkle in the sugar, if using, and crush the fruit to a pulp with a large wooden spoon and fork and/or a potato-masher.

2. Put the bowl in the freezer for 45 minutes. Remove it. Stir and crush the fruit with the wooden spoon and fork.

3. Return the bowl to the freezer for 15 to 30 minutes at a time, repeating the stirring and crushing, until the crushed fruit looks and feels like sherbet, about 1 to 1½ hours total.

4. Whip the cream, if using.

5. Scoop the *cremolato* into individual goblets or bowls, top with the unsweetened whipped cream and serve.

TIP: *Cremolato* goes great with cookies, such as *brutte ma buone* (page 265), or *crostata* (page 292).

Rome's Coffee Cult:
The Mystery of Sant'Eustachio

Eustace may be more myth than martyr. *The Oxford Dictionary of Saints* dismisses his legend as "historically worthless." In Rome he's the object of veneration, not as a saint but as an important deity in the city's coffee cult, for many Romans firmly believe the best coffee in town comes from a roasting establishment and café called Sant'Eustachio, in the Piazza Sant'Eustachio, facing the church dedicated to this mysterious patron of hunters. A Roman general who saw a crucifix between the horns of a stag and converted to Christianity, Eustace refused to sacrifice to the old gods and was therefore martyred by roasting as punishment. With gruesome aptness, his church sited one hundred yards from the Pantheon is filled day and night with the delicious scents of burning oak and roasting coffee beans. For contemporary Romans, the real mystery of Sant'Eustachio revolves not around the saint but the café's legendary *Gran Caffè*, a double-espresso with a fabulously creamy head, thick enough to give you a coffee mousse mustache. In Rome, the foam, or *crema* as it's called, is the ultimate measure of a barman's skill in making espresso, because it's tough to get it just right. It's not so much a question of the foam's taste, it's the technical prowess involved that counts and, to a lesser degree, the aesthetics of the foam and the sensations it produces on the lips and palate. Café Sant'Eustachio's first owners invented the *Gran Caffè* in 1938. Its secret formula has never been divulged. When you step into the café you can't help noticing a series of screens surrounding the coffee machines, like the rood screens separating the sections of a medieval church. Behind them the high priests of caffeine secretly concoct Sant'Eustachio's brew amid steam and tinkling glasses. Current owners Raimondo and Roberto Ricci took over a few years ago, improving the quality of the coffee but leaving the period decor intact: dozens of old hand-cranked coffee grinders, vintage black-and-white photos, a giant clock and a mosaic on the floor showing Eustace's stag and crucifix. The Ricci brothers still import the best coffee beans from around the world, blending then roasting them in a sixty-year-old hand-operated, wood-fueled machine that looks and sounds like the engine of the *African Queen*—or possibly the hollow "brazen bull," in which the ancient Romans roasted old Eustace. Like their forebears, the Ricci brothers won't reveal the recipe for *Gran Caffè*.

Before befriending them, I spent months spying, slyly interviewing their barmen, asking tall friends to peer over the screens. "You have to trick out the machine," whispered one of the café's waiters conspiratorially as I unsuccessfully tried to slip him a hefty tip. "You increase the pressure in the pump to three times normal, raise the heat to 100° C and use a special nozzle to make the coffee foam."

So that was it! This sounded plausible, until I double-checked. The legal setting in Italy for a coffee machine is 1.6 atmospheres and anything 3 or higher will turn it into a whining time bomb.

"Impossible to do that," confirmed a technician at a major Rome hardware and appliance store. As I spoke to him, realizing I'd been duped, a young saleswoman named Simona Patrizi sidled over when she heard me mention Sant'Eustachio's equipment. "I know how they do it," she said proudly. Her boyfriend Fabio ran a place called the Tortuga Bar and, Simona added, his coffee is even better than *Gran Caffè*.

Once Fabio realized I wasn't trying to steal his girlfriend, he showed me the Tortuga Bar technique. "You take light cream, mix it with a little espresso and sugar, beat it and put it in the bottom of the cup, then you make the espresso over it. . . ." I watched and tasted. It was good, but not a *Gran Caffè*.

At the Tre Scalini on Piazza Navona, home of Tartufo ice cream, owner Nando Ciampini assured me that Sant'Eustachio indeed uses cream and sugar to make its mysterious brew. "Haven't you ever heard the spoons tinkling in the cups behind the machines?" he asked con-fidently. "They're beating the cream, sugar and cof-fee together. . . ."

I returned to Sant'Eustachio cocksure I had the secret. To test it, I asked for a *Gran Caffè* with no sugar or cream, expecting them to say it was impossible. "I'm allergic to dairy products," I lied. The barman didn't blink. "No problem. There's no cream in it anyway." As he spun knobs and valves, wielded spoons and followed the mysterious yet familiar secret ritual, I struggled impotently to peek over the rood screen. A perfect *Gran Caffè* appeared sans sugar or cream. "It's the coffee, the water, the machine," the barman said, splaying his arms. "No one can imitate it."

Undaunted, I purchased a half-pound of the house blend containing, said Roberto Ricci, "various Central and South American and other beans." He assured me it was the same blend they used to make *Gran Caffè*. I conveyed it home to experiment with my stovetop Moka—a miserable failure. What if I took the coffee with me to a neighborhood bar and asked the owner to make a Sant'Eustachio-style *Gran Caffè*, I wondered. "Something wrong with the espresso I make here?" asked the barman, reluctantly showing me what he called "Rome's worst-kept secret." He steamed and frothed some light cream with a drop of espresso and sugar, then poured in more espresso. It didn't work. He tried again. But his failed imitations were more hybrid cappuccino than *Gran Caffè*.

I carried the coffee like a babe in swaddling clothes to several other bars and had more or less the same experience. Then, at last, in Trastevere, I found a feisty barwoman at a café near Piazza Trilussa who swore she knew the real secret. "I've seen it. They put powdered milk in the coffee grounds. . . ." She snatched the coffee from me and fussed behind the bar. Needless to say this proved a disaster. I could only deduce that the powdered milk had clogged the filter screen and nozzle.

Ready to give up, I sought enlightenment from another of Rome's top family-run coffee roasting houses, Giovanni De Sanctis. The owner patiently explained that some coffee varieties make more foam than others. "Certain Brazilian mountain and South Indian large-bean robusta varieties will do that . . ."

Well, at last I had the secret, I gloated, they were using foamy beans! Back at Sant'Eustachio's for the hundredth time, feigning innocent curiosity, I asked if I could watch when they did the Friday roast. They gladly consented, ushering me into an inner sanctum. No rood screens here. Not only did I see the *African Queen* or brazen bull in action, I also got an in-depth course on roasting from Rome's greatest freelance coffee toaster, Fausto Frattini. "It's true, some inferior beans make foamy coffee," he agreed, stoking the roaster's engine, stirring the scalding beans, sniffing and tasting them while checking his pocket watch. "But they would never, ever use those beans at this place, believe me. That's not the secret."

As I moped at one of the café's sidewalk tables facing the church of Sant'Eustachio, Raimondo Ricci came out bearing a *Gran Caffè* and sat next to me. He tapped his silver tray and nodded at the sculpture atop the church showing a stag's head with a crucifix between the horns, the café's emblem. "Some things are best left a mystery," he sighed, satisfied. "Drink up!"

La Granita di Caffè della Tazza d'Oro

THE TAZZA D'ORO'S COFFEE ICE

About 1 cup freshly brewed strong Italian espresso made with at least 3 tablespoons top-quality, freshly ground coffee (8 shots)

4 teaspoons sugar

½ cup whipping cream

SERVES 4

The Tazza d'Oro café, owned and operated by the Fiocchetto family, is famous for two coffee-based delights: frothy, remarkably stiff-headed and tiger-striped cappuccino and *granita di caffè*—a coffee ice topped with unsweetened whipped cream. Tazza d'Oro does its own importing and roasting, and both the cappuccino and granita are made with *Miscela Regina*, the secret house blend of top arabicas that hasn't changed since the place opened in 1946. General manager Silvano Giovanucci showed me how his crew concocts granita, an easy, straightforward-enough process—practically the same used for *cremolato* (see page 280). Ideally granita is served *in vetro*—in a narrow glass—in tiny quantities, but many places, including the Tazza d'Oro, serve it in plastic cups for take-out orders. It's strong and undiluted, not your average frozen coffee, with exactly 7 grams (¼ ounce or 1 tablespoon) of finely ground, freshly roasted coffee per cup, packed into the café's bar-style machines. You can make granita successfully with any kind of espresso machine, just don't stint on the quantity or quality of the coffee.

1   Pour the coffee into a Pyrex bowl or other freezer-proof container. Stir in the sugar, beating with a fork. Freeze for 30 to 40 minutes, until the coffee starts to form crystals. Remove the bowl from the freezer and stir with a fork, breaking apart the crystals.

2   Return the coffee to the freezer, removing and stirring it vigorously every 15 minutes or so, until the coffee is thoroughly frozen and splintery like sherbet, about 1 hour.

3   Whip the cream. Fill the bottom of each of four narrow, small glasses with a dollop of whipped cream. Spoon the granita on top. Finish off each glass with 1 heaping teaspoon of whipped cream. Serve immediately.

Tiramisù con le Fragole

FRESH STRAWBERRY TIRAMISÙ

1½ pounds small, fresh sweet strawberries

4 tablespoons superfine granulated sugar

⅓ cup cold water

1 pound mascarpone (2 cups)

2½ cups whipping cream

5 tablespoons Grand Marnier or Cointreau

24 *savoiardi* ladyfingers (see note, page 275)

SERVES 8

*J*ust when you thought you'd eaten your last tiramisù, here's a quintessentially Roman version of this favorite dessert that's light, refreshing and fruity, made with ripe strawberries. The region around Nemi in the Alban Hills southeast of Rome is home to some of the world's best strawberries. But then, so is America. To make this recipe, most Italian cooks, including Anna Fortini, matron of La Taverna dello Spuntino in the town of Grottaferrata a few miles from Nemi, avoid sponge cake, preferring *savoiardi* (Italian ladyfingers), named for the Savoy dynasty that gave United Italy its kings from 1861 to 1946. This is Anna's recipe. She builds her tiramisù up in layers into a dome-shaped dessert on a platter, instead of making it like a pudding cake in a bowl or rectangular Pyrex dish.

1   Rinse the strawberries, drain them in a colander and with a paring knife remove the stems and any imperfections. Reserve 3 whole strawberries to decorate the tiramisù. Cut the remainder into ¼-inch slices. You should have 4½ cups.

2   Combine half of the sliced strawberries (¾ pound or just over 2 cups) with 2 tablespoons of sugar and the water in a medium-sized saucepan. Slowly cook them down over medium-low heat, stirring and crushing with a fork to form a pulpy reduction sauce, about 20 minutes. Set it aside to cool, 15 to 20 minutes.

3   Combine the mascarpone and 1 cup of the cream in a large mixing bowl and whisk until the mixture is smooth, with the consistency of thick frosting. Gently whisk in the remaining 2 tablespoons sugar, cooled strawberry sauce and 1 tablespoon of the liqueur.

4   In another large mixing bowl, whisk together the remaining $1\frac{1}{2}$ cups cream and 4 tablespoons of liqueur until thoroughly blended.

5   To assemble, soak 10 ladyfingers in the mascarpone mixture, turning several times until the mixture has been totally absorbed. With a slotted steel spatula, carefully lift the ladyfingers one by one and arrange eight of them into a flower-petal pattern on a round serving plate at least 9 inches in diameter. With your fingers, break the remaining 2 ladyfingers into four sections each and use these to fill the gaps between the petals in the flower pattern. With a rubber spatula, spread the ladyfingers evenly with about one-third of the mascarpone mixture. Distribute over this about one-fourth of the raw sliced strawberries. Working with one ladyfinger at a time, dip the remaining fourteen cookies into the mascarpone mixture. Build layers with them, alternating with the mascarpone mixture and sliced raw strawberries. Decrease the number of ladyfingers and the quantity of mascarpone mixture and strawberry slices to build a dome. With a rubber spatula, spread any remaining mascarpone mixture over the tiramisù to give the dome a smooth, even appearance. Halve the remaining three whole strawberries and decorate the top with them.

6   Cover carefully with loose plastic wrap and chill for 2 to 3 hours.

7   Serve cool.

Tiramisù alla Velardi

EUGENIO VELARDI'S ULTRA-LIGHT ROMAN TIRAMISÙ

About ½ cup freshly
brewed strong Italian
espresso made with at least
1½ tablespoons of top-
quality, freshly ground
coffee (3 to 4 small shots)

6 large egg yolks, at room
temperature

1½ cups sugar

2 cups mascarpone
(1 pound)

2 cups whipping cream

10 ladyfingers

1 to 2 heaping tablespoons
powdered unsweetened
chocolate

SERVES 8 TO 10

Chef Eugenio Velardi of La Matricianella restaurant
may be known for his amatriciana sauce but he's also
passionate about desserts, especially tiramisù. In 1994, he
won the tiramisù competition in the Umbrian hill town of
Spoleto for this rendition of the famous dessert. Velardi
and countless other Romans believe—right or wrong—
that tiramisù is their city's own, derived from other, older
local spoon sweets such as zabaglione (see page 290) and
zuppa inglese (see page 275). Whether tiramisù first appeared
in the kitchens of Milan or Treviso, as many claim, or in
Rome, it's become a Roman classic among both home
cooks and chefs. This is possibly the airiest version of it I
know, unlike any I've eaten elsewhere. It has no liqueur
and very few cookies. For it you'll need eight to ten glass
goblets, ideally with an 8- to 10-ounce capacity, since
servings are presented individually.

1 Pour the espresso into a shallow bowl and let it cool.

2 Combine the egg yolks and the sugar in a large mixing bowl and mix for 30 to 60
   seconds at low speed. Add the mascarpone and mix until homogenous, 30 to 60
   seconds.

3 In a medium-sized mixing bowl, whip the cream at medium speed until fluffy, peaky
   and about doubled in volume, 5 to 7 minutes. With a rubber spatula, fold the whipped
   cream into the mascarpone mixture until thoroughly blended.

4   Set out ten glass goblets. Pour or ladle about 1 inch of the mixture into each.

5   Break each ladyfinger into three sections. Rapidly dip each piece, one at a time, into the espresso, turning twice with a spoon to moisten without soaking it through. Drop three soaked sections into each goblet. Cover with 1 to 1½ inches of the mascarpone mixture.

6   With a tea strainer or small sieve and a coffee spoon, dust the surface of each goblet with powdered chocolate. Cover the goblets with plastic wrap and chill for 2 hours. Remove the plastic wrap before serving.

NOTE: If you don't have individual glass goblets, you can make this tiramisù in a deep-dish, 11-by-13-inch casserole or Pyrex baking dish.

Zabaglione

SWEET EGG CUSTARD FLAVORED WITH MARSALA

6 egg yolks

3 tablespoons sugar

3 tablespoons marsala

¼ teaspoon ground cinnamon (optional)

SERVES 6

Zabaglione's defining ingredients are eggs—adored by emperors and slaves alike—and marsala, a fortified wine from the city of the same name in Sicily. Despite the southern origin of the wine, zabaglione is as Roman as can be, a favorite homey dessert for the last few centuries. It may have been popular even before the Sicily-based English wine merchant John Woodhouse invented marsala in 1773. In its earliest incarnations, in fact, Roman zabaglione was concocted with brandy or a blend of brandy and white wine, or other sweet liqueurs and fortified wines. Wherever it originated, it has become a pan-Italian perennial and is certainly among the most versatile spoon sweets anywhere, found equally on elegant dinner tables and in the rumpus room. Once upon a time, plenty of Roman families jazzed up their kids' breakfasts with zabaglione served alongside the coffee and hot milk, because zabaglione is so high in energy. Back in the 1970s, my mother always whipped up double batches of zabaglione for me before I ran in races like the Bay to Breakers (in San Francisco) or the Strawberry Canyon Run (in Berkeley). I never even came close to winning but at least I finished, and I sure loved the zabaglione.

You'll need a double boiler to make this recipe. If you don't have one, nest two steel pots together. Pour 1 to 1½ inches of water into the larger, bottom pot. Make the zabaglione in the smaller top pot.

1   Put the yolks in the top pot of a double boiler and pour in the sugar. Beat vigorously with a fork until the eggs and sugar are homogenous and turn almost white, 2 to 3 minutes.

2   Place the double boiler over medium-low and heat it evenly, lowering the heat to keep the water from coming to a boil.

3   Stirring the egg-and-sugar mixture gently clockwise with a wooden spoon, drizzle in the marsala. Keep stirring until the zabaglione thickens into light custard, with a dark golden color, about 3 to 4 minutes.

4   Spoon the zabaglione into individual goblets. Optionally, sprinkle with a tiny pinch of ground cinnamon. Serve zabaglione warm or cover it with plastic wrap and chill for 1 hour before serving.

NOTE: Save your egg whites from this and other recipes and use them to brush the crust of *Crostata alla Romana* (page 292) or *Torta Ebraica di Ricotta* (page 294) or make *Brutte ma Buone* (page 265). Brushing with egg white speeds up the browning process, thereby helping to protect the dough and filling from overcooking. You can also freeze egg whites and keep them for months.

Crostata alla Romana con Marmelata di Visciole

TRELLIS-CRUST PIE WITH SOUR CHERRY JAM

1 cup (2 sticks) unsalted butter, chilled

3½ cups all-purpose flour

¾ cup sugar

3 egg yolks

Zest of 1 lemon

1 cup sour cherry or other high-quality, low-sugar, dense jam (apricot, peach, blackberry)

1 egg white

SERVES 8

A favorite of home cooks because it's so easy to make, *crostata* is also sold by every Roman pastry shop—and most trattorias and cafés—in town. A more or less literal translation of the name would be "mostly crust." This is a thick, buttery platform for jam, the denser the jam the better. Sweet-toothed adults breakfast on *crostata*. Kids snack on it. Everyone gobbles it for dessert. The beauty of this simplest of fruit pies is that it can be made with any kind of fruit jam or conserve in any season, though the *alla romana* designation goes to those made with the city's favorite flavor of jam, sour cherry. If you want to get fancy you can top the finished pie with diced fresh fruit, such as strawberries, apricots or plums.

There's nothing better than a slice of buttery-sweet *crostata* and a shot of strong espresso. The secret of this recipe, made by family friends in Rome and by my mother in California, is the lemon: It makes the crust in itself an irresistible, zesty delight.

HAND-MIXING METHOD:

1 Cut the chilled butter into pats. Pour the flour into a mound in a large mixing bowl, make a well in the center, sprinkle in the sugar and drop in the butter and the egg yolks.

2 Mince or grate the lemon zest. Stir the zest into the mixture with a wooden spoon or spatula.

3 Pinch and squeeze the dough with your fingers, pushing away and gathering back until the dough cleans the side of the bowl and is the consistency of modeling clay, about 7 minutes.

1   Cut the butter into pats and let it soften to room temperature. Mince or grate the lemon zest.

2   Combine the softened butter, egg yolks, flour, sugar and lemon zest in a food processor or standing-mixer bowl. Pulse with the processor for 30 to 60 seconds. Alternatively, mix with the standing mixer at low speed for 30 seconds, increasing the speed to medium-low for 30 seconds.

3   Transfer the grainy dough to a flour-dusted board or marble slab and finish kneading by hand for 1 to 2 minutes.

TO FINISH:

4   Separate the dough into two unequal parts, roughly one-third and two-thirds. With a rolling pin flatten the larger piece to about ¼ inch thick.

5   Butter a 7-by-12-inch shallow pie pan or Pyrex baking dish or 9-inch round pie pan. Stretch the sheet into it and up the sides. Fold any excess dough over the edge. With the tines of a fork, poke holes in the dough to allow steam to escape. Trim off and reserve any excess dough.

6   Preheat the oven to 350° F.

7   With a rubber or wooden spatula, evenly spread a ¼-inch-thick layer of jam over the dough.

8   Pinch the remaining small piece of dough into pecan-sized balls. Roll them out with your palms and fingertips. Use a rolling pin to flatten them into a dozen or so ⅓-inch-wide strips of varying lengths. Build a trellis with the strips over the jam. Join the ends to the piecrust by pinching firmly at the rim. With the tines of a fork, score the rim all the way around.

9   Lightly beat the egg white with a fork or whisk. Use a pastry brush to apply it to the trellis and edge. Bake until the crust is golden, 30 to 35 minutes.

10   Let the *crostata* cool in the pan for 1 hour. Slice and serve at room temperature.

TIP: By brushing the trellis and crust edge with egg white, you speed up the process of getting the crust golden, protecting the dough and jam from overcooking.

Torta Ebraica di Ricotta

JEWISH-ROMAN RICOTTA CHEESECAKE WITH SOUR CHERRY JAM OR CHOCOLATE

FOR THE CRUST:

½ pound (2 sticks) unsalted butter, at room temperature

Zest of 1 lemon or 12 drops vanilla extract

3 large eggs

½ cup superfine granulated sugar

3½ cups all-purpose flour

1 teaspoon salt

FOR THE FILLING:

2 small eggs

2 cups ricotta (about 1 pound), preferably Italian ewe's-milk ricotta

4 tablespoons superfine granulated sugar

½ cup sour cherry or other high-quality, low-sugar jam, or 1 cup dark chocolate, broken into chunks, semisweet chocolate chips, or high-quality chocolate syrup

SERVES 6 TO 8

Affable young pastry chef Stefano Ceccarelli runs a popular cake shop in the Via del Portico d'Ottavia called La Dolce Roma next door to his parents' restaurant Giggetto, a Roman institution since the 1920s. Stefano makes desserts for the restaurant, including this Jewish cheesecake in the style of the former Ghetto, where his family has lived for generations. *Torta ebraica di ricotta* is more pie than cake, with a lot of delicious crust. "Roman cheesecake should look not like the cupola of Saint Peter's," says Stefano, sculpting architecture in the air with his hands, "but like the Pantheon's dome." Others less familiar with Rome's monuments might compare this ancient Roman dessert, which originally was sweetened with reduced grape must, to a flying saucer. It's surprisingly airy and not cloying. To transform it into a Roman chocolate cheesecake, use chocolate chips and/or chocolate syrup instead of the jam.

1   With a hand mixer, whip the butter in a large mixing bowl to a light, peaky consistency, about 5 minutes. Alternatively, use a food processor and process the butter for about 1 minute.

2   Mince or grate the lemon zest.

3   Beat the eggs and sugar together in a small mixing bowl until foamy but not stiff. Mix in the lemon zest.

4   Add the flour and salt to the whipped butter. Mix or process at low speed until homogenous, 20 to 30 seconds. Incorporate the beaten egg-and-sugar mixture by hand with a rubber spatula, or process for about 1 minute.

5   Transfer the dough to a flour-dusted work surface and knead gently, squeezing with your fingers, until the dough feels silky. Roll the dough into a compact ball, put it in a clean bowl, cover with a dishcloth and chill for 1 hour.

6   Preheat the oven to 425° F. Butter and flour a 9-inch round, shallow pie pan, preferably with a removable bottom or a pressure ring, or a 10-inch tart pan with removable bottom.

7   Divide the dough into two unequal pieces, roughly one-third and two-thirds. Use a rolling pin to roll out the larger piece of dough into a ¼- to ⅓-inch-thick disk approximately 11 inches in diameter. Transfer the rolled dough to the pie pan, lining the bottom and sides. Trim off any excess dough and add it to the remaining dough. Poke holes through the piecrust with the tines of a fork.

8   Bake the crust for 15 to 20 minutes, until firm and golden. Remove the pan from the oven and let it cool for a few minutes.

9   Roll out the remaining piece of dough to a thickness of about $1/8$ to $1/4$ inch and a diameter of about 10 inches. Set it aside in a cool spot.

10 To make the filling, beat one of the eggs in a large mixing bowl. Add the ricotta, sugar, and 6 tablespoons of the jam, or $3/4$ cup of chocolate syrup or all of the chocolate chunks or chips. Stir thoroughly with a rubber spatula until smooth and homogenous.

11 Spread the remaining 2 tablespoons of the jam or $1/4$ cup of the chocolate syrup over the prebaked piecrust. With a large spoon, make a mound of the ricotta mixture on top. Smooth the mound down with a rubber spatula.

12 Set the second disk of dough on top of the mixture to form a low-profile dome. Crimp the edge all around with your thumbs or the back of a wooden spoon. Trim any excess dough.

13 Separate the yolk of the remaining egg and eliminate about half of the white. Beat the egg thoroughly and brush it onto the top crust.

14 Bake for 10 minutes. Lower the heat to 375° F. and finish baking for 20 to 30 minutes, until the top crust is golden. Let the pie cool in the pan.

15 Slice and serve at room temperature.

SOURCES

Retail, mail-order and Internet sources for Roman and Italian food items:

A. G. Ferrari
(locations nationwide)
www.agferrari.com
Olive oils, olives, Italian cheeses including mozzarella and various types of pecorino, pancetta, pastas, vinegars, porcini and other specialty foods.

B&L Specialty Foods
P.O. Box 80068
Seattle, WA 98108
(800) EAT-PASTA
Olive oils, olives, Italian cheeses including mozzarella and various types of pecorino, pancetta, pastas, vinegars, porcini and other specialty foods.

Convito Italiano
1515 Sheridan Road
Wilmette, IL 60091
(847) 251-3654
Fax: (847) 251-0123
E-mail: information@convitoitaliano.com
www.convitoitaliano.com
Olive oils, including several from Rome's region, Gaeta olives, Italian canned tomatoes including San Marzano, dried porcini in bulk and in packages, farro, fresh vacuum-packed chestnuts, Rustichella capers in sea salt, noniodized sea salt, semolina, Pecorino Romano, *peperoncini* in bulk and in jars, pancetta.

The Cooks' Garden
PO Box 535
Londonderry, VT 05148
(800) 457-9703
Fax: (800) 457-9705
E-mail: info@cooksgarden.com
www.cooksgarden.com
Italian seeds for puntarella and other chicories, Romanesco broccoli, arugula, tomatoes and herbs.

Corti Brothers
5810 Folsom Boulevard
Sacramento, CA 95819
General information: (916) 736-3814
Deli: (916) 736-3802
Produce department: (916) 736-3804
Meat department: (916) 736-3805
Anchovies, Italian cheeses, olive oils, vinegars, capers, risotto rice, mushrooms and other specialty foods.

Dean & Deluca Mail Order
560 Broadway
New York, NY 10012
(800) 221-7714
Catalogue requests: (800) 221-7741
www.deandeluca.com
Some products are available only seasonally. Various pecorino cheeses, dried porcini, fresh chestnuts and whole organic chestnuts in a jar (available starting late August, early September), farro, anchovies packed in olive oil, risotto rice, sea salt and other specialty foods.

Esperya USA
3 Westchester Plaza
Elmsford, NY 10523
(914) 592-5544
Fax: (914) 592-1787
E-mail: customerservice.usa@esperya.com
www.esperya.com
Farro, chestnut flour, durum wheat flour and other specialty items.

Formaggio Kitchen
244 Huron Avenue
Cambridge, MA 02138
(617) 354-4750
Fax: (617) 547-5680
E-mail: ihsan@formaggiokitchen.com
www.formaggiokitchen.com
Cheeses, olive oils, vinegars, mushrooms and other specialty foods.

G. B. Ratto International Grocer
821 Washington Street,
Oakland, CA 94507
In state: (800) 228-3515
Out of state: (800) 325-3483
(510) 832-6503
Fax: (510) 836-2250
Olive oils, olives, dried porcini, pastas, flours, polenta, vinegars and other specialty foods.

Greenleaf
1955 Jerrold Avenue
San Francisco, CA 94124
(415) 647-2991
Fax: (415) 647-2996
E-mail: ajp@greenleafsf.com
Fresh seasonal produce, including Italian chicory and arugula.

Hobbs' Applewood Smoked Meat Company
1201 Andersen Drive
San Rafael, CA 94901
(415) 453-0577
Fax: (415) 453-1653
E-mail: tino187@aol.com
Domestic pancetta and Parma ham (prosciutto).

Indian Rock Produce
530 California Road
Quakertown PA 18951
(215) 536-9600
(800) 882-0512
Fax: (215) 529-9448
E-mail: irp@indianrockproduce.com
www.indianrockproduce.com
Fresh Italian peas, fava beans, tomatoes, arugula and chicory are available year-round. Puntarella is available from late August through May.

Jamison Farm
171 Jamison Lane
Latrobe, PA 15650
(800) 237-5262
Fax: (724) 837-2287
E-mail: sukey@jamisonfarm.com
www.jamisonfarm.com
A prime U.S. source for suckling lamb (*abbacchio*).

King Arthur Flour Co.
The Baker's Catalogue
P.O. Box 876, Norwich, VT 05055-0876
Orders: (800) 827-6836
Customer care fax: (800) 343-3002
E-mail: customercare@kingarthurflour.com
E-mail (for baking questions):
bakers@kingarthurflour.com
www.kingarthurflour.com
A prime source for durum wheat flour, semolina and occasionally chestnut flour. Also stocks a wide variety of noniodized sea salts.

Manganaro Foods
488 Ninth Avenue
New York, NY 10018
(212) 563-5331
Fax: (212) 239-8355
Olive oils, olives, Italian cheeses, pastas, vinegars, porcini and other specialty foods.

Manicaretti Italian Food Imports
5332 College Avenue
Oakland, CA 94618
(510) 655-0911
(800) 799-9830
Fax: (510) 655-2034
E-mail: mail@manicaretti.com
www.manicaretti.com
Farro, anchovies, capers, olive oils, olives, risotto rice, polenta, Rustichella dry and egg pastas, vinegars and other specialty items.

Mozzarella Company
2944 Elm Street
Dallas, TX 75226
(214) 741-4072
(800) 798-2954
E-mail: info@mozzco.com
www.mozzco.com
A prime retail and mail-order source for domestic fior di latte (cow's milk) mozzarella and ricotta made either from cow's milk or goat's milk in the traditional Italian manner, using the whey from the mozzarella curds. They also make capriella (50 percent cow's and 50 percent goat's milk) mozzarella.

MURRAY'S CHEESE
257 Bleecker Street
New York, NY 10014
(212) 243-3289
Fax: (212) 243-5001
Italian cheeses, including mozzarella and various
varieties of pecorino, Parmigiano-Reggiano.

ORNAMENTAL EDIBLES
3622 Weedin Court
San Jose, CA 95132
(408) 946-SEED
Fax: (408) 946-0181
E-mail: info@ornamentaledibles.com
www.ornamentaledibles.com
Italian chicory, arugula, tomato and other vegetable and
herb seeds.

R. M. FELTS PACKING CO.
P.O. Box 25
Surry, VA 23883
(800) 222-4267
Fax: (804) 294-5378
Great bacon and smoked hog's jowls similar to Roman
salt-cured guanciale.

THE ROCKRIDGE PASTA SHOP
5665 College Avenue
Oakland, CA 94618
(510) 547-4005
E-mail: lsikorski@markethall.com
Farro, fresh and dried pasta, olive oils, vinegars, risotto
rice, porcini and other specialty foods.

SALUMERIA BIELLESE
378 8th Avenue (& 29th Street)
New York, NY 10001
(212) 736-7376
Fax: (212) 736-1093
This is the prime U.S. source for guanciale (cured pork
jowl) and pancetta. They sell and ship (2 to 3 days
regular or overnight) whole jowls weighing
approximately 1.5 pounds.

SHEPHERD'S GARDEN SEEDS
30 Irene Street
Torrington, CT 06790
(860) 482-3638
E-mail: mmgrow@shepherdseeds.com

www.shepherdseeds.com
Italian seeds for puntarella and other chicories,
Romanesco broccoli, arugula, tomatoes and herbs.

SULTAN'S DELIGHT
P.O. Box 090302
Brooklyn, NY 11209
(718) 745-6844
(800) 852-5046
Shelled fava beans.

TIERRA VEGETABLES
13684 Chalk Hill Road
Healdsburg, CA 95448
(707) 837-8366
Fax: (707) 433-5666
evie@tierravegetables.com
www.tierravegetables.com
Seasonally available Italian chicories and peppers both
sweet and spicy.

TODARO BROTHERS
557 Second Avenue
New York, NY 10016
(212) 679-7766
Fax: (212) 689-1679
E-mail: todarobros@msn.com
www.todarobros-specialty-foods.com
Farro, pancetta, olive oils, olives, Italian cheeses, pastas,
vinegars, porcini, risotto rice and other specialty foods.

TOMALES BAY PRODUCE AND COWGIRL CREAMERY
P.O. Box 717
Point Reyes Station, CA 94956
(415) 663-9335
Fax: (415) 663-5418
Fresh produce and artisan-made cheeses, including
many Italian varieties.

VIVANDE
2125 Fillmore Street
San Francisco, CA 94115
(415) 346-4430 or (415) 346-2877
Olive oils, olives, Italian cheeses including mozzarella,
pastas, risotto rice, durum wheat flour, vinegars, porcini
and other specialty foods, plus Italian herb and lettuce
seeds and seasonal produce.

WALLY'S
2107 Westwood Boulevard

Los Angeles, CA 90025
(800) 8-WALLYS
Olive oils, olives, Italian cheeses, pastas, vinegars, porcini and other specialty foods.

WHOLE FOODS MARKETS
(locations nationwide)
www.wholefoods.com
Olive oils, olives, Italian cheeses, pastas, vinegars, porcini and other specialty foods.

WILLIAMS-SONOMA
Catalogue Sales
P.O. Box 7465
San Francisco, CA 94120
(800) 541-2233
Fax: (415) 421-5153
www.williamssonoma.com
Olive oils, vinegars, mushrooms, Parma ham, pancetta, cheeses, fresh pasta, vegetables and other specialty foods and kitchen tools.

ZABAR'S MAIL ORDER CATALOGUE
2245 Broadway
New York, NY 10024
(212) 787-2003
(800) 221-3347
E-mail: info@zabars.com
www.zabars.com
Olive oils, olives, Italian cheeses, pastas, vinegars, porcini and other specialty foods.

ZINGERMAN'S
422 Detroit St.
Ann Arbor, MI 48104
(888) 636 8162
(734) 477-6986
Fax: (734) 477-6988
www.zingermans.com
Farro, pancetta, *peperoncino,* olive oils, olives, Italian cheeses, pastas, vinegars, risotto rice, porcini and other specialty foods.

SOMETIMES A CHALLENGE TO FIND:

Abbacchio (suckling lamb): Jamison Farm

Anchovies and capers packed in salt: Convito Italiano, Corti Brothers, Dean & Deluca Mail Order, Manicaretti Italian Food Imports, Todaro Brothers, Zingerman's

Chestnuts and chestnut flour: Convito Italiano, Dean & Deluca Mail Order, Esperya USA, King Arthur Flour Co., Zingerman's

Durum wheat flour: Dean & Deluca Mail Order, Esperya USA, King Arthur Flour Co., Vivande

Farro: Convito Italiano, Dean & Deluca Mail Order, Esperya USA, Manicaretti Italian Food Imports, Todaro Brothers, The Rockridge Pasta Shop, Zingerman's

Gaeta olives: Convito Italiano

Guanciale: R. M. Felts Packing Co., Salumeria Biellese

Mozzarella and ricotta: A. G. Ferrari, B&L Specialty Foods, Mozzarella Company, Murray's Cheese, Tomales Bay Produce and Cowgirl Creamery

Pecorino Romano: A. G. Ferrari, B&L Specialty Foods, Dean & Deluca Mail Order, Formaggio Kitchen, Murray's Cheese, Todaro Brothers, Zingerman's

Peperoncino: Convito Italiano, Dean & Deluca, Tierra Vegetables, Zingerman's

Puntarella and chicory: Indian Rock Produce, Tomales Bay Produce and Cowgirl Creamery, Vivande

Risotto rice: Corti Brothers, Dean & Deluca Mail Order, The Rockridge Pasta Shop, Todaro Brothers, Vivande, Zingerman's

Sea salt: Convito Italiano, Dean & Deluca Mail Order, King Arthur Flour Co., Zingerman's

Seeds: The Cooks' Garden, Ornamental Edibles, Shepherd's Garden Seeds, Vivande

BIBLIOGRAPHY

Artusi, Pellegrino. *The Art of Eating Well.* Trans. Kyle M. Phillips III. New York: Random House, 1996.

Belli, Giuseppe Gioachino. *Sonetti.* Milan: Grandi Classici Oscar Mondadori, 1990.

Boni, Ada. *Il talismano della felicità.* Rome: Editore Colombo, 1999.

———. *La cucina regionale italiana.* Rome: Newton, 1995.

———. *La cucina romana.* Rome: Newton & Compton Editori, 2000.

Capatti, Alberto and Massimo Montanari. *La cucina italiana, Storia di una cultura.* Rome: Editori Laterza, 1999.

Carnacina, Luigi and Luigi Veronelli. *La cucina rustica regionale.* 4 Vols. Milan: Biblioteca Universale Rizzoli, 1977.

Carnacina, Luigi and Vincenzo Buonassisi. *Roma in cucina.* Milan: N.p., 1968.

Dalby, Andrew. *Empire of Pleasures.* London: Routledge, 2000.

Dalby, Andrew and Sally Grainger. *The Classical Cookbook.* Malibu: J. Paul Getty Museum Press, 1996.

Dickens, Charles. *American Notes for General Circulation* and *Pictures from Italy.* London: Mandarin, 1991.

Di Ravello, Roberto. *Giggetto: l'osteria romana, una tradizione.* Tarquinia, Italy: STEG srl, 1995.

Fabrizi, Aldo. *Nonna Minestra.* Rome: N.p., n.d.

Farmer, David Hugh. *The Oxford Dictionary of Saints.* Oxford: Clarendon Press, 1978.

Giaquinto, Adolfo. *Cucina di famiglia e pasticceria casalinga.* Rome: N.p., 1922.

Gozzini Giacosa, Ilaria. *A Taste of Ancient Rome.* Chicago: The University of Chicago Press, 1992.

Grant, Mark. *Roman Cookery.* London: Serif, 1999.

Hare, Augustus J. C. *Walks in Rome.* New York: George Routledge & Sons, N.d.

Jannattoni, Livio. *La cucina romana e del Lazio.* Rome: Newton & Compton Editori, 2000.

Limentani Pavoncello, Donatella. *Dal 1880 ad oggi, La cucina ebraica della mia famiglia.* Rome: Carucci Editore, 1982.

Malizia, Giuliano. *La cucina romana.* 2nd edition. Rome: Tascabili Economici Newton, 1995.

Mariani, John. *The Dictionary of Italian Food and Drink.* New York: Broadway Books, 1998.

Metz, Vittorio. *La cucina del Belli.* Milan: SugarCo, 1984.

Padulosi, S. and K. Hammer, J. Heller, eds. *Hulled Wheats.* Rome: IPGRI, 1996.

Pellati, Renzo. *Tutti i cibi dalla "a" alla "z."* Milan: Mondadori Oscar Guide, 1999.

Ragusa, Vittorio. *La vera cucina casareccia a Roma e nel Lazio.* Rome: Editrice IEDEP, N.d.

Rendina, Claudio. *Roma di Belli.* Rome: Edizioni della Città, 1994.

Roden, Claudia. *The Book of Jewish Food.* New York: Alfred A. Knopf, 1996.

Root, Waverley. *Food.* New York: Simon & Schuster, 1980.

Serra, Anna and Piero. *A Roma se magna così.* Monteruscello, Italy: Salvatore Di Fraia Editore, N.d.

Soyer, Alexis. *The Pantropheon.* New York and London: Paddington Press Ltd., 1977.

Tropea, Ivana. *Cucina romana.* Florence: Edizioni del Riccio, 1984.

Zanazzo, Giggi. *Proverbi romaneschi.* Modena, Italy: Editrice Europa, 1886.

Zanini De Vita, Oretta. *Il Lazio a tavola.* Rome: Alphabyte Books, 1994.

INDEX